IMAGES
of America

LAKEWOOD PARK

On the cover: **Dick Clark Brings His Show to Lakewood Ballroom, 1959.** A television and radio personality, game show host, and businessman, Dick Clark is best known for hosting *Bandstand* in 1956, then *American Bandstand* when the show went national in 1957. On a Friday evening in July, Dick Clark, new to the record-producing business, brought Chubby Checker to Lakewood Park to promote the up-to-then unknown singer. Checker's hit "The Twist" had not been released, and his appearance fee was merely the national exposure he was getting with Dick Clark. (Courtesy of the Guinan family.)

IMAGES
of America

LAKEWOOD PARK

The Guinan Family

ARCADIA
PUBLISHING

ISBN 978-0-7385-6578-1

Published by Arcadia Publishing
Charleston, South Carolina

Printed in the United States of America

Library of Congress Control Number:2009920841

For all general information contact Arcadia Publishing at:
Telephone 843-853-2070
Fax 843-853-0044
E-mail sales@arcadiapublishing.com
For customer service and orders:
Toll-Free 1-888-313-2665

Visit us on the Internet at www.arcadiapublishing.com

CONTENTS

ACKNOWLEDGMENTS

Despite a disastrous fire that destroyed our grandparents' home and department store in 1945, pictures of Lakewood Park remained at the Guinan summer bungalow or in married sons' homes. After going through Lakewood memorabilia following my mother's death and listening for years to the stories of my dad and uncles, I felt compelled to collect all the history and record it in book form.

With the encouragement of several people, including Shirley Ryan, the best genealogist and living historian on the Mahanoy City area, I solicited the help of Richard Guinan Jr.'s daughter Kathryn (Kathy) Connolly and Frank Guinan's daughter Janet Cunningham to help with the project. For their research and writing I am most grateful. My uncle Lawrence (Larry) Guinan, age 90, patiently answered my questions and retold stories until I got them right, and my cousin Ceci Connolly lent her journalistic editing to the introduction. Although most of the pictures and postcards belong to family members, the following people must be thanked for rooting in attics and basements to find the pictures I wanted to tell the story of Lakewood: Mary Ellen Koval-Steeves, Marjorie Fletcher, Joseph Moore, Dale Freudenberger, Mary Althoff Koch and her sister Lois, Marle Becker for his help in contacting Bob Buchanan and John Kenley, the Knights of Lithuania and members Jim and Dot Setcavage, Helen McBrearty, Paula Duda Holoviak, Donald Coombe, Carolyn Jenkins, Marie Mokol Marlow, the Mayesky family, and Francis and Barbara Pedriani. Thanks also to the late Bob Skeath for his scrapbook memories, Tom Whalen for his keen eye in identifying people, my husband for proofreading, John "Puck" Sullivan for his wonderful eyewitness accounts, and, most importantly, Krista Gromalski, my local editor, who checked my style and grammar before it was submitted to our publisher.

Each person who reads this book has their own memories of Lakewood—picnics, rides, a dance, a kiss, and, many times, a spouse. I sincerely hope you will share those memories with me at peggrig@frontiernet.net. Unless otherwise noted, the images in this book are courtesy of the Guinan family.

—Peggy Grigalonis

INTRODUCTION

Louis Armstrong, Glenn Miller, and the Dorsey Brothers were regulars at Lakewood Park. Rudy Vallée, Vaughn Monroe, and Paul Whiteman broadcast live from its ballroom. Frank Sinatra and Doris Day were merely backup singers with the big bands. Bill Haley, Teresa Brewer, and Dick Clark brought rock and roll to swooning teenagers.

This is the story of Lakewood Park, a 70-year journey as thrilling as the amusement rides within it. From its World War I beginnings as a picnic site for weary coal miners to the raucous ethnic festivals of the 1970s, Lakewood served as a popular leisure-time mecca for the people of northeastern Pennsylvania and beyond.

Unlike many corporate amusement parks, Lakewood was owned and managed by the same family from 1916 until its closing in 1984. Today the park's original carousel is housed in a museum in Grand Rapids, Michigan, and its magnificent ballroom has been burned to the ground.

The 88-acre park, situated two hours north of Philadelphia in the heart of Pennsylvania coal country, was the brainchild of the Guinan brothers. Sons of an Irish immigrant miner and his wife, Richard and Daniel Guinan became entrepreneurs at an early age.

Richard Sr., after spending time as a boy in the mines, opened his first business driving a coffee and tea cart around the Mahanoy City area. With the help of his bookish brother, he built two department stores, one in Mahanoy City and another in neighboring Mount Carmel.

Daniel I, meanwhile, became a banker, real estate developer, school superintendent and congressional candidate. Living with the Richard Guinan Sr. family, he became the family's mentor in finance and politics and the Guinan boys' beloved uncle who traveled with them throughout the United States.

As the United States' involvement in World War I was about to begin and the coal towns were flourishing, the brothers purchased a vast tract of farmland in Ryan Township with the idea of developing an amusement park. Within the first five years, Lakewood featured women's and men's bathhouses, a boathouse and dock, campgrounds, picnic pavilions, water pump stations, food stands, an icehouse, and a large dance pavilion.

Each day from May to September, patrons boarded trains in towns such as Tamaqua and Shenandoah for the short ride to the Lakeside Junction railroad station. Swimming meets, diving competitions, fireworks, alligator wrestlers, and celebrities like Buster Crabbe (Tarzan) attracted bathers and spectators to the new park. Professional swim coaches arrived from Florida to train the local kids.

In 1925, the Lakewood Ballroom—known to most as the dance hall—was erected. Big bands traveling between Chicago and New York City began making weekly stops at the growing dance capital. Thursdays became dance night, date night, and the night to plan for all week in the coal region and beyond.

The early sound system comprised a microphone and two small speakers. But the hall—with its vaulted ceiling and wooden arches—provided excellent natural acoustics for the bands and their soloists.

As the new ballroom was being built, the man-made lake was divided into a pool—three times the length of an Olympic pool—and an adjacent lake for canoes. A toboggan, 33-foot-high diving tower, stationary rafts, and sprinklers were added.

In those early years, the children of the founders were being trained. A program for the ballroom of 1925 to 1929 details the management team: Daniel Guinan II (age 15), assistant ballroom manager; Richard Guinan Jr. (13), interior decorator; and Francis Guinan (11), ticket collector. Apparently Larry, at age 9, was deemed too young to work! After college, Daniel II and Richard Jr., joined by their two younger brothers, took on the management of the park.

As the park grew so did the surrounding community of Park Crest. Some of the earliest settlers were the men and women who manned the amusement rides: the Fogarty family, whose son John ran the park's train, Susie Burke, operator of the carousel, and his brother Red Burke, always at the controls of the Hey Dey.

Young entrepreneurs like the Mayesky and Althoff families built homes across the road from the park. A horse stable was built by the Reed family in Park Crest, and Peter and Olga Lastowsky (Chopsy's) built a variety store and operated the fishpond in the park.

Ethnic music and food are part of the fiber of the coal region. Building on the success of Lithuanian Day, believed to be the longest-running ethnic festival in Pennsylvania, Lakewood organized several other ethnic festivals—Ukrainian, Italian, Russian, Bavarian, and Irish—each drawing crowds from surrounding states.

In 1948, a 750-seat, air-conditioned theater was built for the legendary John Kenley, producer and founder of New York City summer stock plays. Only the stars came in for the week's show; the house actors were young talents like Tom Poston of Bob Newhart fame. Each week, the house actors performed one play onstage while rehearsing for the next week's play across the walk in the ballroom. Highlights include performances by Lana Turner and apprentice Alan Alda.

Donald Coombe remembers locals were a supporting cast to the Lakewood Theater. In Coombe's words, Kenley bought his gas and joined in the conversation at Brownie's Gas Station. One day he asked Joe "Brownie" Mayesky to pick up Shelley Winters in Philadelphia to bring her to the theater for her appearance in the play *Born Yesterday*. Folks at the time assumed that Kenley asked Mayesky because he drove a flashy yellow convertible. Theater records indicate the date as June 6, 1950. Winters had broken all records at the Paramount Theatre in New York right before coming to Lakewood. Many of the stars stayed in local homes because they were not provided with a car. Jackie Cooper lived over Witkowski's Bar for a week, enjoying center stage at the bar and at the theater.

The theater, much like the ballroom, brought a dose of big-city glamour to rural Pennsylvania. By day, the stars sunbathed at the Lakewood pool, and in the wee hours, they frequented the local bars and restaurants—at least 15 of them—located within walking distance of the park and open after the dances. Bars like Applegate's, Margaret's, Witkowski's, Ogrodnick's, and the Log Cabin served homemade food and white lightning moonshine.

Early images included in this collection are the park grounds before the pool was constructed, the original toboggan, the ornately carved horses from the original carousel, Dick Clark greeting the crowds, and the ballroom decorated for the Bavarian Oktoberfest festival. Autographed pictures of big band leaders and Broadway stars include a photograph of local natives Tommy and Jimmy Dorsey, Theresa "Mom" Dorsey, and Julia Guinan and her four sons on the occasion of Mom Dorsey's 80th birthday bash at the Lakewood Ballroom.

When it closed in 1984, Lakewood Park had hosted Xavier Cugat, Guy Lombardo, Clarabell, Zippy the chimpanzee, and Sally Starr. Red Buttons and Veronica Lake had acted in its theater, Jack Palance kissed babies, Frankie Laine danced in a marathon, Muhammad Ali appeared at a fund-raiser, governors spoke at its banquets, romances flourished on its dance floor, and high school students held their proms there, riding the amusements in gowns and tuxedoes. Wrestling alligators, bathing beauties, dance marathons, the Grand Irish Jubilee, and the Bavarian Festival—it all happened at Lakewood Park.

One

IN THE BEGINNING

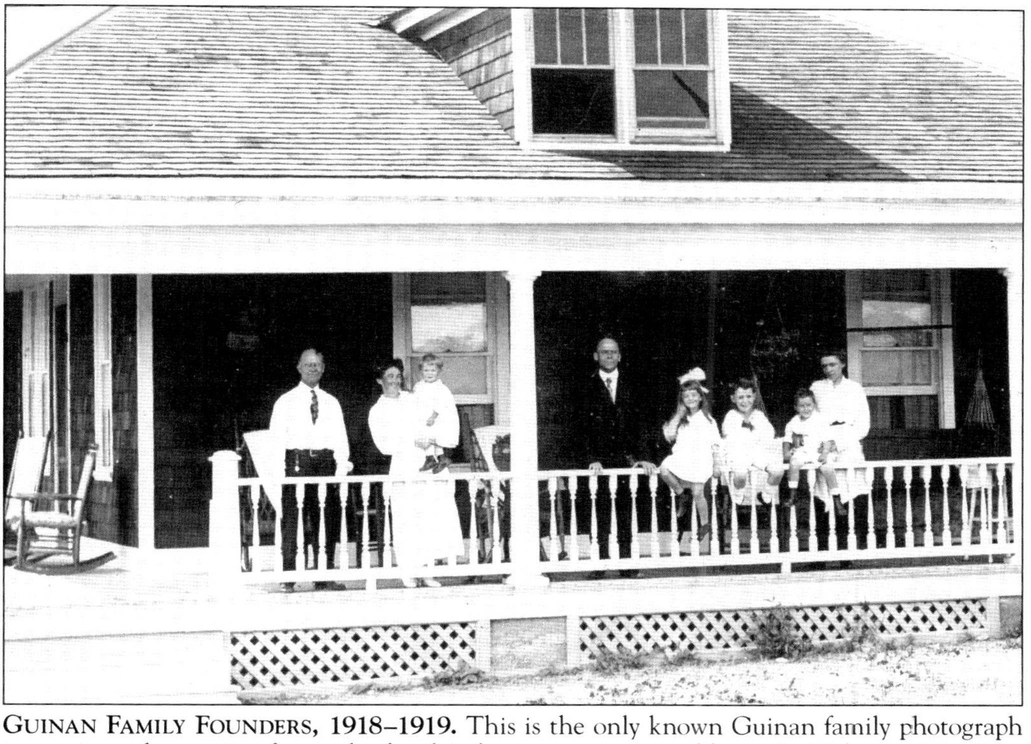

GUINAN FAMILY FOUNDERS, 1918–1919. This is the only known Guinan family photograph to survive a devastating fire to the family's department store and home in Mahanoy City. The photograph was taken on the porch of the Guinans' summer bungalow in nearby Barnesville. Pictured are, from left to right, Richard Guinan Sr.; Julia Guinan, wife of Richard; Francis (Frank) Guinan (in mother Julia's arms); Daniel Guinan I, brother of Richard, Richard and Julia's children Catherine, Daniel II, and Richard Jr.; and nursemaid, housekeeper, and friend Kate Bier. Richard and Julia's youngest son, Larry, was born in 1919. Catherine, their oldest, died shortly after this photograph was taken.

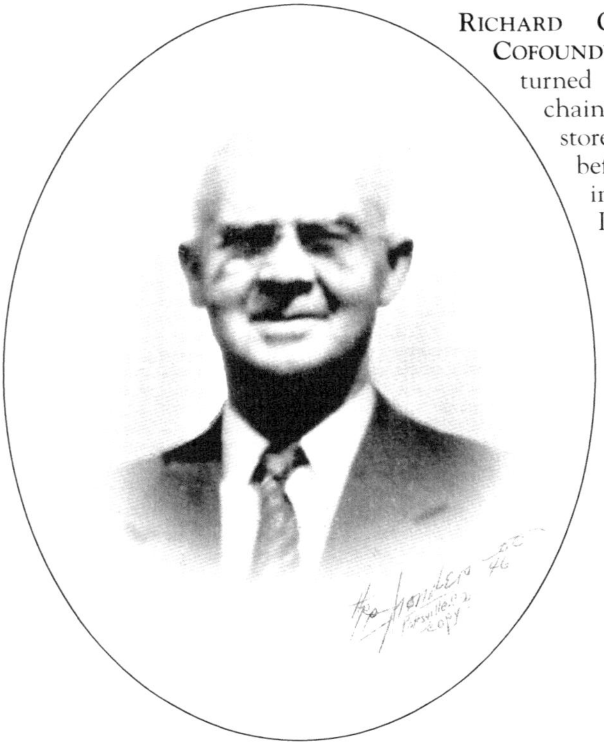

RICHARD GUINAN SR., LAKEWOOD PARK COFOUNDER. Richard Guinan Sr. had already turned a coffee cart business into a small chain of successful three-story department stores in Mahanoy City and Mount Carmel before creating Lakewood Park in 1916 in Barnesville with his brother Daniel. It was the brothers' combined talents, along with the warmth, legendary generosity, and kindness of Richard's wife, Julia, that drew crowds to their many endeavors.

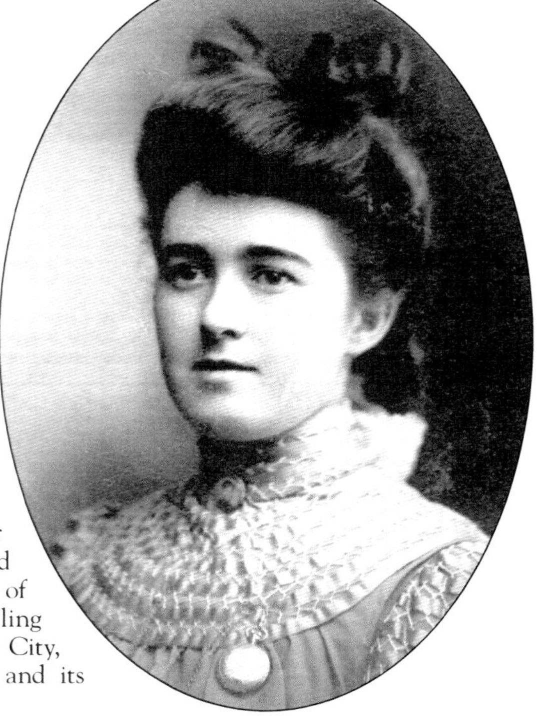

JULIA GUINAN. A schoolteacher before her marriage to Lakewood Park cofounder Richard Guinan Sr., Julia Guinan managed a family of five children, was in charge of buying and selling at Guinan's Department Store in Mahanoy City, and kept daily records of Lakewood Park and its dance hall.

DANIEL GUINAN I, LAKEWOOD PARK COFOUNDER. Daniel Guinan I was an educator, superintendent of schools, real estate investor, politician, and banker who loved to travel with his nephews to Atlantic City, Florida, and national parks in the West. Of all the Guinan boys' memories, their admiration and love for their uncle Daniel is what they remember most.

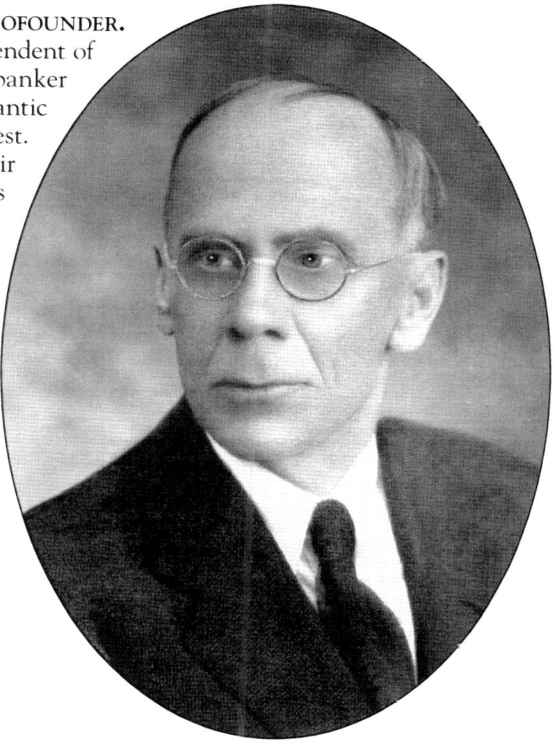

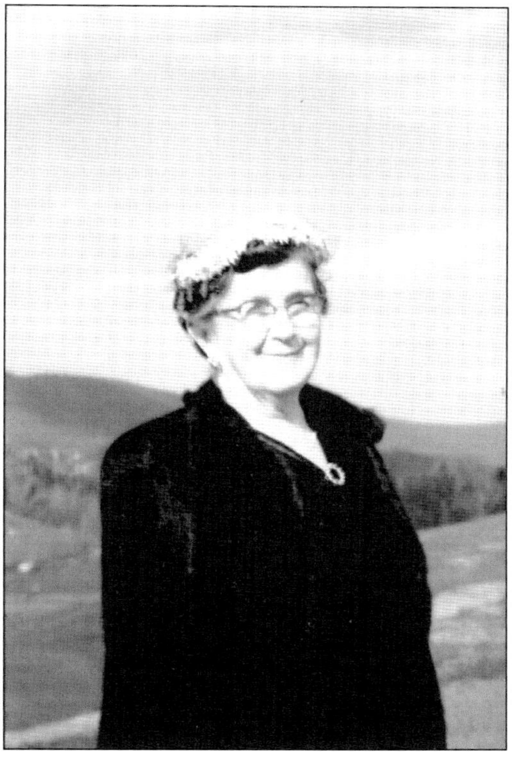

GENEROUS JULIA GUINAN. Julia Guinan was renowned for her generosity to her store customers. She frequently sent a first communion dress or piece of furniture as a gift to her most loyal patrons. Seeing a need for a Catholic church in the area surrounding Lakewood Park, Julia donated a former tennis clubhouse for use as a chapel. As the congregation grew, Julia donated land for a church to be built. During the early years of the church, the pastor lived at the Guinan bungalow as the family's guest.

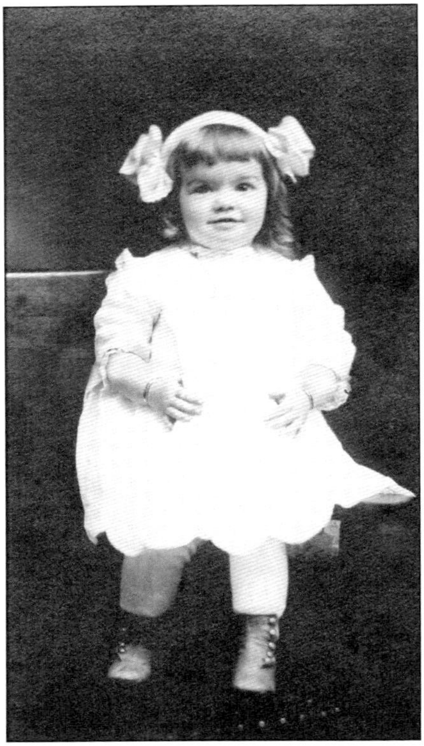

CATHERINE GUINAN. The oldest child of Richard and Julia Guinan, Catherine Guinan was born in 1910 and died at the age of eight from appendicitis. Kate Bier, Julia's housekeeper and lifelong friend, always said that Julia was never the same after the death of her only daughter.

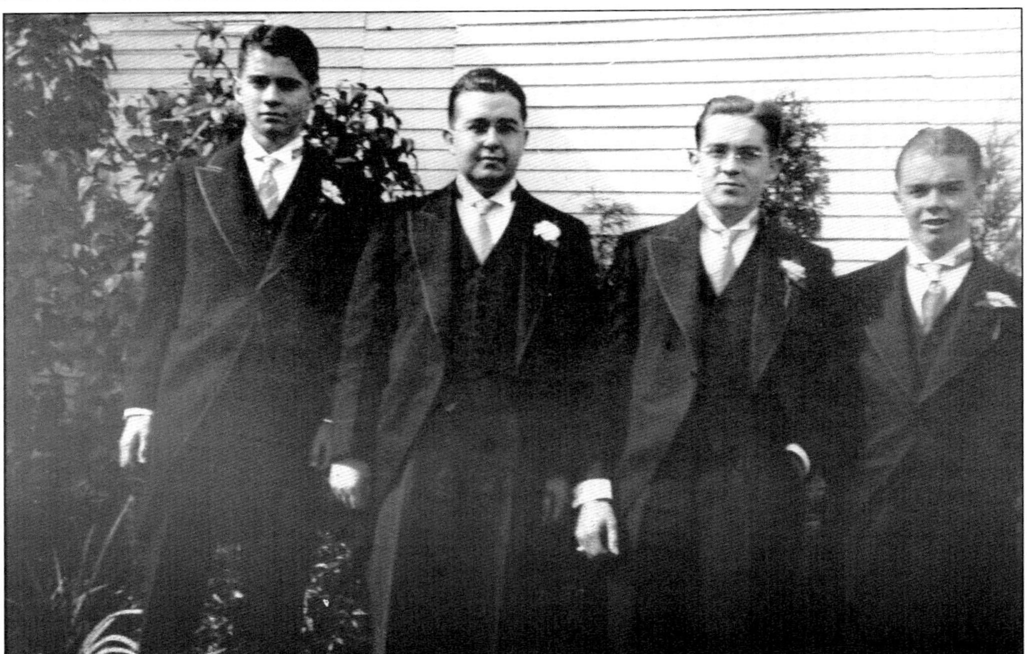

THE FOUR SONS, 1937. Pictured outside the Lakewood Ballroom on the occasion of Richard Guinan Jr.'s marriage to Josephine Kurtz are the four surviving children of Richard and Julia Guinan: from left to right, Larry, the youngest; Daniel II, the oldest; Richard Jr.; and Frank.

DANIEL GUINAN II FAMILY, 1957. Richard and Julia Guinan's oldest son, Daniel Guinan II, is pictured with his wife, Margaret, and two children, Peggy and Danny. Guinan was postmaster of Mahanoy City and served on the Pennsylvania National Bank Board of Directors most of his adult life. At Lakewood Park, Guinan booked entertainment, promoted the park in advertising, wrote and published the weekly *Melodyland*, brought Broadway to Lakewood, and made investment decisions for the family.

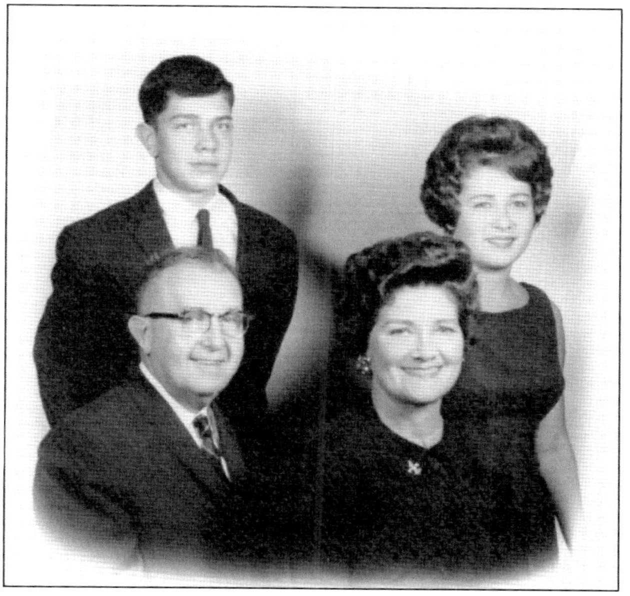

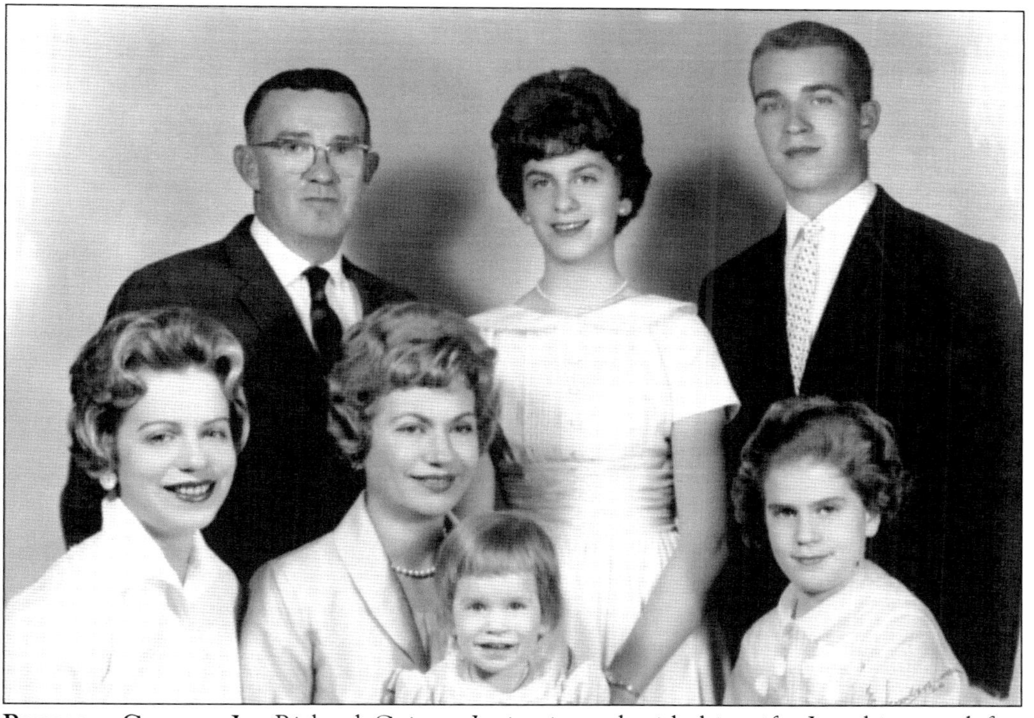

RICHARD GUINAN JR. Richard Guinan Jr. is pictured with his wife, Josephine, and five children, from left to right, Kathy, Patricia (P. J.), Mary, Elizabeth (Liz), and Richard (Richie). Upon graduation, he immediately moved to Mount Carmel and took over the reins of the newly opened department store. His reputation was that of a fair and compassionate businessman, and, endowed with the entrepreneurial spirit of his father, he devoted himself to his family, the amusement park business, Mount Carmel's industrial community, and the Liberty State Bank, serving as bank president for a time.

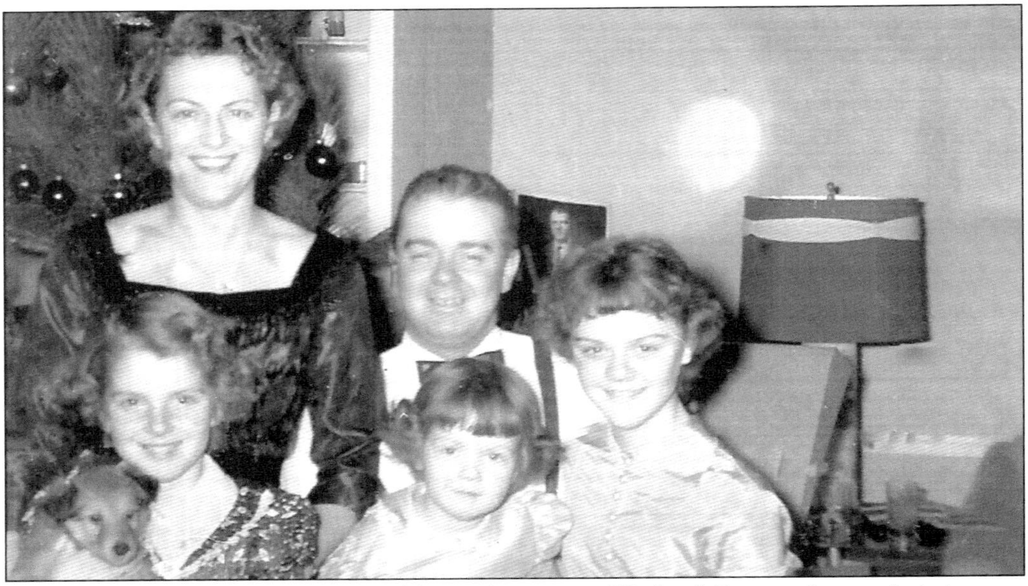

FRANK GUINAN. Frank Guinan and his wife, Patricia Wayland Guinan, began their journey together in the Washington, D.C., area. Frank graduated from Catholic University Law School in 1940 while Patricia worked in the banking industry. Soon afterward, the couple settled near West Palm Beach, Florida, only to return to Mahanoy City a year later to help with the family business. Frank and Patricia are pictured with their children, Janet Cunningham, Nancy Guinan, and Patti Lucyk.

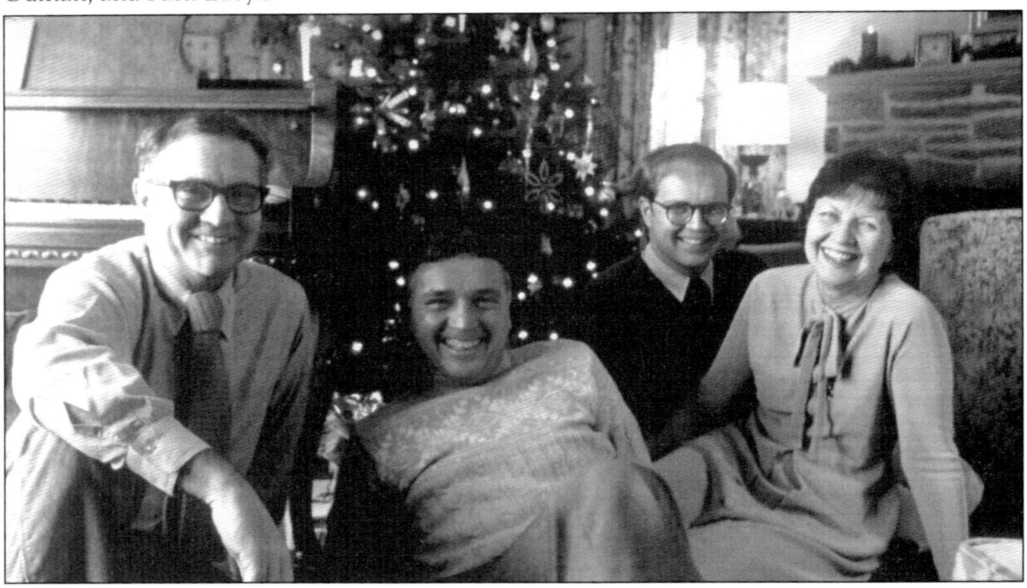

LARRY GUINAN. Pictured here from left to right are Larry Guinan, Eddie Fanelli (Marjorie's brother), Larry and Marjorie's son Jack, and Marjorie Fanelli Guinan. Like his brothers before him, Larry went to Catholic University, where he studied liberal arts. At the outbreak of World War II, Larry joined the U.S. Navy, ending the war as a lieutenant, senior grade. Upon returning home, Larry worked at the Guinan's Department Store, Mahanoy City, until its closing. He lives today near Lakewood, where his memories of the park are still vivid.

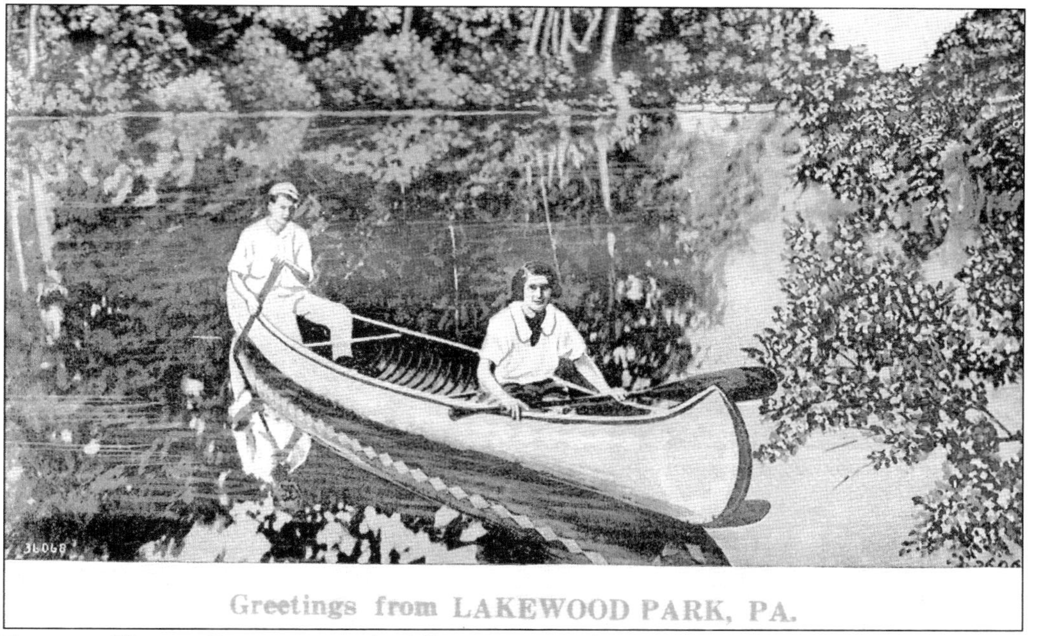

EARLIEST KNOWN POSTCARDS. The following series of postcards, from around 1917, is the only known record of Lakewood Park's original design by Richard and Daniel Guinan. Most visitors walked from the railroad stop on the southern end of the park to the man-made lake where boating and picnicking were popular.

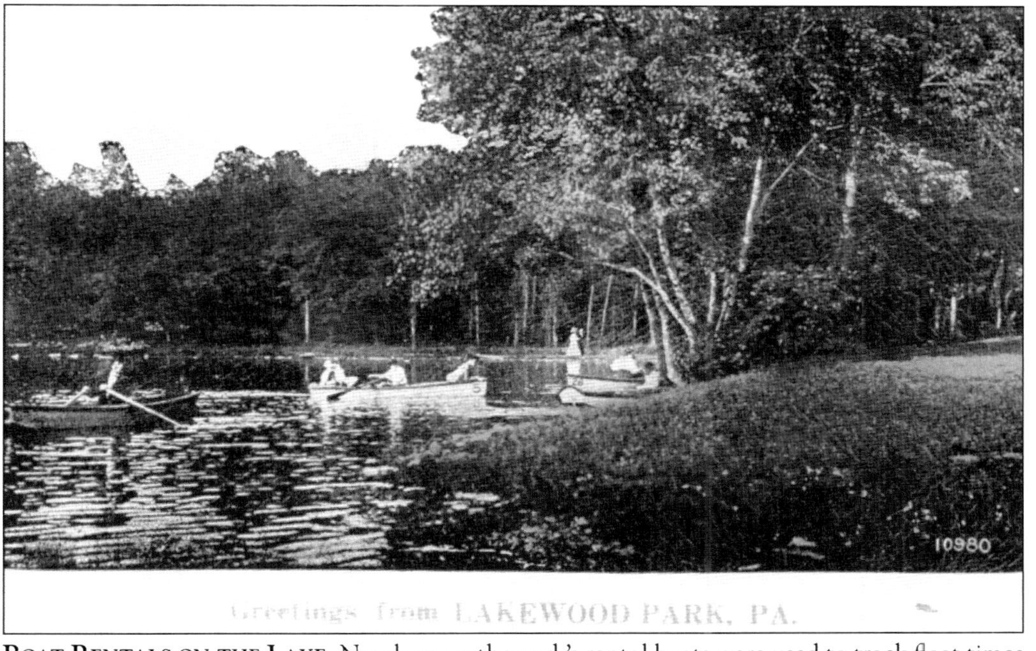

BOAT RENTALS ON THE LAKE. Numbers on the park's rental boats were used to track float times and to call boaters in when their rides were finished. Park visitors often dressed formally for a day in the country. In this *c.* 1917 photograph, one gentleman wears a high top hat (foreground), while a woman in a long dress strolls with her beau (background).

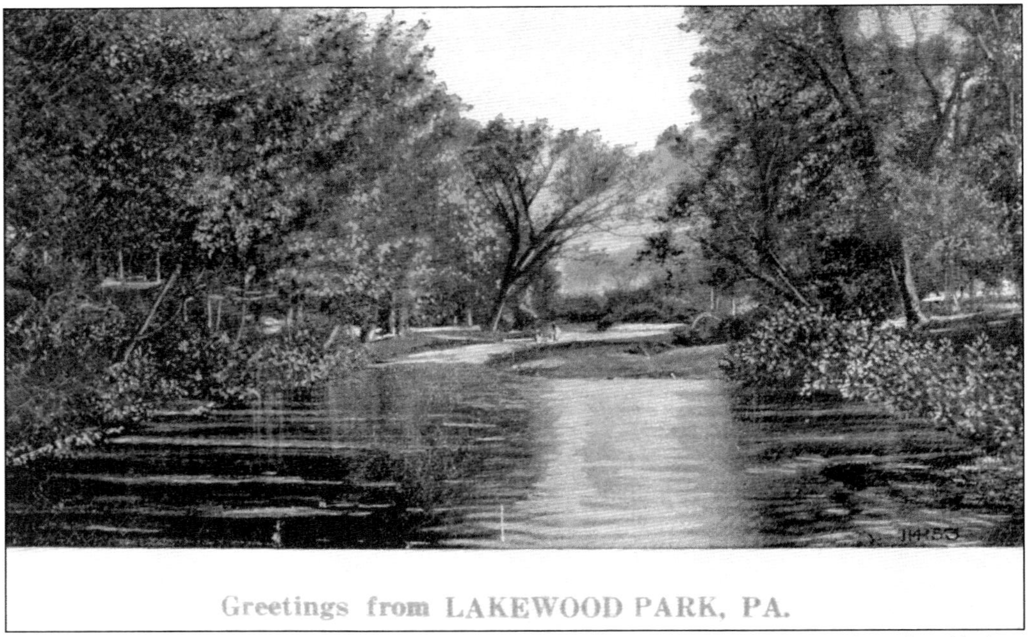

STREAM THROUGH KIDDIELAND. The stream that flowed through Lakewood Park added to the bucolic scene enjoyed by thousands of visitors. Throughout the park's history, picnickers kept their watermelons cool in the stream, and on ethnic celebration days, such as the annual Lithuanian Day held every August, teams competed in games of tug-of-war across its water.

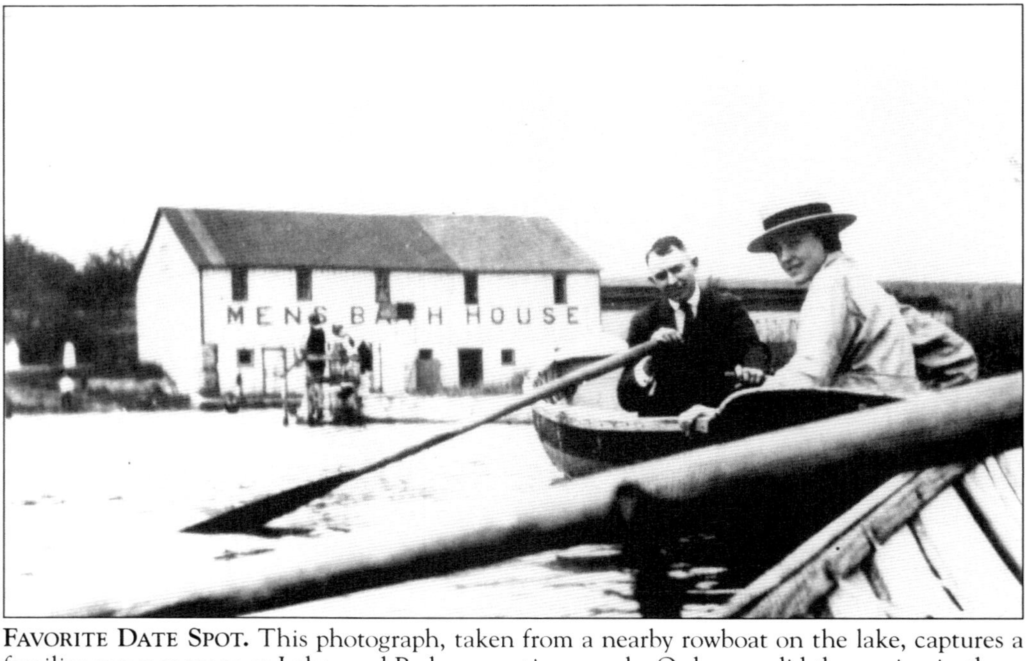

FAVORITE DATE SPOT. This photograph, taken from a nearby rowboat on the lake, captures a familiar summer scene at Lakewood Park: a courting couple. Only men did the rowing in those days, fully dressed in suit and tie.

EARLY ADVERTISING LITHOGRAPH, C. 1916. This photograph of an original lithograph was discovered in 2003 when Janet Cunningham and her husband George were cleaning the attic of their Barnesville home. The Cunninghams live in the bungalow of Janet's grandparents Richard and Julia Guinan. The lithograph (42 inches by 32 inches) was professionally restored and placed under protective glass. It is now a focal point and historical conversation piece that is displayed proudly in the Cunningham home.

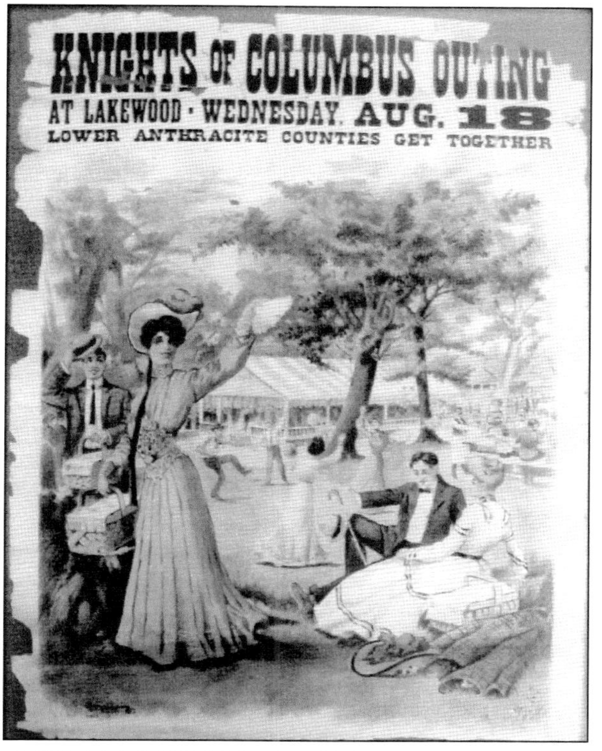

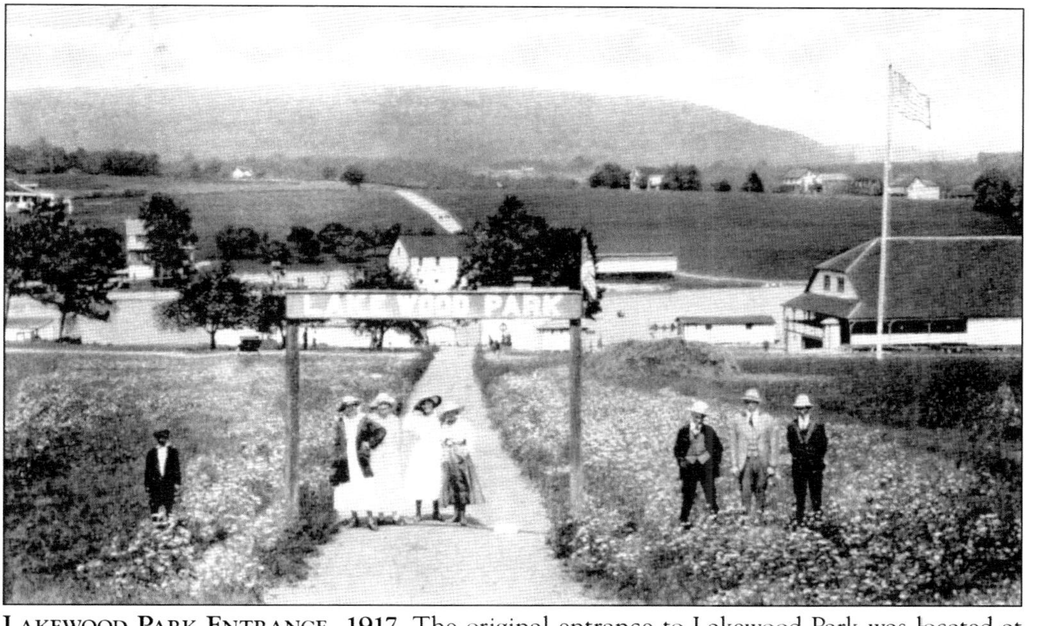

LAKEWOOD PARK ENTRANCE, 1917. The original entrance to Lakewood Park was located at the southern end of the park near the Pennsylvania and Reading Railroad tracks. The path led to the picnic groves, lake, and bathing areas. The building with the flag in front (right) is the original dance hall, or, as it was called then, the dance pavilion. A boathouse and bathhouses for changing clothes and showering were located along the lake.

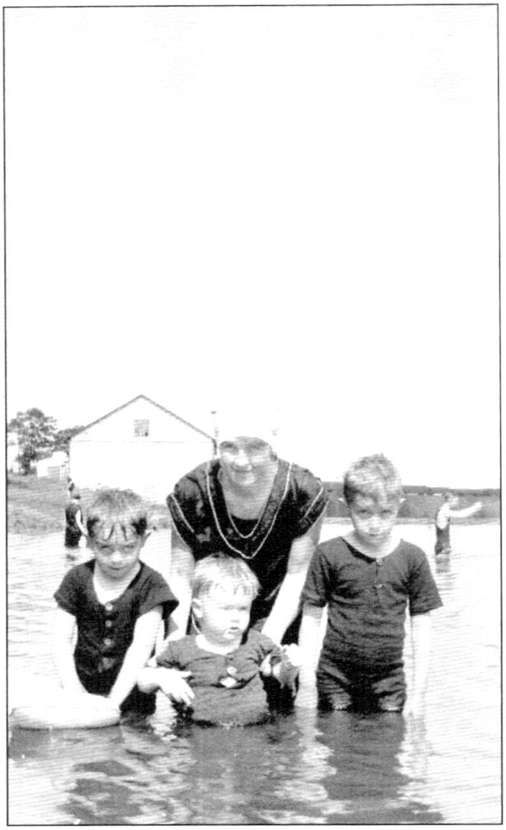

LAKEWOOD BEFORE THE POOL. Julia Guinan (in bathing cap), wife of Lakewood Park cofounder Richard Guinan Sr., enjoys a dip in the lake with three of her sons, from left to right, Richard Jr., Frank, and Daniel II. The men's bathhouse is visible in the distance.

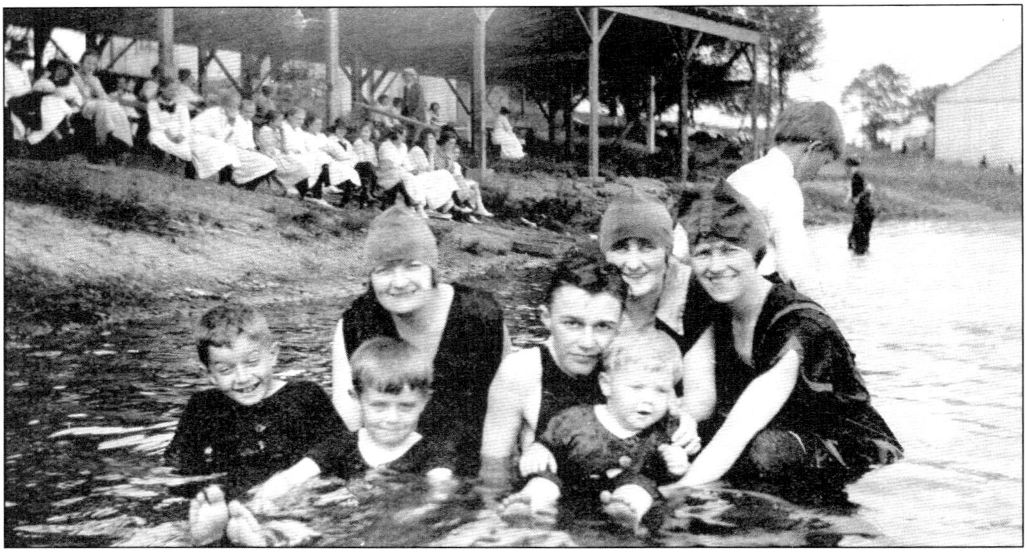

SWIMSUIT FASHION. Unlike today's swimwear, swimming suit fashion of the early 1900s was typically black, heavy, and woolen. The Guinans' three oldest boys (front row) swim with unidentified adults. In the background, numerous park visitors sit in the shade almost totally covered in their dress whites.

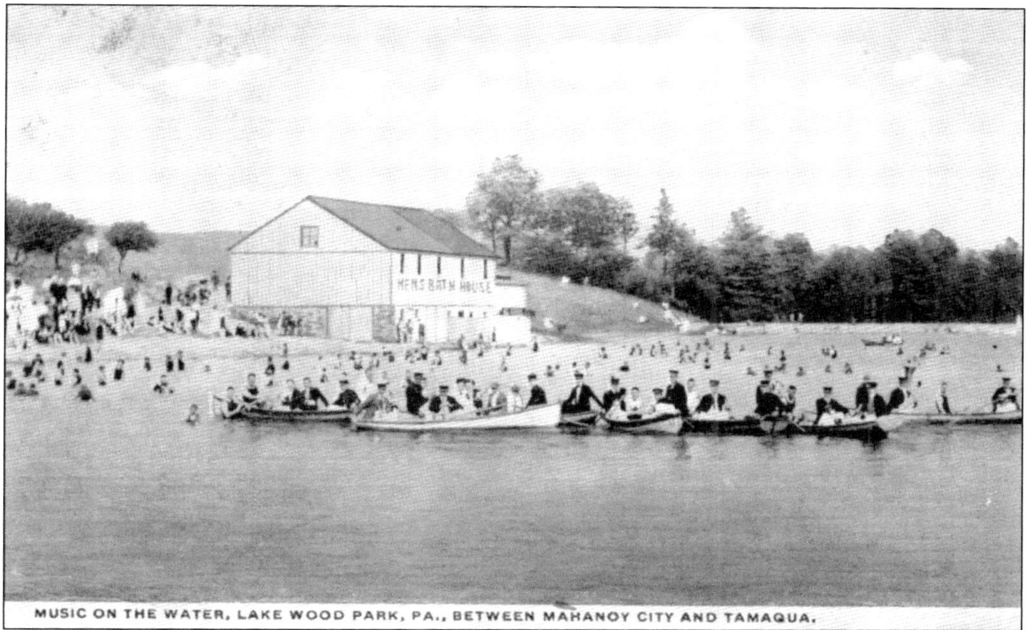

MUSIC ON THE WATER, C. 1919. Many of the men and women from communities near Lakewood Park enjoyed the facility's popular musical performances. Pictured are a flotilla of musicians entertaining park visitors.

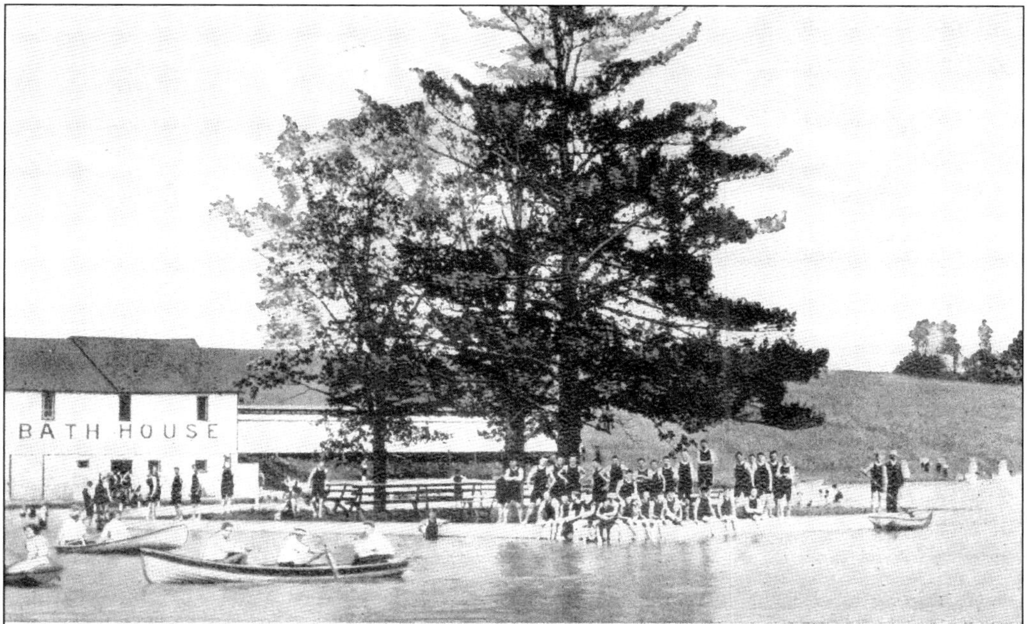

PARK IMPROVEMENTS. Lakewood Park's facilities were constantly being updated. Around 1919, an island was built in the middle of the lake using concrete and sand. It was used by both swimmers and boaters. Within a few years, the island became the site of the diving tower and pit area in the new swimming pool.

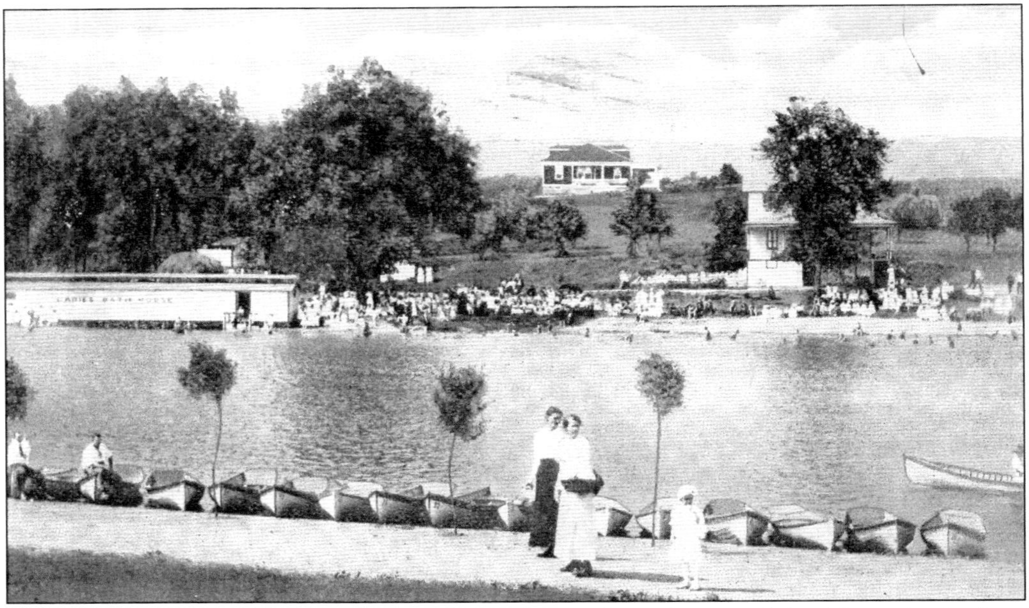

LAKEWOOD PARK, 1920S. This postcard provides northward views of the lake with the boat launch in the foreground. The ladies' bathhouse and swimming area are visible in the middle, and the newly built Guinan family bungalow is visible on the hill in the distance. The home in the middle right was the homestead of Daniel Flynn, who sold the original site to the Guinans and a local contractor named Campion.

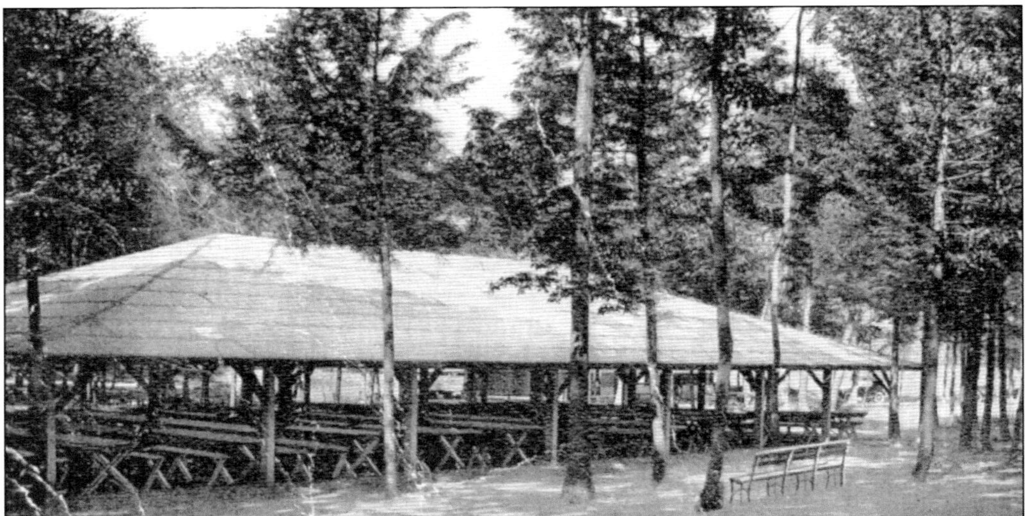

LUNCH BUILDING. By 1919, large sheds were built to afford park guests shade and protection from the rain. Approximately 50 picnic tables were provided under this shed, which was a popular location for family reunions and outings of groups such as Boy Scout troops, churches, and fraternal organizations. The picnic tables were available free of charge on a first-come basis. Local resident Bernie Marchalonis remembers sleeping on top of the tables to guarantee a picnicking spot for his family's Lithuanian Day ethnic celebration. Many families camped out prior to a large gathering and chained their tables together to reserve them for the following day.

FUN ON THE SLIDING BOARD. Times were simpler 90 years ago. Children dressed in white to picnic in the grass and to ride Lakewood Park's sliding board. Despite the heat, teenage boys wore jackets, shirts, and ties to a summer outing; girls wore cotton leggings (stockings).

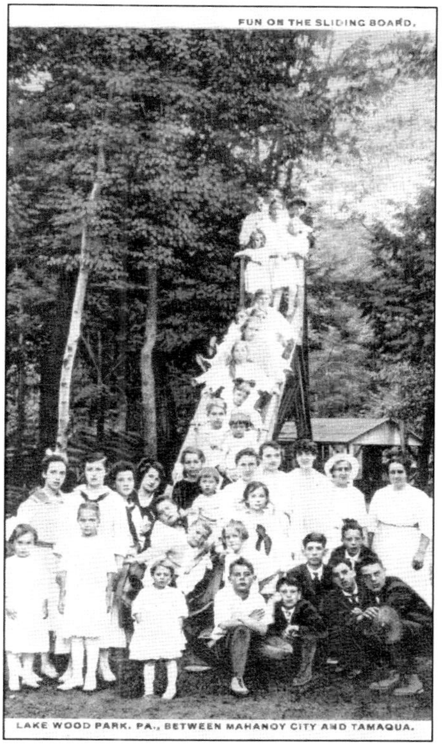

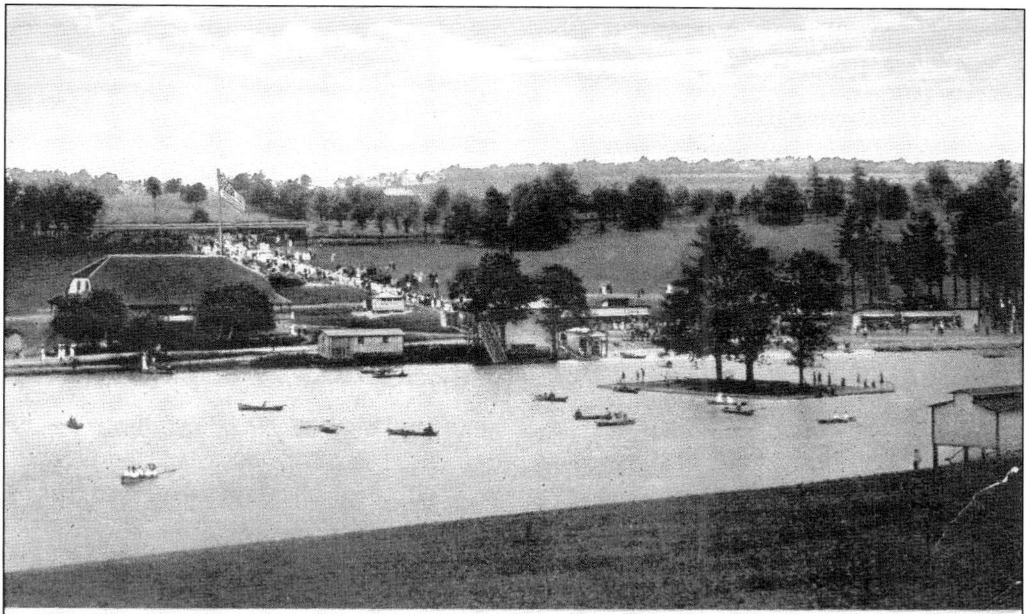

PICTURESQUE PARK. This postcard provides a sweeping view of Lakewood Park in 1919, with its large lake and man-made island in the right center. The building at left center with the flag on top is the original dance hall where many famous big band musicians performed. To the right of the hall is the walkway leading from the railroad station to the lake.

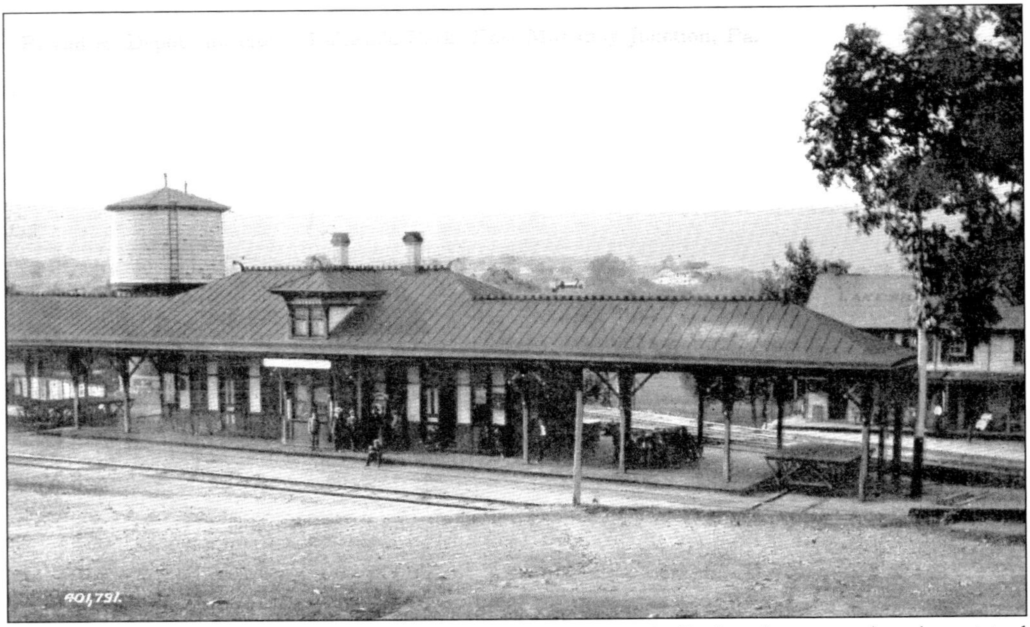

Pennsylvania and Reading Railroad Junction, 1908. Railroad transit played a critical role in the development of Lakewood Park and its counterpart, Lakeside Park, both situated within a mile of each other. It was a short walk down a scenic path from the railroad station to either park. As Lakewood's popularity grew, the train stopped at Lakewood Park, eliminating the need for visitors to walk the path.

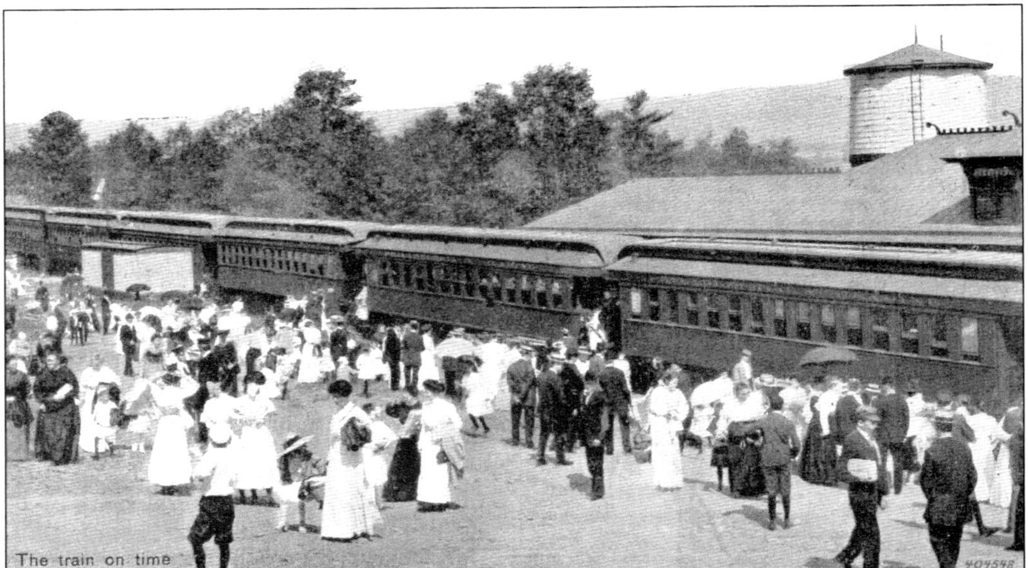

On Track to Lakewood. These passenger railcars are typical of the kind advertised in local newspapers as an easy method of transport for park visitors. Nine passenger cars were added to the Reading and Northern Railroad to comfortably carry thousands of park visitors from the Pennsylvania anthracite coal mining towns of Mount Carmel, Shenandoah, and Mahanoy City. Special trains also ran from nearby Tamaqua. (Courtesy of Dale Freudenberger.)

TRAIN SCHEDULE. This train schedule for the annual Father Mathew Pioneer Corps picnic appeared in the local newspaper, the *Record American*, on July 20, 1921.

FATHER MATHEW PIONEER CORPS ANNUAL OUTING

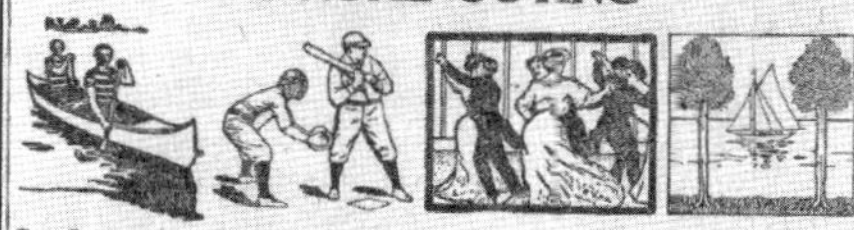

Lakewood Park **July 21, 1921**

TRAIN SCHEDULE
TO LAKEWOOD

Leave	A.M.	A.M.	P.M.	P.M.	P.M.
St. Nicholas	8.45	10.15	12.30	3.15	6.10
Mahanoy City	s9.00	s10.25	s12.45	s3.25	s6.20
Buck Mountain . . .	s9.10	s10.33	s12.55	s3.33	s6.28
Lakewood, arrive . .	9.19	10.43	1.05	3.43	6.36

FROM LAKEWOOD

Leave	P.M.	P.M.	P.M.	P.M.
Lakewood	5.10	7.00	8.20	10.00
Buck Mountain	s5.21	s7.11	s8.31	s10.11
Mahanoy City	s5.27	s7.17	s8.37	s10.17
St. Nicholas	5.37	7.23	8.43	10.23

Note—"s" indicates Stop. Special Trains will stop at Lakewood Park. Baggage car for baskets on train leaving Lakewood at 7:00 P. M.

SPORTING EVENTS

The following program has been arranged by the Sporting Committee:

1—Potato Race (for Ladies) . . . . Start 1.30 P.M.
2—Bag Race (for Men) . . . . Start 1.45 P.M.
3—Three-legged Race (for Men) . . . . Start 2.00 P.M.
4—Fifty-yard Dash (for Ladies) . . . . . Start 2.15 P.M.
5—Tug of War (for Men) . . . . Start 2.30 P.M.
6—Baseball Game—Town vs. Township—Start 2.45 P.M.

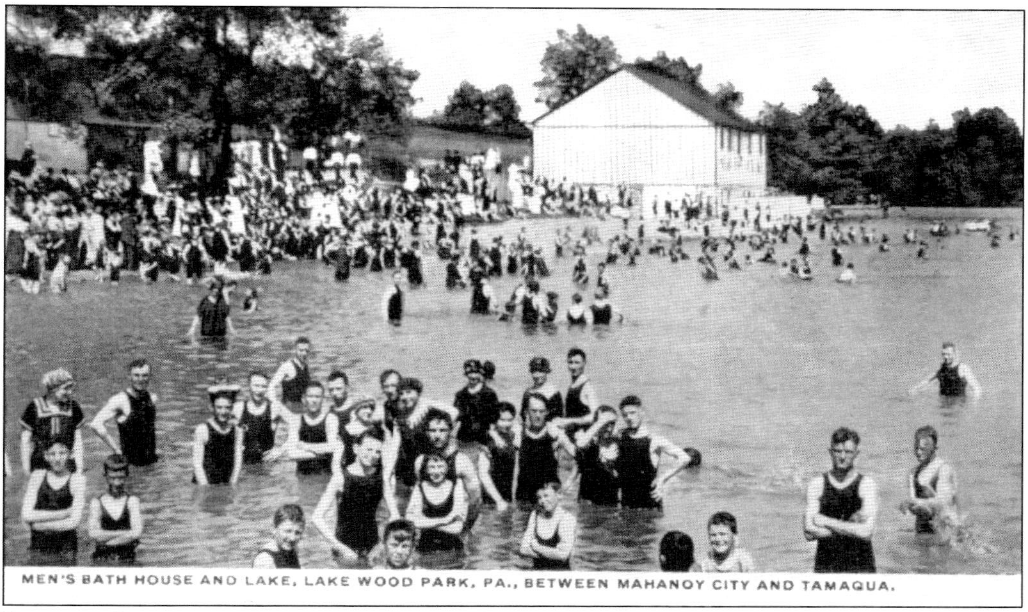

PIONEER OUTING. Centenarian John "Puck" Sullivan, coal region historian, tells about his experience as a kid in the 1920s this way in the *Evening Herald*: "Most kids in my day got to the park once a year which was when your church held a picnic. Our church affair, always held in mid July was called the Pioneer Outing. We saved up for it by picking and selling huckleberries which earned us enough for the swimming pool, the rides, doggies, Larkin's Ice Cream and Ryan's temperance. That was in addition to all the fine fare in the family picnic basket."

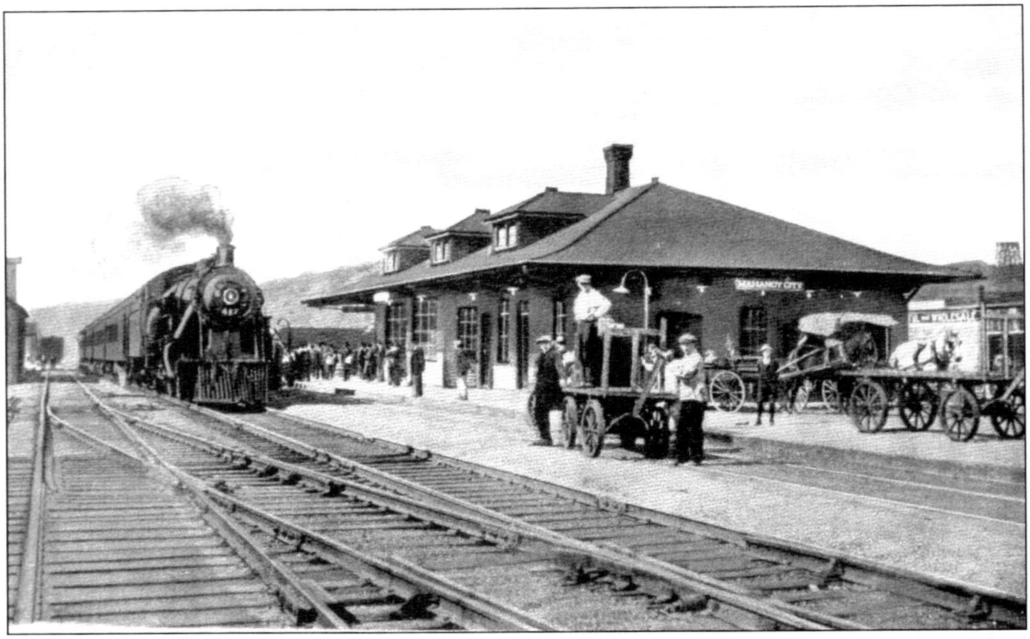

TRAIN. Pictured is the Pennsylvania and Reading Railroad station in Mahanoy City, located on an elevated platform near Main and Centre Streets, where passengers boarded for the five-mile ride through the Vulcan Tunnel and on to Lakewood Park. Riders were always reminded to keep their arms inside the cars when approaching the tunnel.

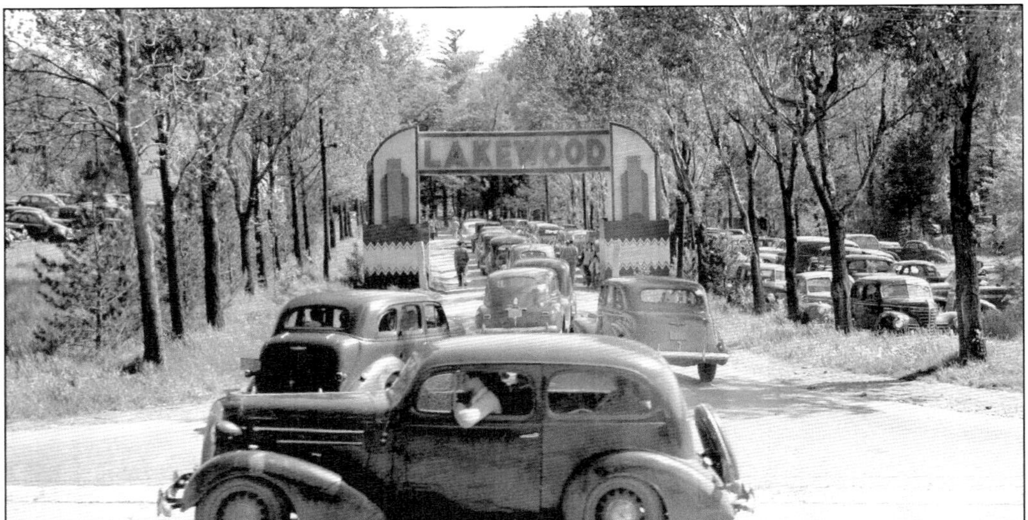

TRAFFIC COMING TO THE BOXING MATCHES. Puck Sullivan describes the boxing matches during the 1930s as something not to be forgotten. Under the leadership of A. P. "Beaut" McLaughlin and Herbie Noakes, Lakewood's were among the best fight cards ever presented. One of the greatest was the battle royal between two of the toughest men to set foot inside any ring, Iron Mike Kushwara of Morea Patch and Matt Rice of Gilberton. Rice won. According to Sullivan, "No one thrilled us more than the immortal Pat Igo, Shenandoah's 'Bertin Harp,' who was always colorful."

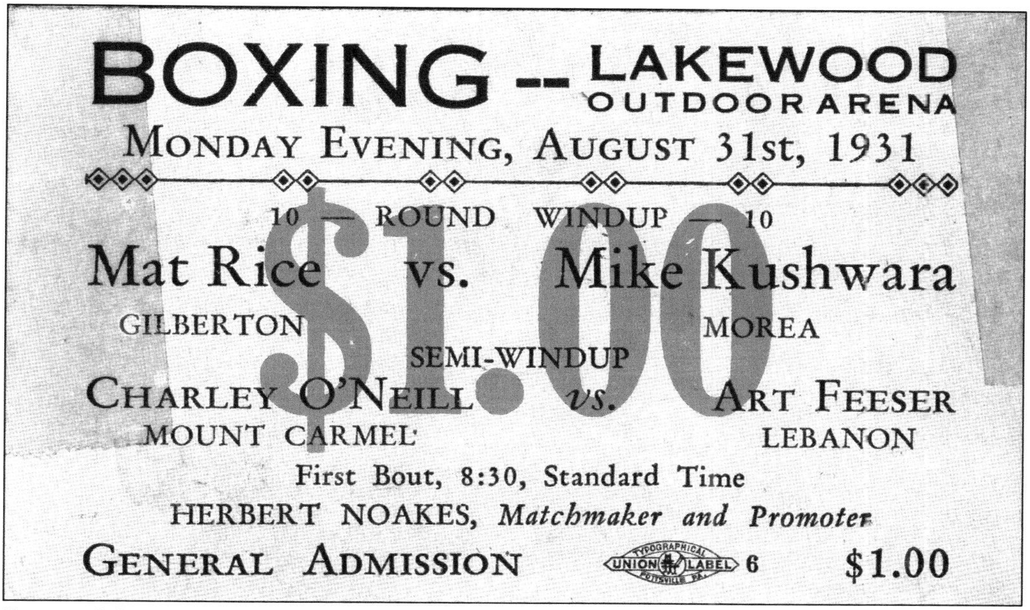

BOXING MATCHES, EARLY 1930S. Boxing matches were Lakewood Park attractions that drew large crowds. In a ring located across from the roller coaster, Iron Mike Kushwara and many other boxers fought all willing challengers.

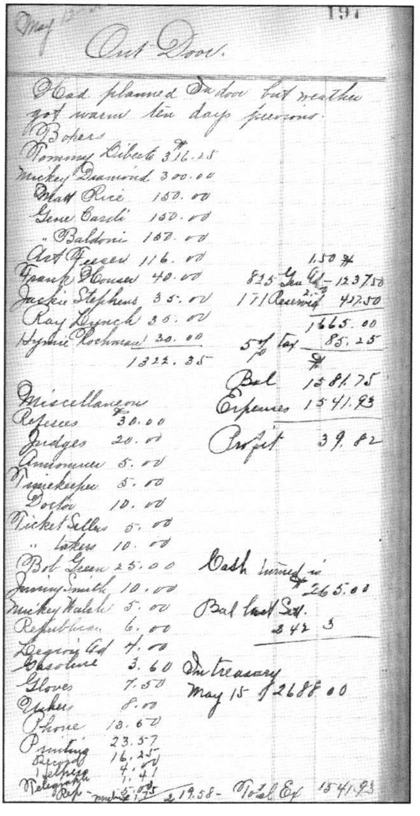

JULIA'S DIARY. Throughout her married life, Julia Guinan kept a diary of park business and activities. The most detailed entries occurred from May to September, summer season at Lakewood. This entry from Guinan's ledger features a boxing card, from May, recording expenses for the announcer, judge, referee, doctor, and ticket seller. Profit for the evening was $39.

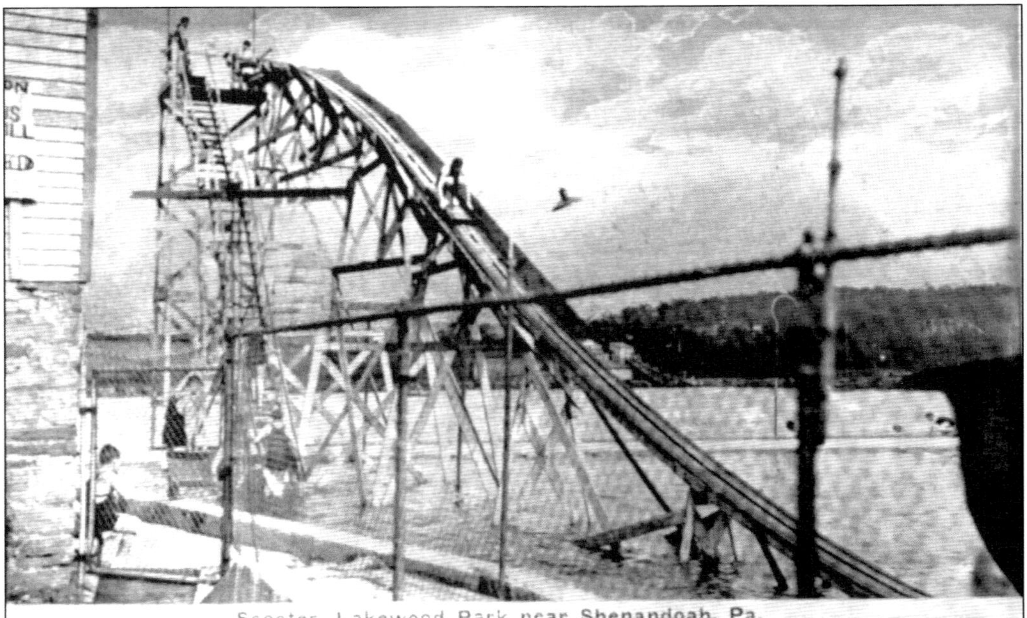

THE TOBOGGAN, C. 1929. Referred to as the scooter when it was first installed, the toboggan ride was located in the Lakewood Park pool for 30 years. Riders had to be strong enough to carry the heavy wooden toboggans up at least 30 steps. After the thrilling descent, riders were treated to a 100-foot glide over the water. Amazingly, no one was ever injured on the toboggan.

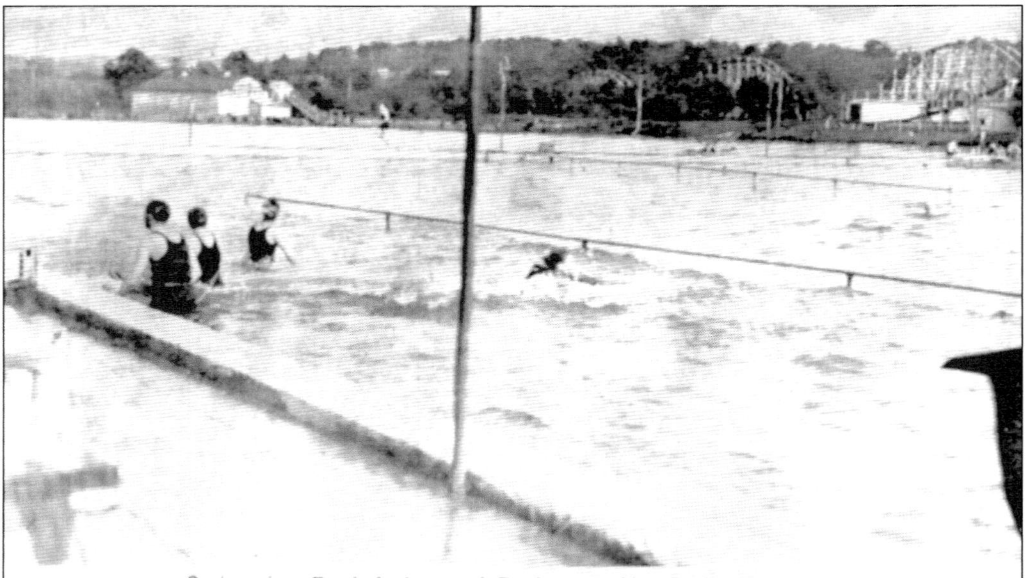

PREDECESSOR OF THE FLUME. Riders and swimmers at the bottom of Lakewood's toboggan attraction had to hurry out of the way or risk getting hit from the next descending toboggan. Invented in the early 1920s, the toboggan was the early predecessor of today's amusement park flume rides. Visible in the distance are the roller coaster and the icehouse, where frozen lake water was harvested during winter and stored for use all summer.

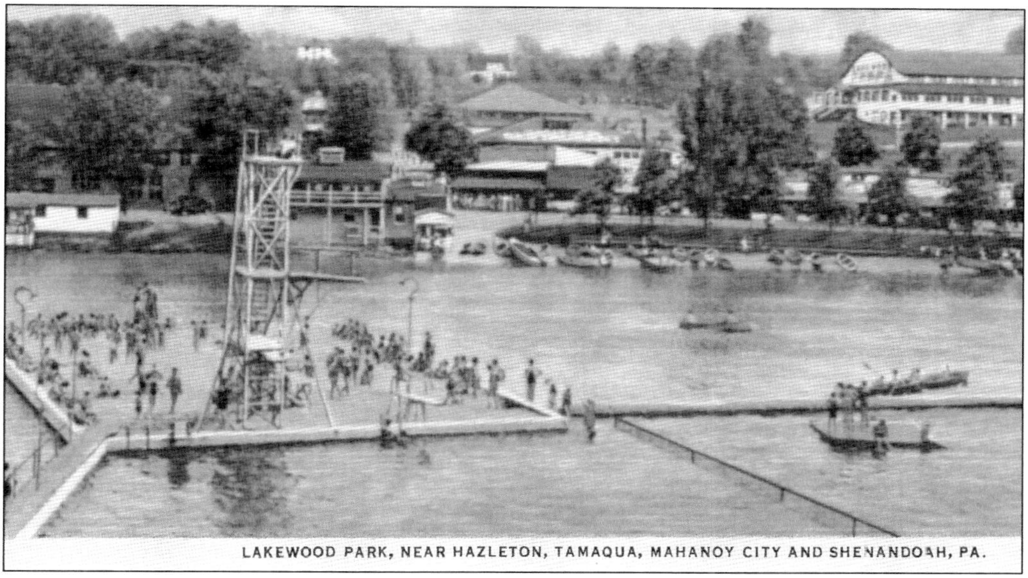

HEYDAYS OF THE 1940S. This classic postcard image features many popular highlights of Lakewood Park. On the left is the island with the diving tower. At front right is a raft used by swimmers for floating and for enjoying a playful water game that involved jumping up and down on the raft in an attempt to knock other swimmers into the pool. Directly behind the raft, the wall separating the pool from the lake is visible. Boats line the lake's shore and the midway, featuring food and carnival stands.

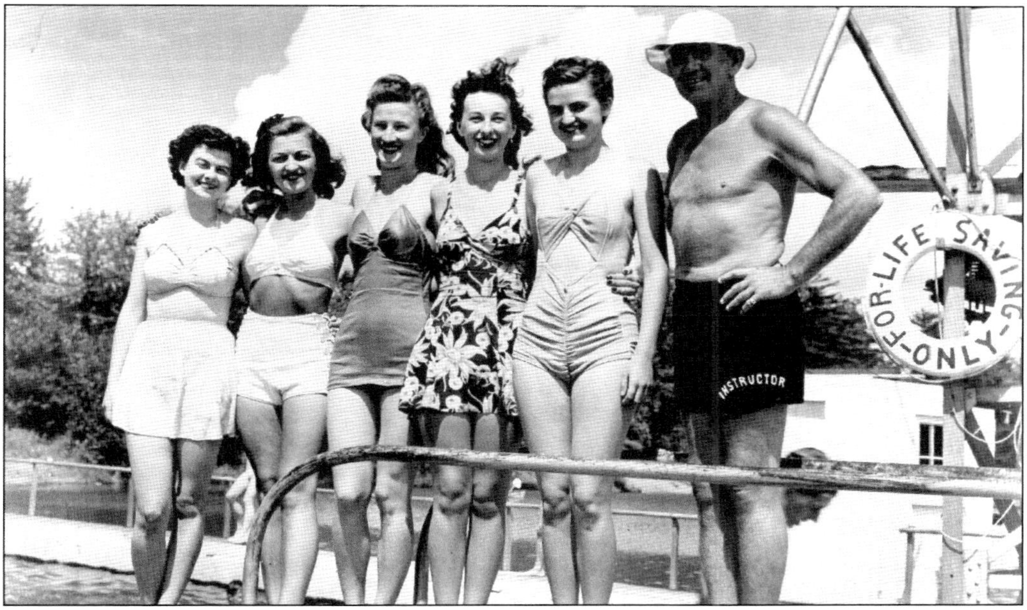

JACK NOLL, LATE 1940S. Jack Noll, pictured at right in his familiar hat, became synonymous with the Lakewood Park pool. Throughout the 1920s and 1930s, Noll taught generations of youngsters to swim, held competitive swim meets, promoted diving contests, and, with his wife, Theresa, organized the Water Rats—a swimmers' fun club. Here Noll is seen with a group of unidentified bathing beauties who swam for Lakewood.

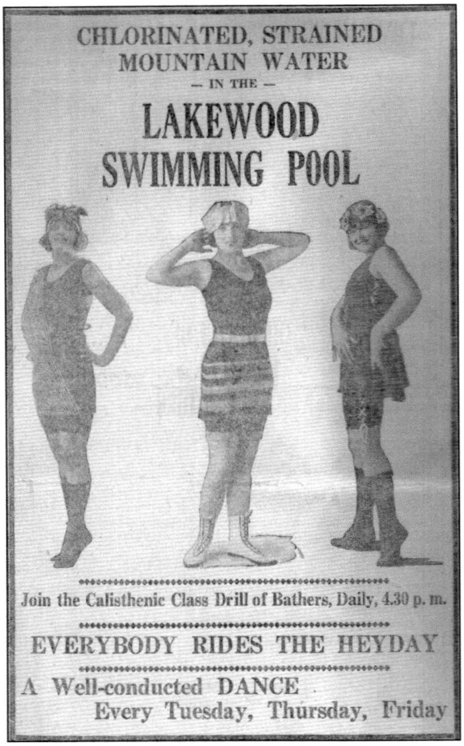

CALISTHENICS. This unique advertisement provides evidence that ladies did not just bathe at Lakewood Park. Calisthenics in the water, an early precursor of water aerobics, was promoted at Lakewood in the 1920s and 1930s.

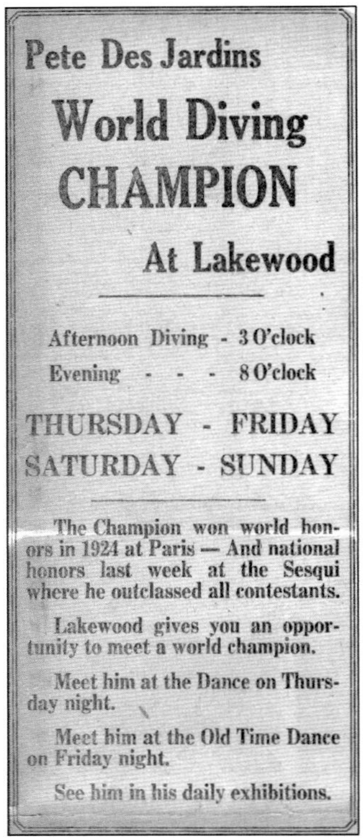

NATIONAL DIVING CHAMPIONS. Along with local diving standouts the Ferguson girls, Lakewood Park booked nationally known diving champions to perform at the pool. This newspaper advertisement promoting Pete Des Jardins ran in the *Record American* in August 1926.

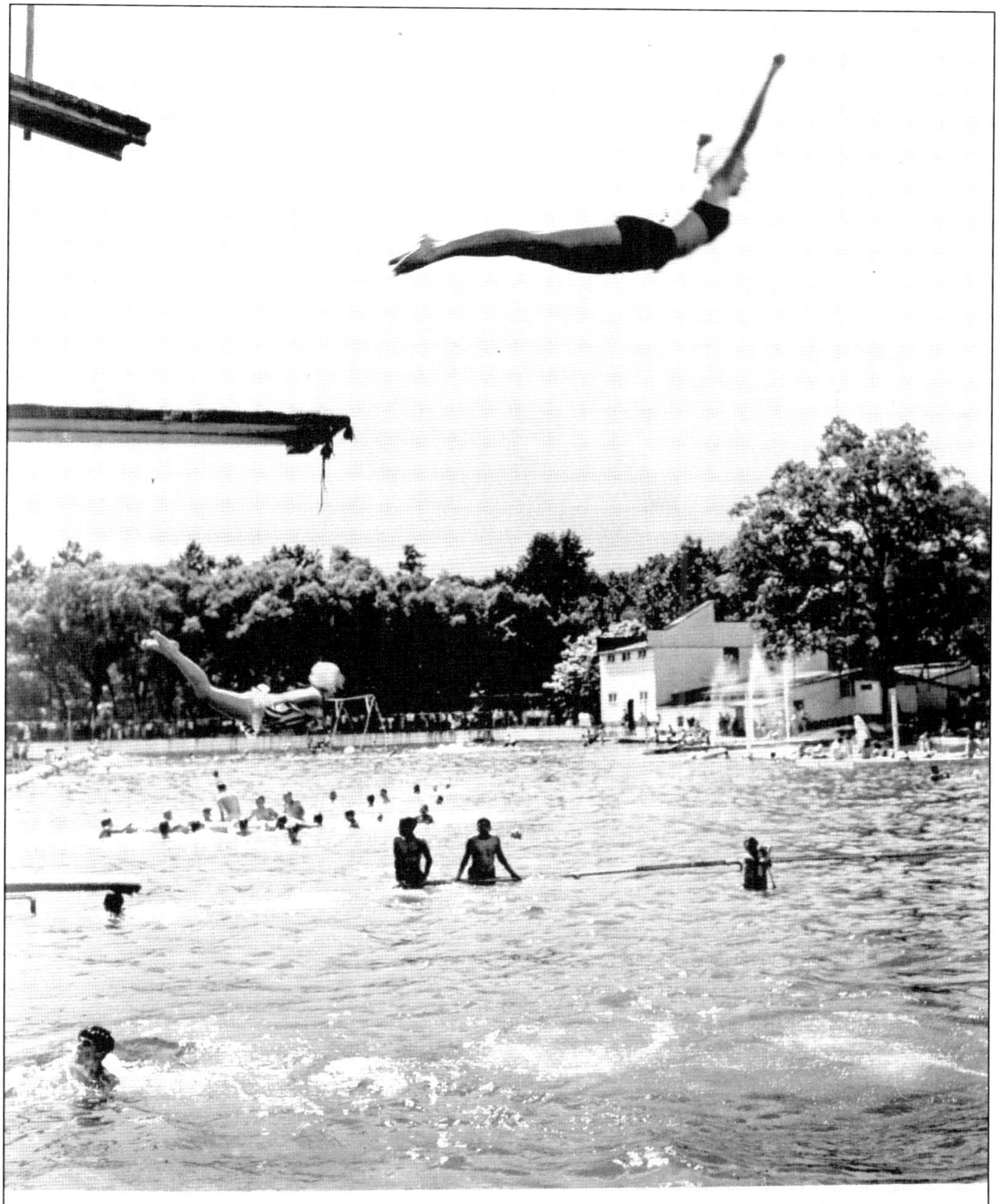

VIEW OF LAKEWOOD PARK SWIMMING POOL, MAHANOY CITY

DARING DIVERS. This professional photograph, promoting the Lakewood Park pool, features two divers, one from the 10-foot board and the other from the 5-foot board. Higher on the tower were the 20-foot and 34-foot platforms. At left (foreground), on the eastern end of the pool, is "the pit" where divers plunged into 10 feet of water. In the middle, a group of swimmers enjoy one of two floating rafts.

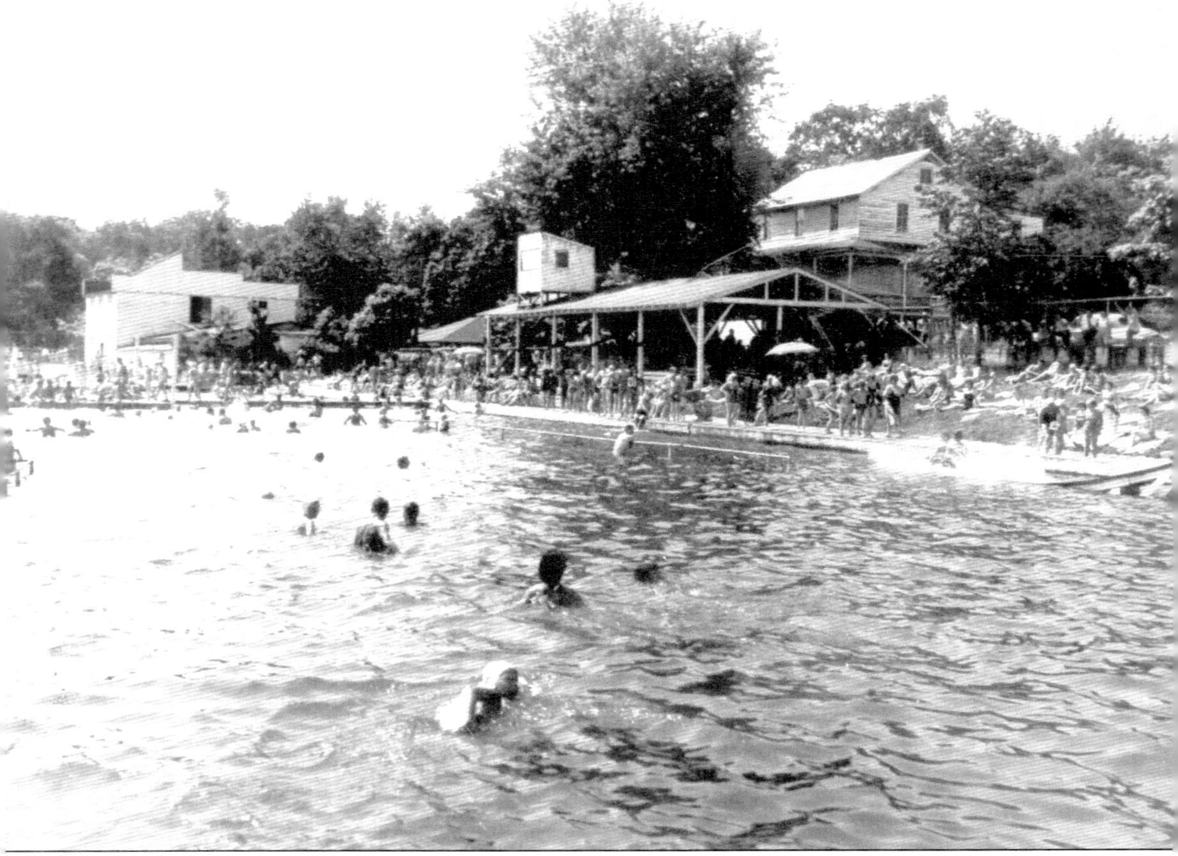

LAKEWOOD POOL, LATE 1940S. This promotional photograph shows the full 150-yard length and 50-yard width of the Lakewood Park pool. At right, a corner of the toboggan ride, originally called the scooter, is visible. In the middle is a stationary raft used for sunning and water games. In the middle right, picnicking pavilions provide popular spots for swimmers and spectators. In the foreground, Kathy Guinan Connolly swims her daily laps (25 lengths of the pool).

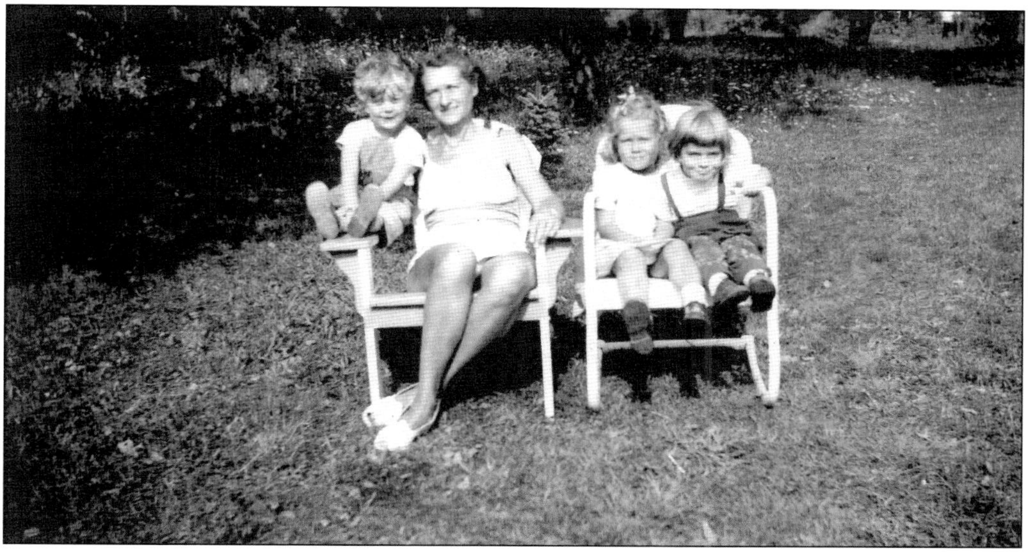

"Aunt Theresa" Noll, c. 1948. Theresa Noll, known as "Aunt Theresa" to the Guinan family, was a beloved friend for generations. She is seen here with, from left to right, Danny, Peggy, and Mary Guinan. Noll was hike leader, initiation master, and storyteller extraordinaire. She taught the Lakewood Park Water Rats to catch insects with their hands and determine who liked butter by placing a buttercup flower under the chin. She initiated the Water Rats, making members eat "worms" that were noodles and "bugs" that were Rice Krispies. The Water Rats club existed for 40 years.

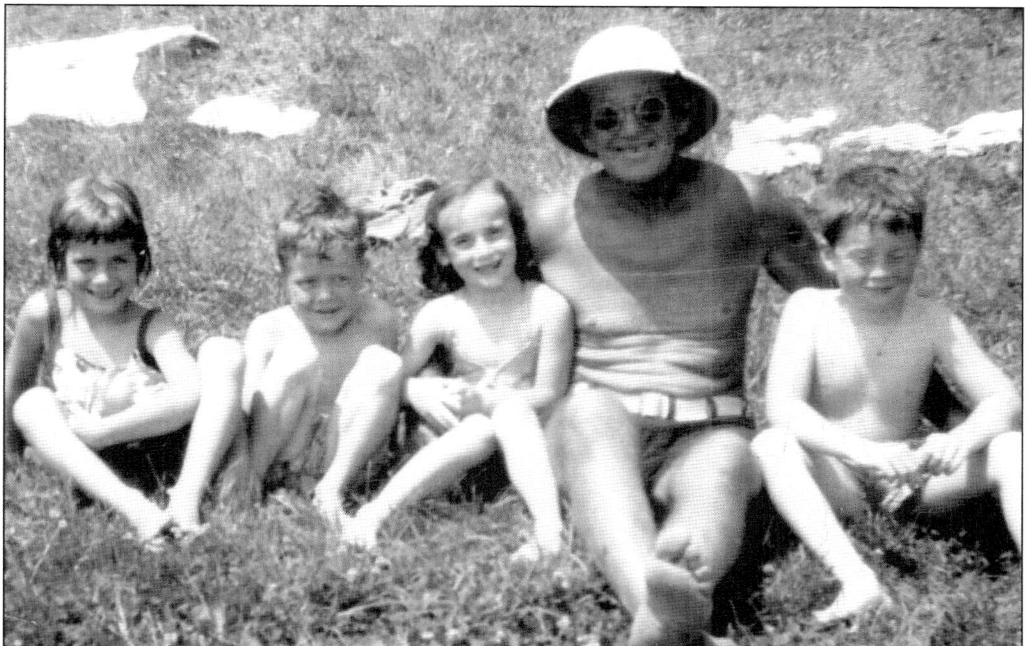

Jack Noll and the Water Rats. Always kind, giving, and full of fun, Jack Noll traveled to Lakewood Park each summer to teach the youngest to swim. Pictured are, from left to right, Mary and Danny Guinan, Kathy McGroarty, Jack Noll, and Jack Guinan.

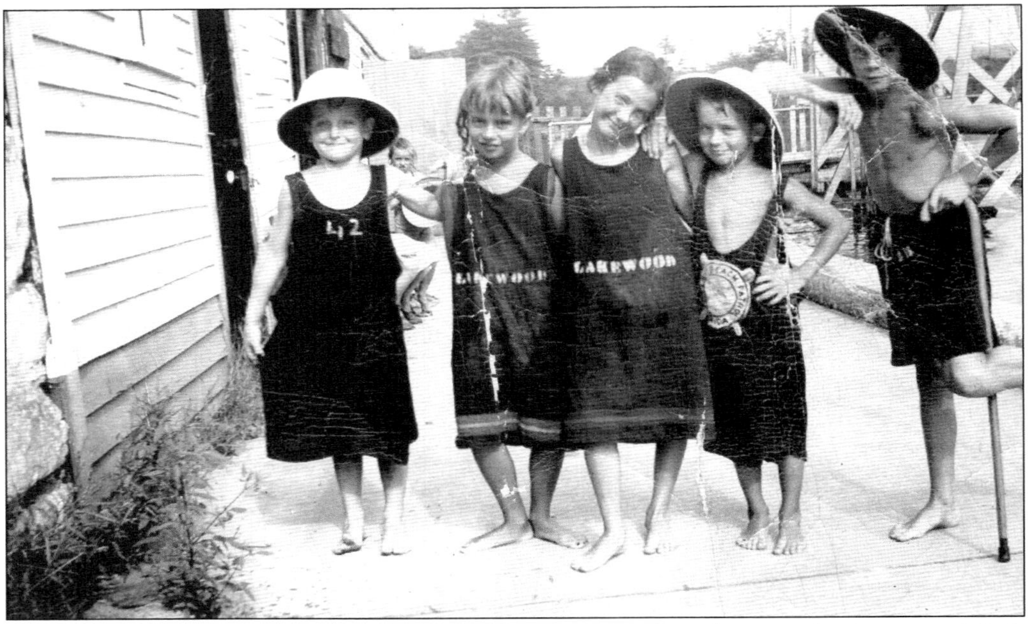

The Water Rats. Members of the Water Rats pose in their long woolen Lakewood Park bathing suits and hard lifeguard hats. To become a member of the club, children had to swim well, know water safety, hike several miles, and endure the good-humored initiation rituals of "Aunt Theresa" Noll.

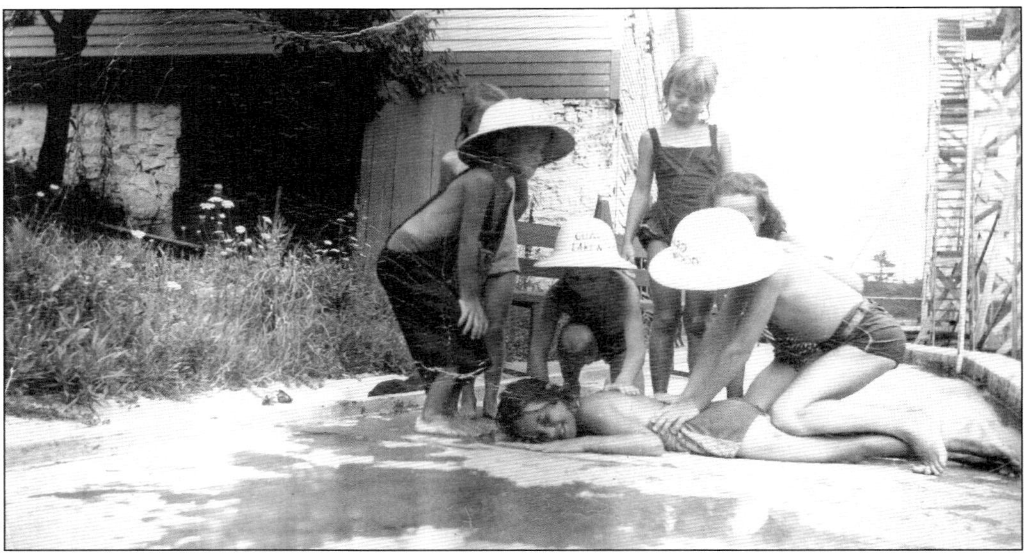

Water Safety. Although the Water Rats was a fun club, members were expected to learn the latest lifeguard rescue techniques. Joe McGroarty is pictured practicing a method used to pump air into a drowning victim, played by his sister Mary.

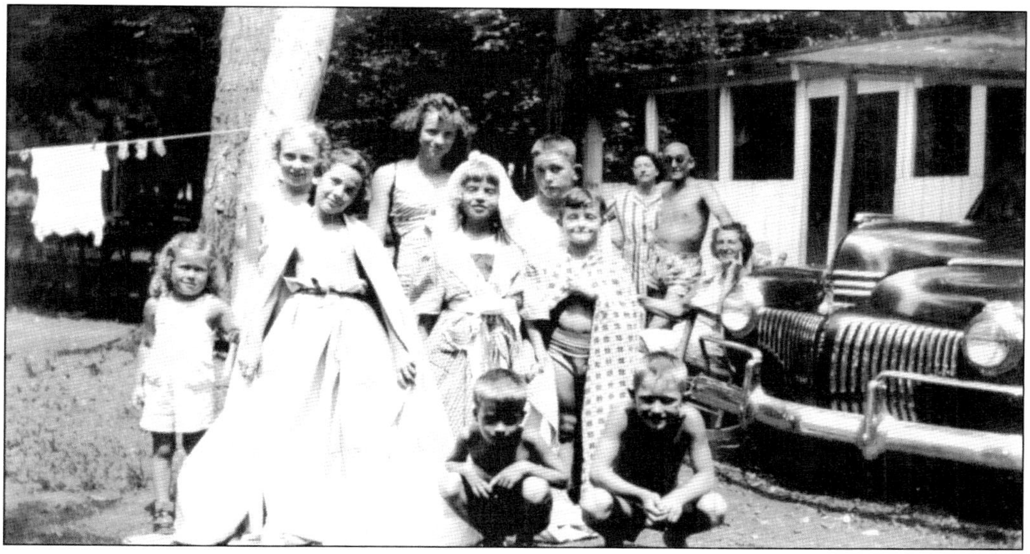

PARK GROUNDS NEAR THE NOLLS' BUNGALOW, C. 1946. Key to the fun of the Water Rats were its founders, Jack and Theresa Noll, who traveled each summer from Florida to Lakewood Park in Barnesville. Along with swimming, Theresa encouraged acting. Pictured getting ready to perform are, from left to right, (first row) Richie Guinan and unidentified; (second row) Peggy Guinan, Mary McGroarty, Kathy Guinan, and Gerald "Chester" McGroarty; (third row) Lucille Costa, Joannie Costa, and unidentified. Standing in the background are an unidentified individual and Jack Noll with Theresa Noll (seated).

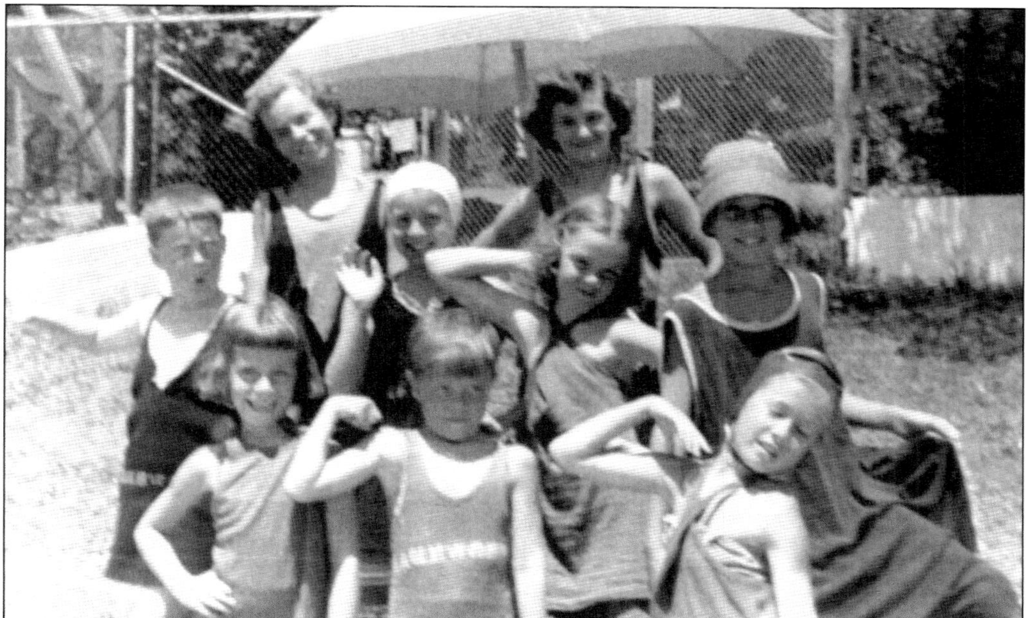

THE POOL, C. 1950. A new generation of Water Rats ham it up, dressing in old-time Lakewood Park woolen bathing suits. Pictured are, from left to right, (first row) Mary, Danny, and Peggy Guinan; (second row) Jack Guinan, Lucille Costa, and Patti and Richie Guinan; (third row) Kathy Guinan and Barbara "Pepsi Joe" Pedriani.

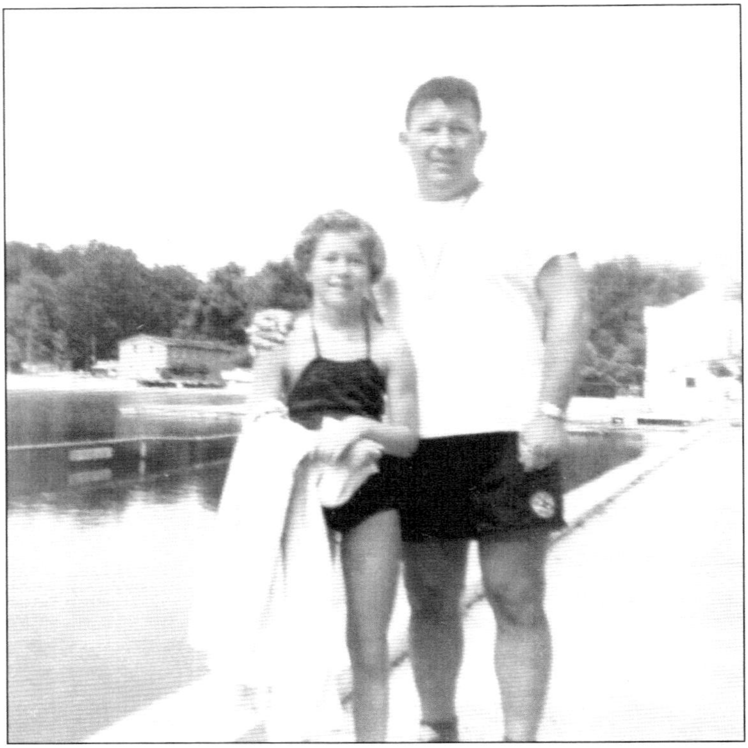

SCRAPPER FARRELL, 1954. From the mid-1950s to the 1970s, the chief lifeguard, water safety instructor, and overall man in charge was Ed "Scrapper" Farrell, pictured here with Peggy Guinan. Football coach at nearby Shenandoah High School, Farrell ran the pool with firmness and an equal amount of good humor.

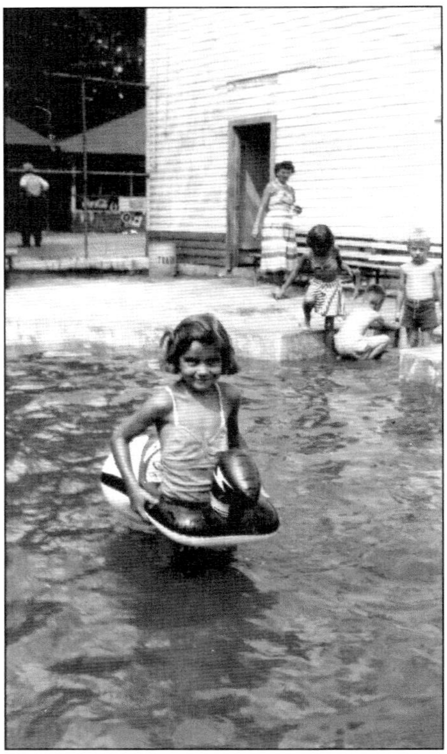

KIDDIE POOL. Toddlers as well as many beginning swimmers enjoyed the kiddie pool at Lakewood Park located next to the large complex. A cement circle with water six inches deep, a fountain in the middle, and sand all around was the perfect spot for moms and their children to spend the afternoon. Here Kathy Whalen Wufsus wades in the waters of the pool with the bathhouse behind her. No doubt her mother was close by. (Courtesy of Kathy Whalen Wufsus.)

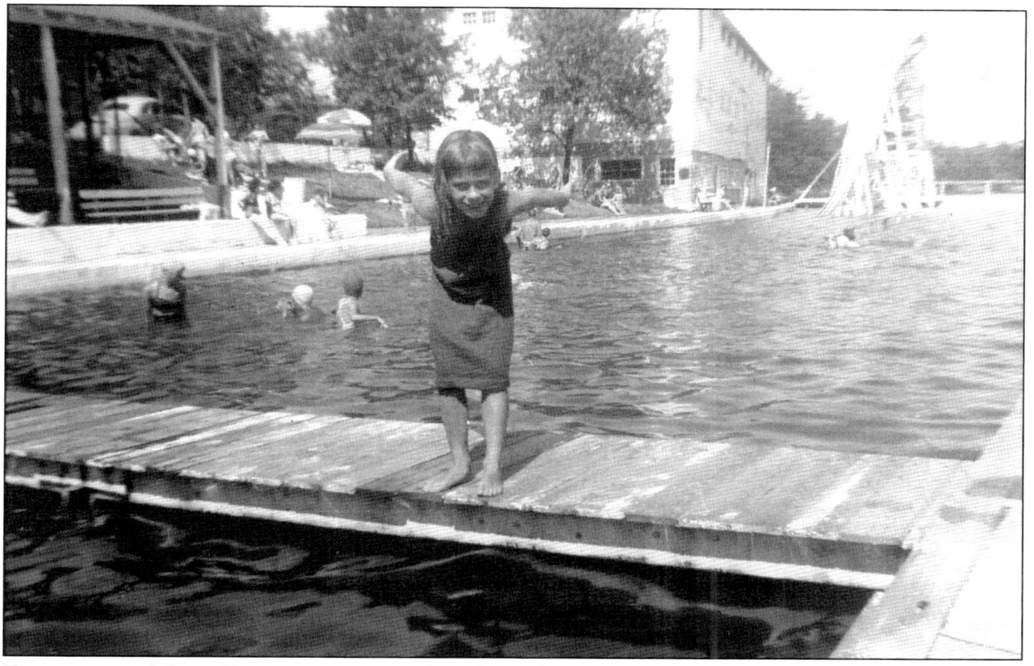

FOUNTAINS. Mary Guinan poses as if to do a shallow racing dive off the Lakewood pool's fountain area. The toboggan ride is visible in the distance.

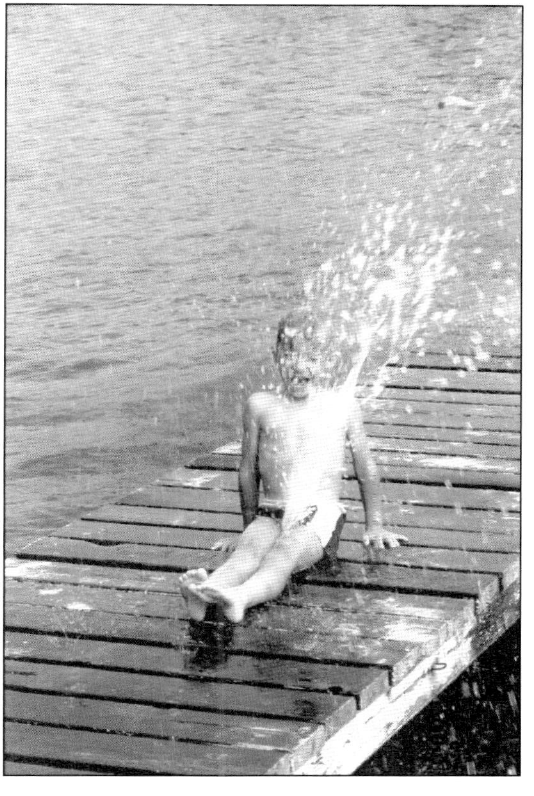

FOUNTAINS, 1968. Young children at the Lakewood pool preferred the shallow area, which featured a walk-in entrance. There they could sit, stand, or splash. Next to the children's area were the shooting fountains where the brave could run through the water or, as Steve O'Pake tried to do, stop the water from coming up! (Courtesy of Mark Purcell and Mickey DeCesare.)

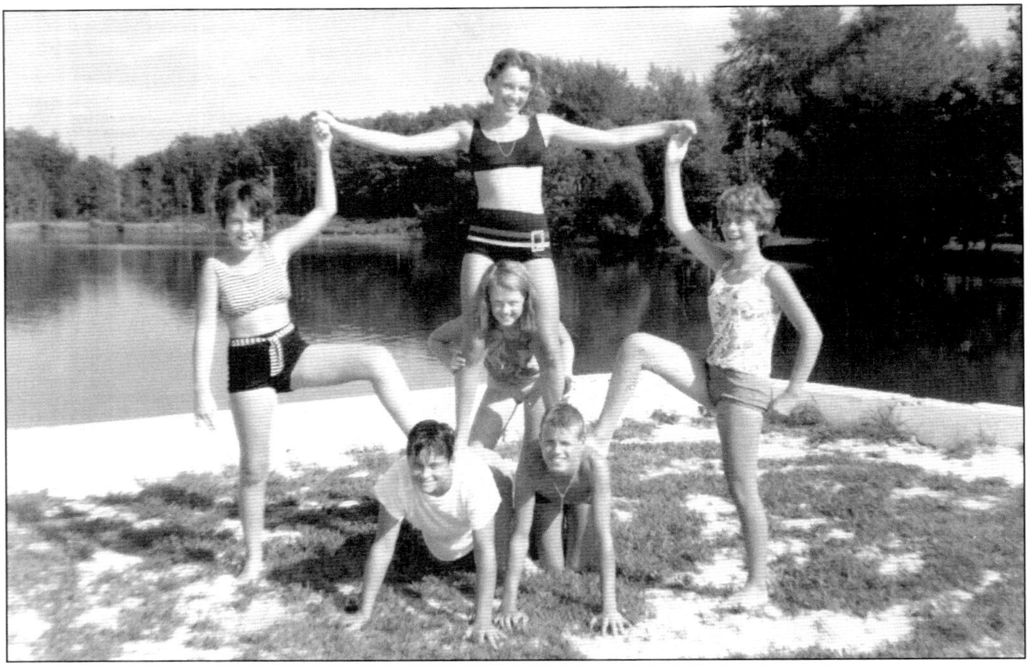

PYRAMIDS ON THE ISLAND. The soft sand on the island provided the best spot to construct human pyramids. Pictured from left to right are (kneeling) Damien Peca and Jimmy Moss; (standing) Scrapper Farrell's daughters Kathy and Mary Pat and Guinan cousins Nancy and Liz.

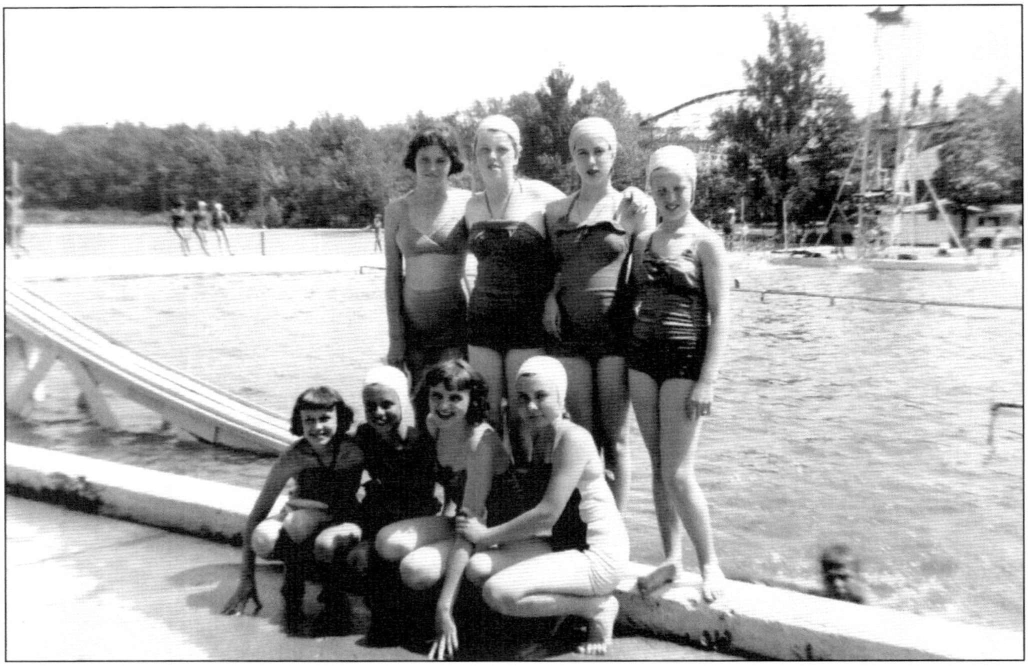

SCHOOL OUTINGS. During the 1940s and 1950s, it was common for schools to have end-of-the-year picnics at Lakewood Park. Pictured in the pool at their June 1952 picnic are a group of eighth-grade friends from Our Lady of Mount Carmel Grade School.

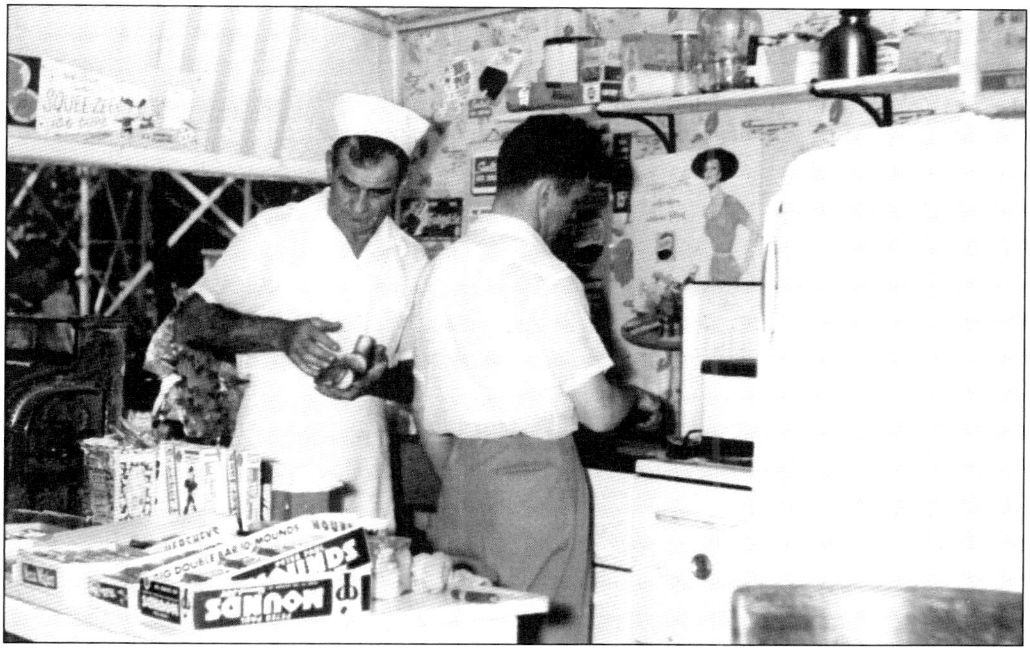

FOOD STANDS. Despite the many picnickers who enjoyed the groves at Lakewood Park, several families maintained food concession stands for hungry swimmers and day visitors. Besides selling hamburgers, hot dogs, and french fries, concessions offered a crowd favorite: homemade soup. Pictured above and below is what was, throughout the years, either the Joseph Klitsch or the Maurer's stand along the stream across from the train ride station.

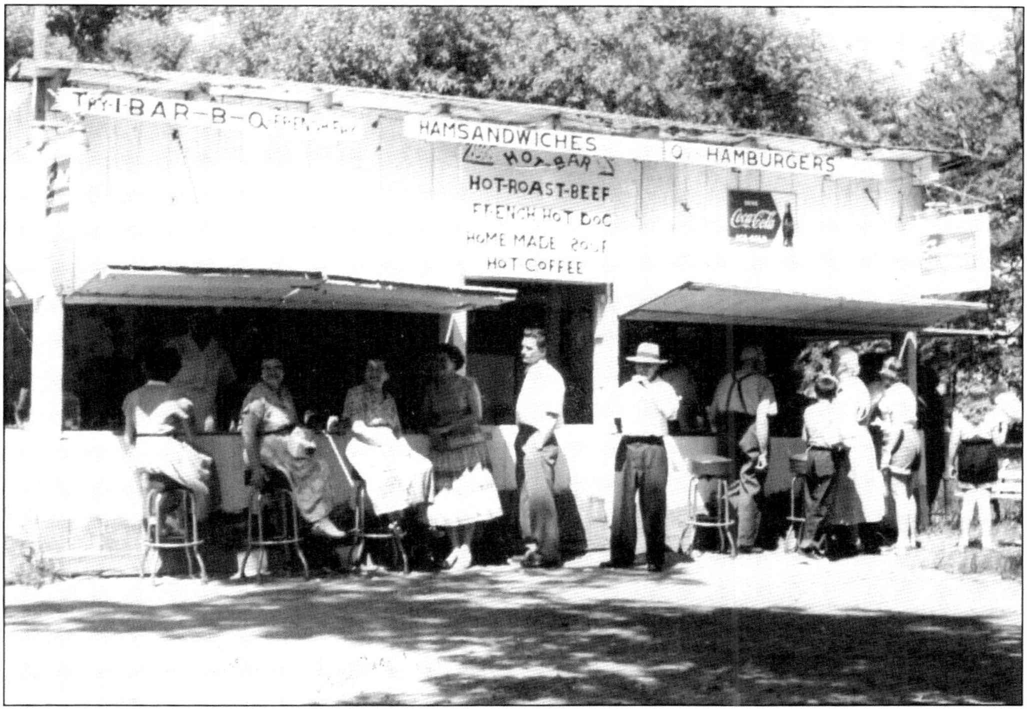

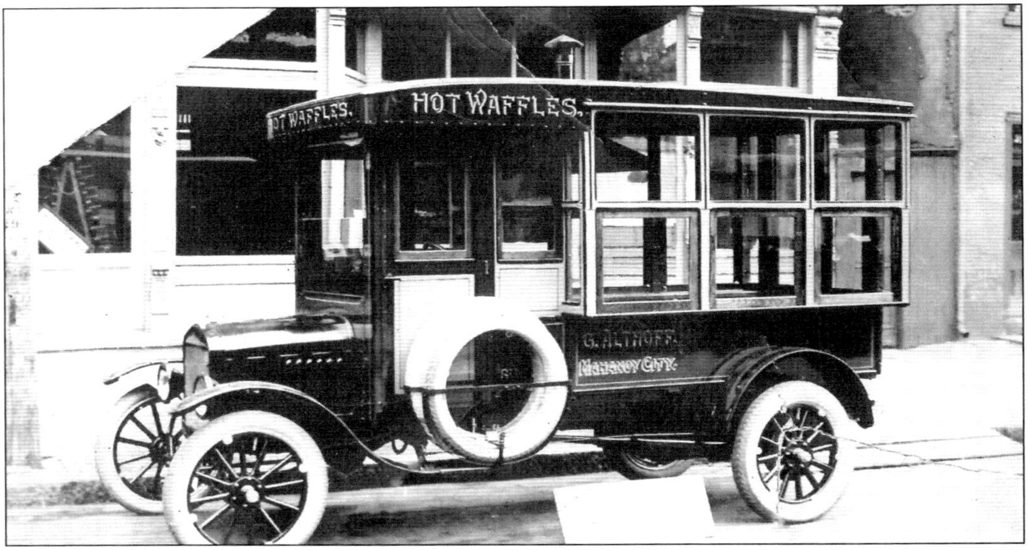

ALTHOFF WAFFLE WAGON, 1920S. As essential to Lakewood Park as the pool, dance hall, and rides were the Althoff waffle and ice-cream stands. According to Mary Althoff Koch, who found this photograph among her brother George Jr.'s possessions, their father started the business in the motorized cart above. Founder George Althoff Sr.'s name and the business's location, Mahanoy City, are visible on the side of the car, under the window. Lakewood Park housed four Althoff waffle stands, each selling original-recipe products known to be fresh and delicious. (Courtesy of Mary Althoff Koch.)

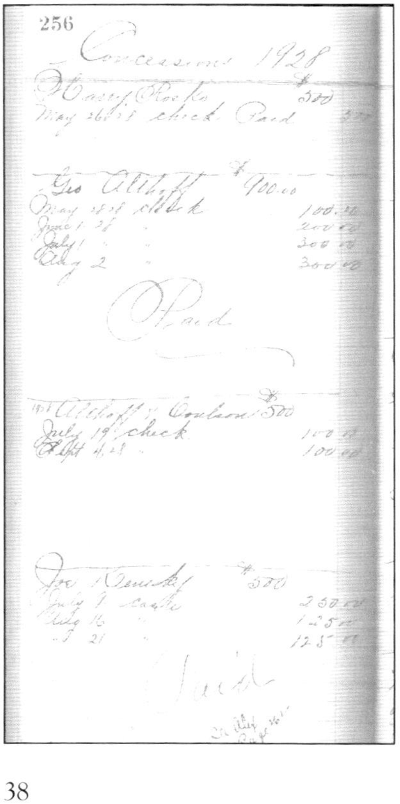

LEDGER OF JULIA GUINAN, 1928. The oldest ledger kept by Julia Guinan, in 1928, includes the name of concessionaire George Althoff Sr. Lois Althoff Musser remembers that Althoff's family, including five children, lived in a bungalow along the lake where they fished out a window, watched fireworks on the island, and took swimming lessons from Johnny Weissmuller (of Tarzan fame), remembered by Betty Althoff Goepfert. Mr. and Mrs. George Althoff Sr., son George Jr., and daughter-in-law Bernice Ansbach maintained concession stands in Lakewood until its closing in the 1980s—approximately 60 years.

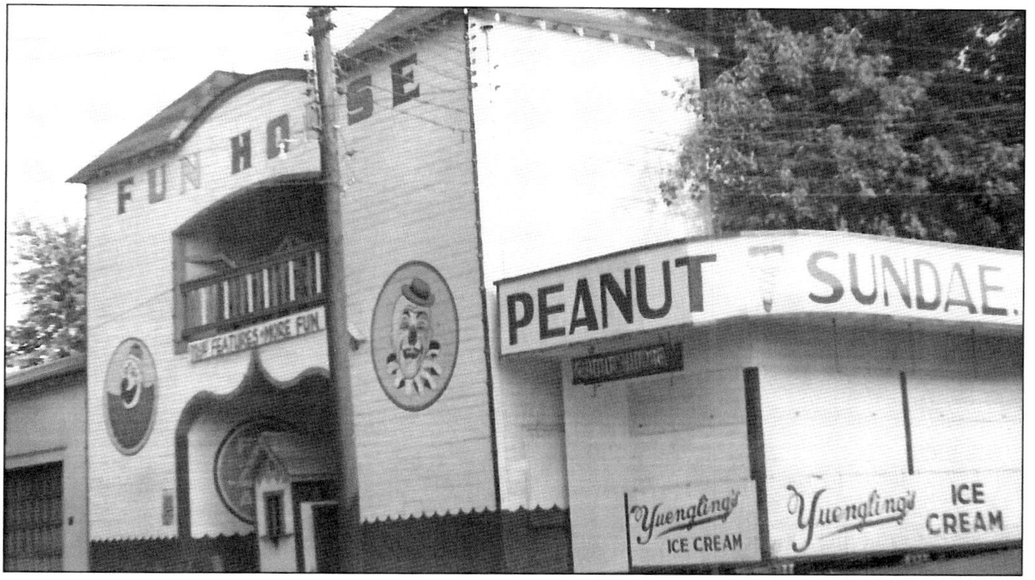

PEANUT SUNDAE STAND AND THE FUN HOUSE, 1940S. According to Mary Althoff Koch, the Althoffs' first concession stand was the large one near the skating rink, where waffle batter and candy apples were made. From there, products were carried to four stands around the park. The stand in this photograph (above right) was built last, during the 1940s. Mary and her sister Lois fondly remember their half-hour breaks from work at the stands, when they skated, enjoyed the rides, or attended a dance. (Courtesy of Mary Althoff Koch.)

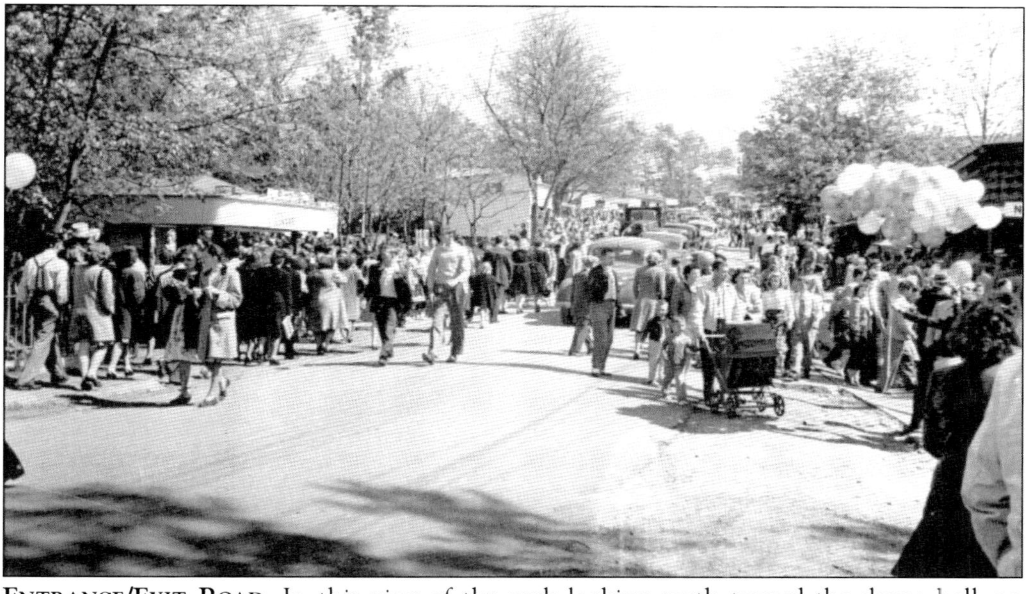

ENTRANCE/EXIT ROAD. In this view of the park looking south toward the dance hall, an Althoffs' concession stand can be seen (left). A fourth Althoff location was a restaurant across from the pool and offered light lunch and candy products. A former employee, Joanne Brentari, remembers working at Althoff's as a 13-year-old and not being strong enough to cut the ice cream. She depended on a muscular teenage boy to cut it for her, bring her change, and walk with her as she turned in the money at the end of the day.

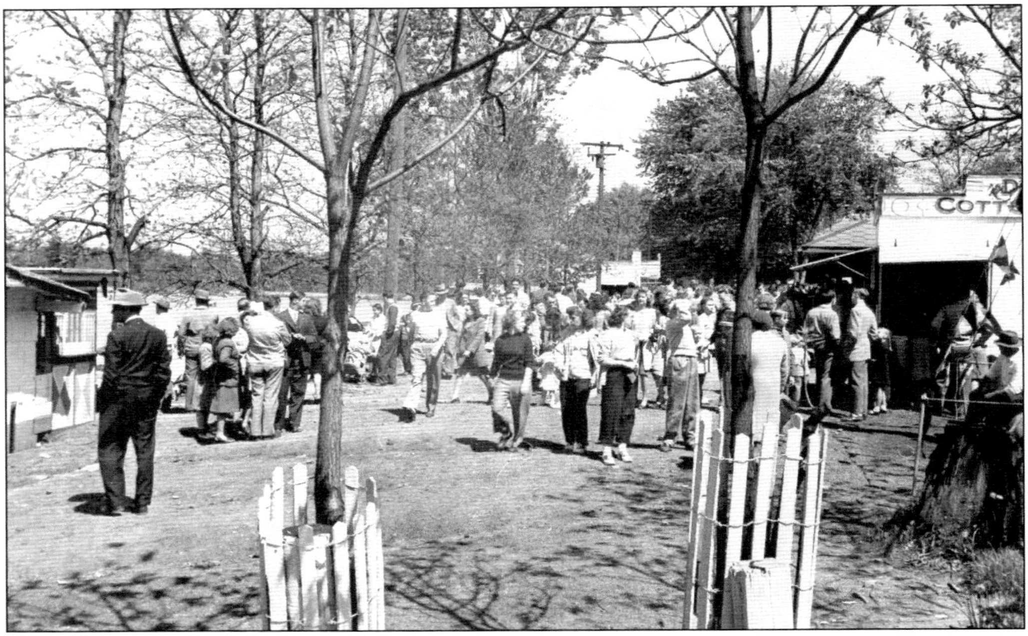

The Midway, 1940s. The park's midway was always jammed with visitors. On the lake (left) were boats and benches. Carnival stands (right) included the fishpond, taffy stand, and the Penny Arcade. During the annual Bavarian Festival, bread baking and crafts were displayed here. During the Grand Irish Jubilee, bands entertained under the trees.

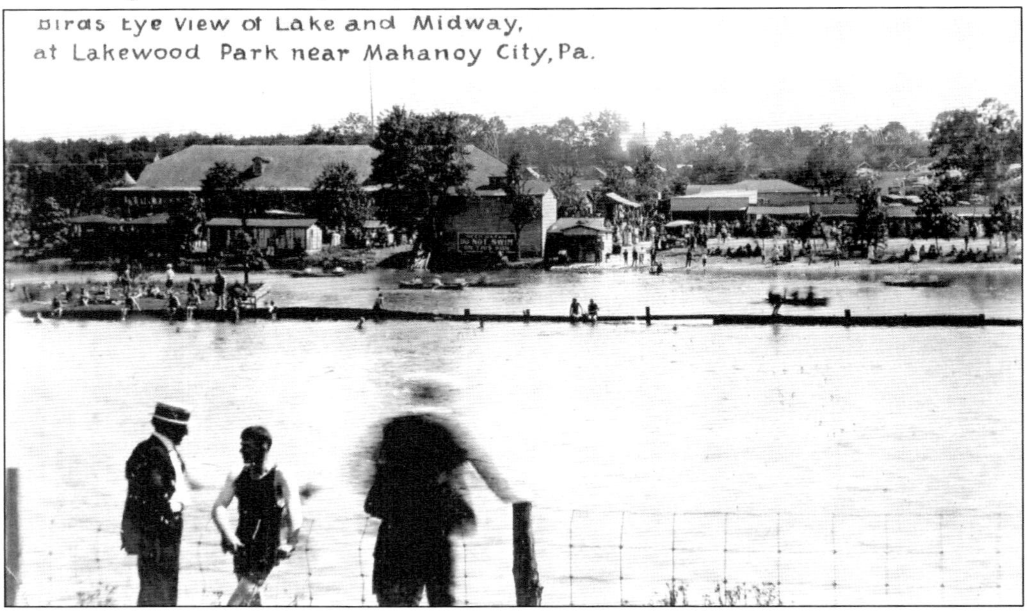

The Midway, View from the Pool. Looking south from the pool fence, the eastern end of the midway is anchored by the original dance pavilion on the left. Along the water, the boathouse and launch are visible with the Do Not Swim sign. Behind the pavilion, the large wooden roller coaster had not been built, but tents from early campers can be seen in the distant middle. To the right are the many lakefront stands and amusements.

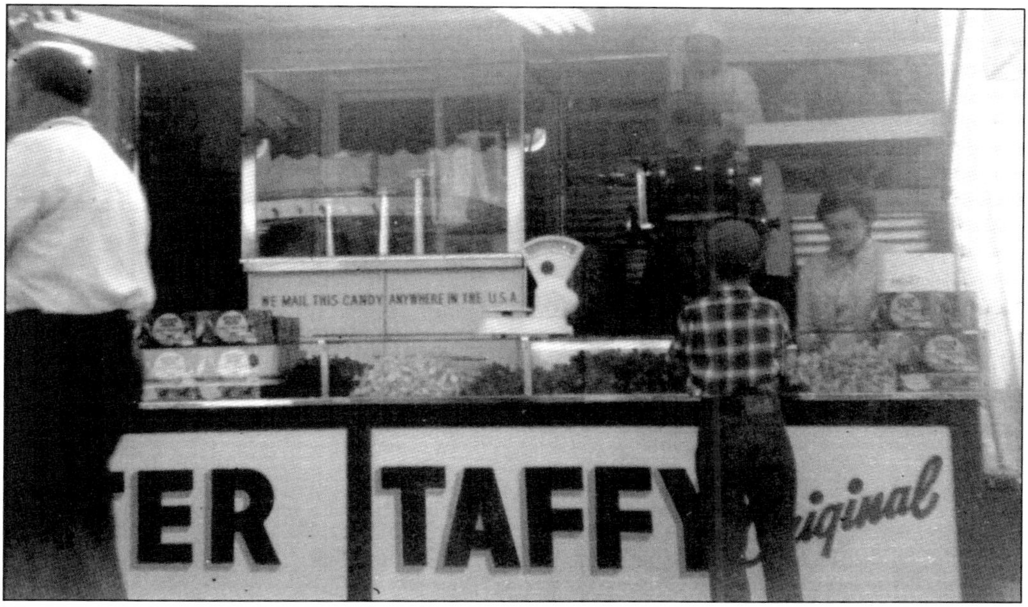

TAFFY AND COTTON CANDY. This photograph shows a typical concession stand along the park's midway. Stands were owned by local families and were reminiscent of those along the boardwalk in Atlantic City. Saltwater taffy and cotton candy were made fresh at Lakewood Park while visitors watched. It was along the midway that the Althoffs lived and the gypsies had a tent.

July 1926 Double Page Advertisement

Smith's Restaurant Full course Dinners Every Day .60 Can you beat it? Have you Scooted lately? Take a ride on the Scooter for the ride of your life C.J. Smith Proprietor	**REGAL & BLUM** We operate The Gift Store and toy shop Watch and clock Store Devil's bowling Alley Grocery and Pillow Store Bottle Ball Game
Are you going to build at Park Crest or Vicinity? If so, let us estimate for you Park Crest Builders and Supply Co.	STEP ON IT And away you go on the Miniature Speedway Ride the ever popular FERRIS WHEEL W.O. Lord Prop.
EAT at KLEIN & BRUGAS STAND on the midway Hot dogs right off the griddle	Horse Horses Horses Treat the kiddies to a ride on our pretty ponies See our—coyotes, prairie dogs and a nice Lady Baboon ----------Mc Master Riding Academy---------
Carson's on the Midway Novelties Cigars Cigarettes	Stines's Place Midway and Main Road
Minature Railway Take a ride through the grove. At the end enjoy Liberty Root Beer from the Big Barrel Robert Walker, Prop.	The Whip and the Merry Mix Up On the midway Kenesky and Alex. Prop.
Heisroth Novelty Stand on the Midway Only exclusive Novelty Stand in the Park Novelties Souvenirs Etc.	Other Proprietors: Long's Jumping Horses, Kolb's Stand, Lakewood Restaurant-Gastin's, Corn Game Boettinger's Mac's Place McInerney's, Starkey's Stand, George Althoff's Waffles and Ice Cream

LIST OF CONCESSIONAIRES. Pictured here is an adaptation of a full two-page advertisement in the local newspaper in July 1926. It is a partial list of attractions on the midway along the lake.

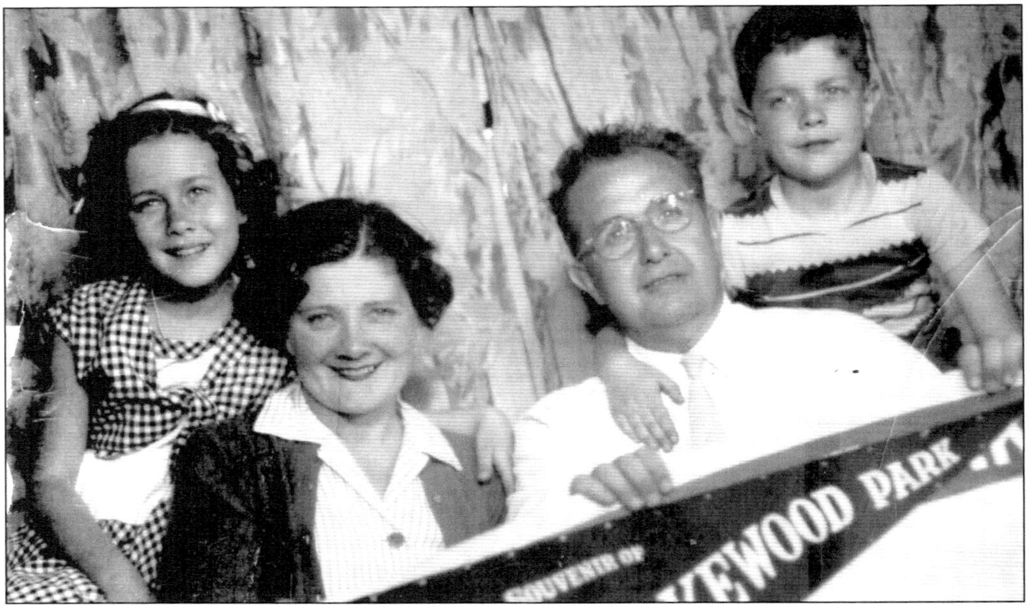

PENNY ARCADE, EARLY 1950S. Located on the park's midway, the Penny Arcade housed a myriad of skill and chance games where tickets were exchanged for prizes. The most popular entertainment at the arcade was a booth where visitors had their photographs taken on either a boat or horse (below). Pictured are, from left to right, Peggy, Margaret, Daniel II, and Danny Guinan.

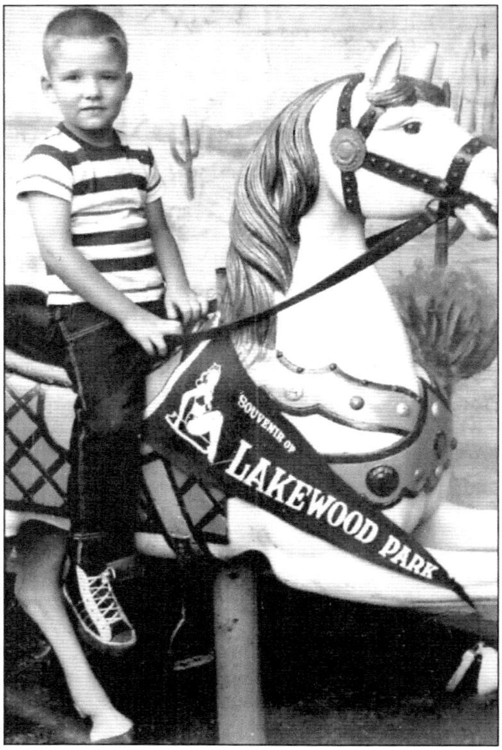

VISITOR PHOTOGRAPHS. Pictured is eight-year-old Frank R. Kline in the late 1950s seated on a photograph prop at the Penny Arcade. The real carousel ride, with hand-carved horses, was located 50 yards down the midway.

PENNY ARCADE, 1944. John and Elizabeth Thomas and their daughter Shirley celebrate Memorial Day 1944 by getting their picture taken at Lakewood Park. (Courtesy of Shirley Thomas Ryan.)

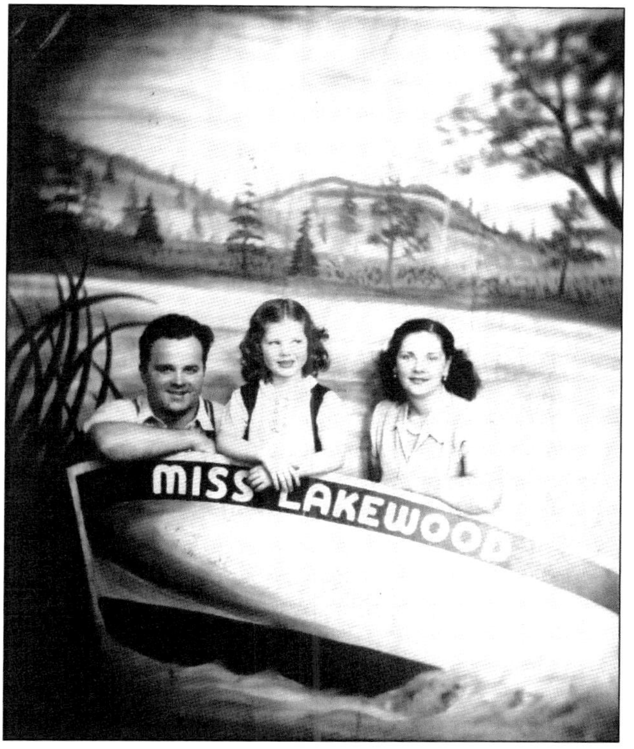

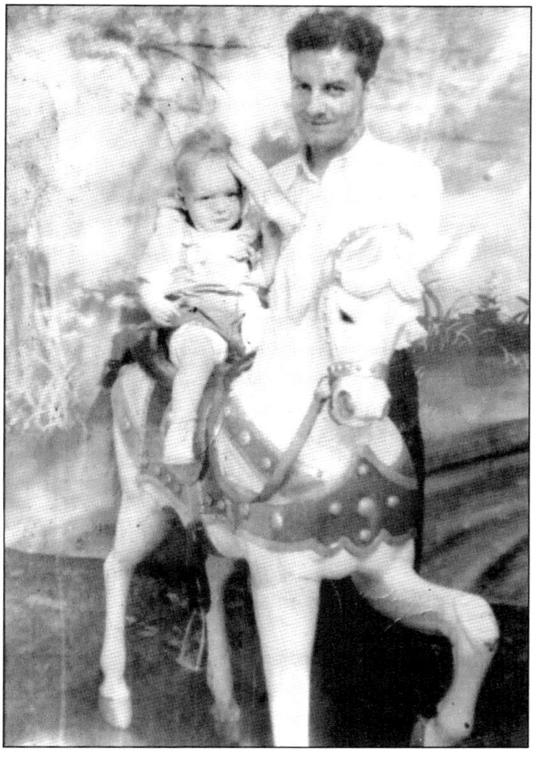

PENNY ARCADE, C. 1940. Paul R. Ryan attempts to get his son Paul J., age one, to smile for the camera around 1940. (Courtesy of Paul J. Ryan.)

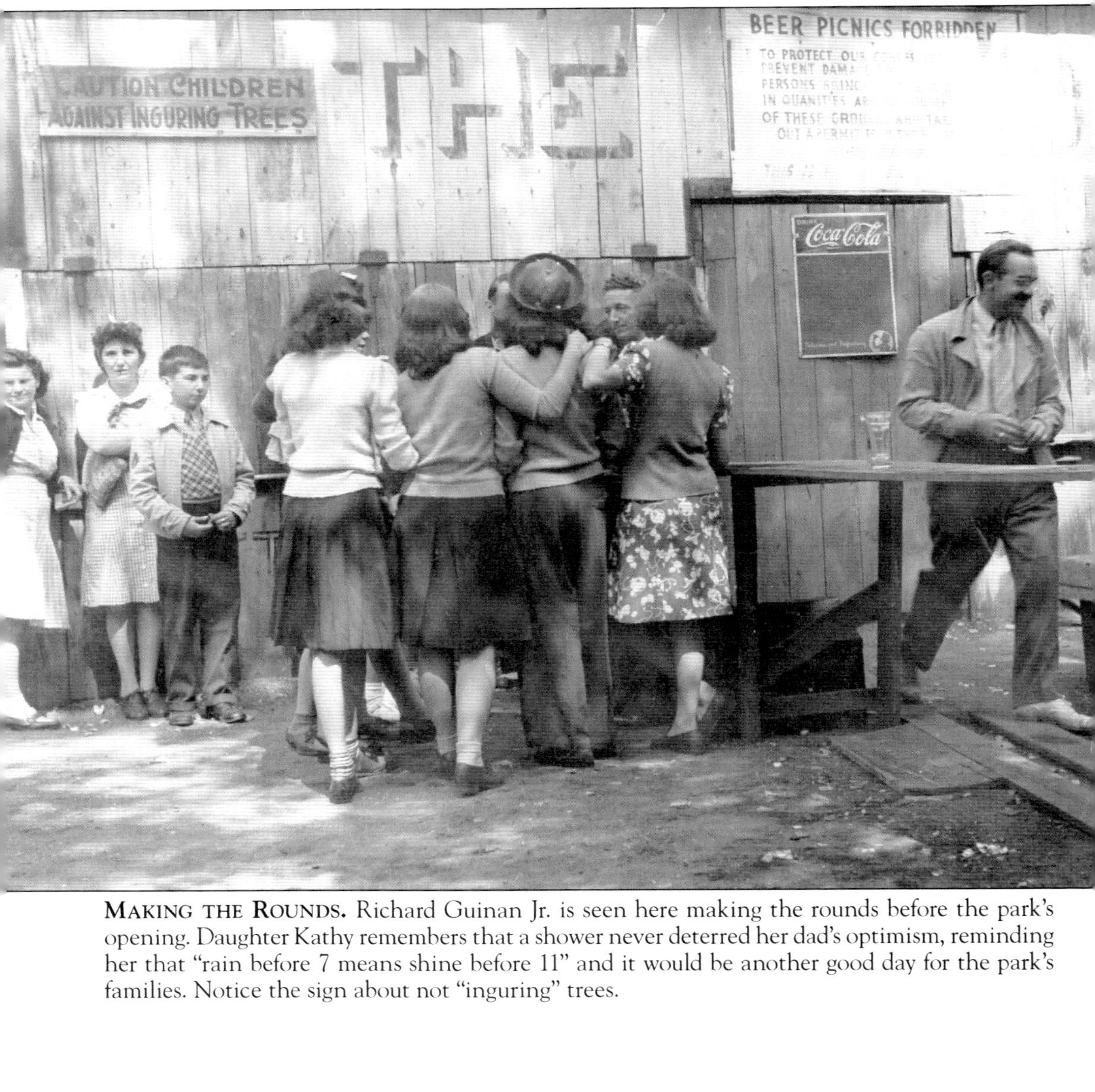

Making the Rounds. Richard Guinan Jr. is seen here making the rounds before the park's opening. Daughter Kathy remembers that a shower never deterred her dad's optimism, reminding her that "rain before 7 means shine before 11" and it would be another good day for the park's families. Notice the sign about not "inguring" trees.

Two

THE RIDES

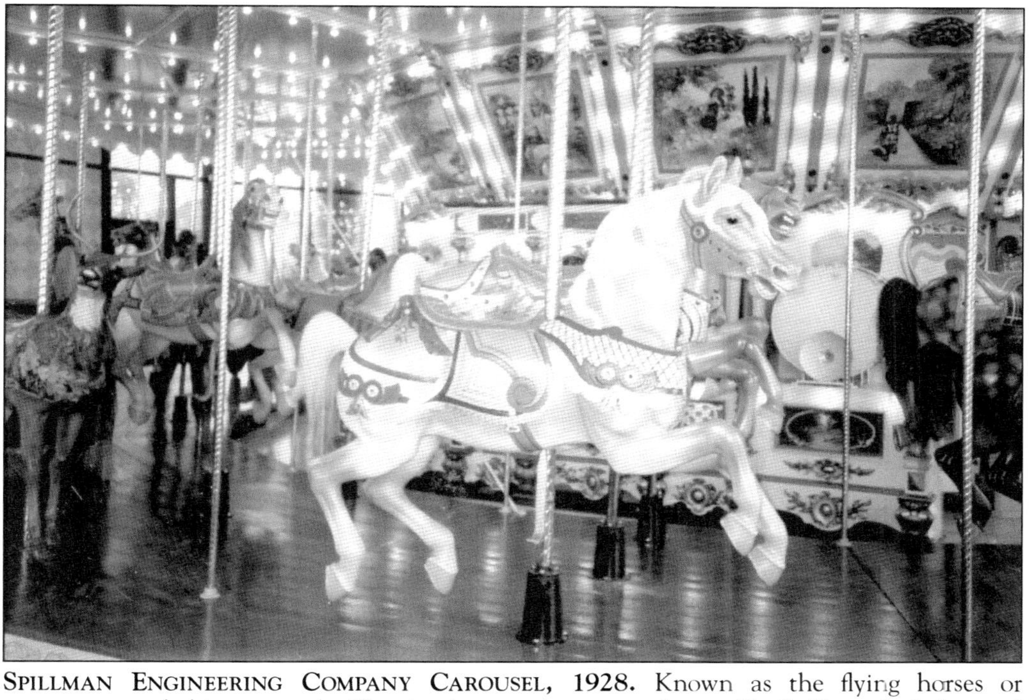

SPILLMAN ENGINEERING COMPANY CAROUSEL, 1928. Known as the flying horses or merry-go-round, this spectacular 52-animal carousel was manufactured by Spillman for Lakewood Park. The ride operated until 1984 when the park closed. It is one of only three ever manufactured and features German hand-carved horses, giraffes, goats, and lions; 1,200 lights; gleaming brass poles; magnificent artwork on its interior and exterior screens; and music by a Wurlitzer organ. The flying horses ride was sold in 1984 to the Van Andel Museum, Grand Rapids, Michigan, and is open to visitors who want to experience a ride on this fabulous work of art.

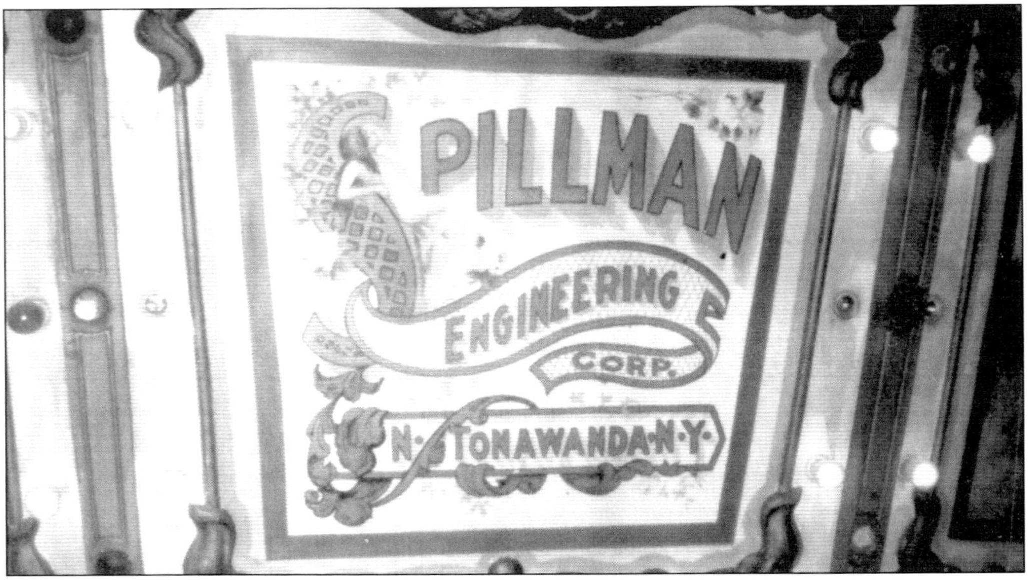

CAROUSEL QUALITY AND ARTISTRY. The Spillman name on a carousel meant hand-carved animals and horses that "jumped." For the Lakewood Park carousel, the Spillman masters created 44 horses, 6 menagerie animals, and 2 chariots (carved seats lined with velvet) to accommodate 50 riders. Spillman designed each of the horses to appear to be leaping. To create this effect on the standing horses, the company cut off the horses' legs and added jumper legs. The carousel at Lakewood Park was always referred to as the flying horses.

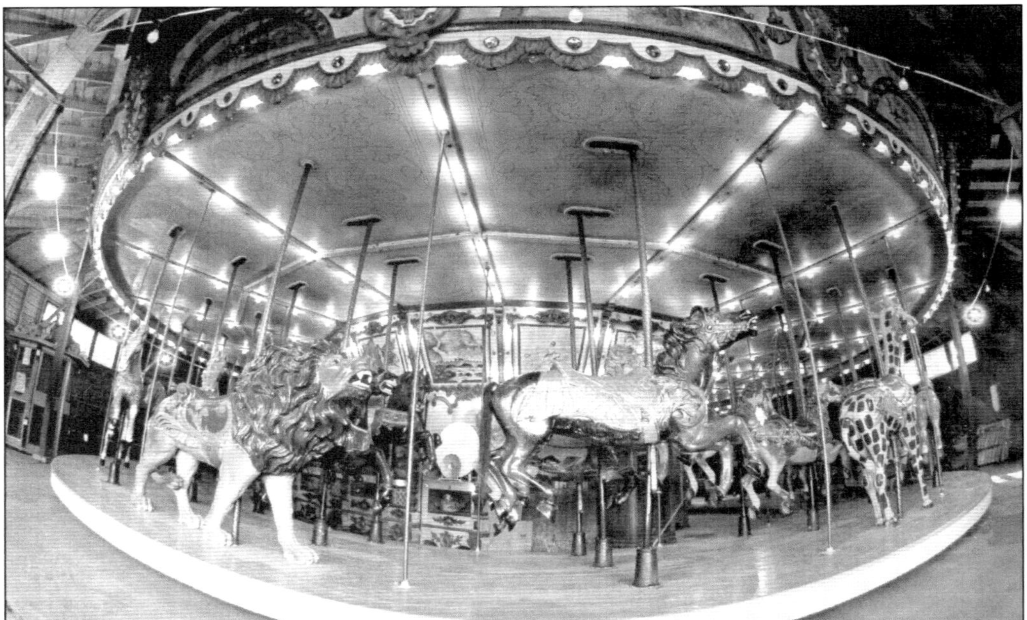

A FISHBOWL VIEW. This professional shot taken at Lakewood Park provides a unique view. The diameter of the carousel is 55 feet. Embellished panels, murals, and mirrors circled above all of the animals. The Wurlitzer 157 band organ was a nickelodeon-type built in 1908 with a large drum and cymbal.

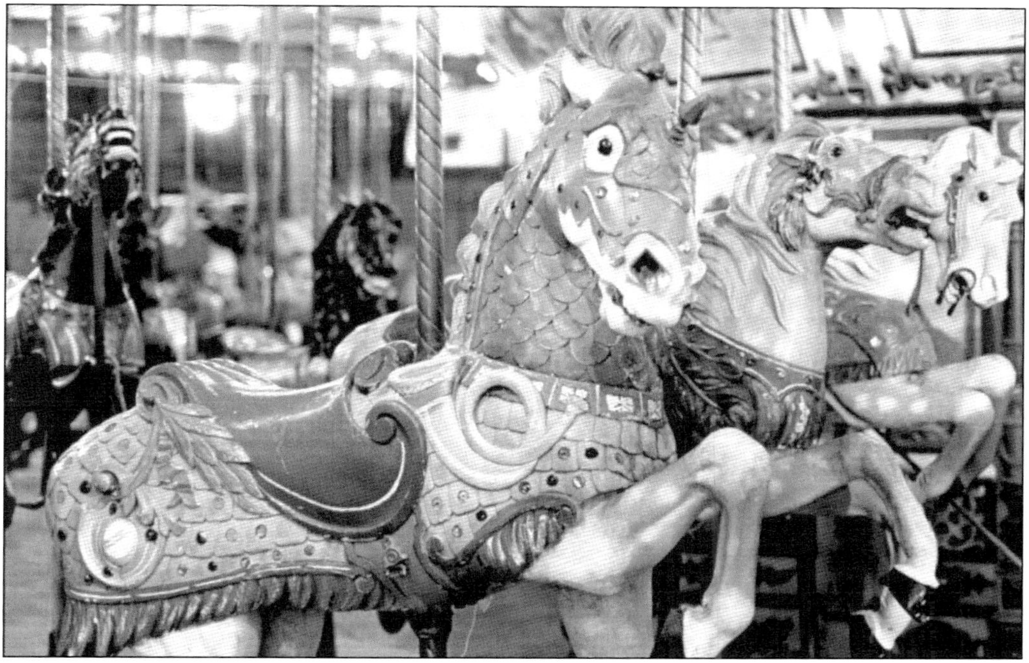

The Lead Horse. This Lakewood Park carousel horse features magnificent jewels for eyes, armor decoration, a natural horsehair tail, and a brass pole. The original horses had leather harnesses and stirrups that could not be replaced, in later years, for insurance reasons.

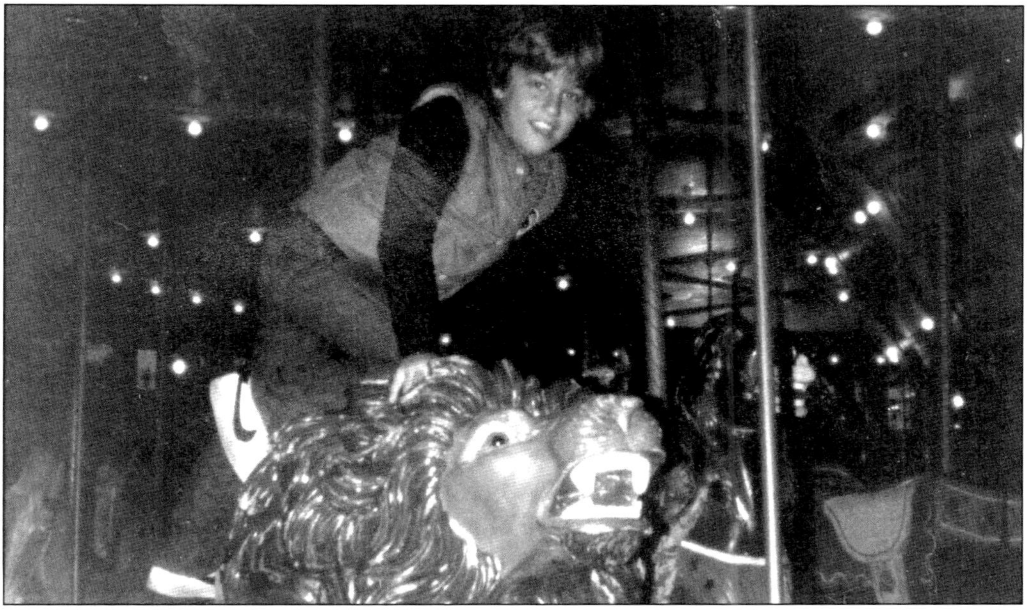

Catching the Brass Ring. Michael Grigalonis Jr. rides a lion to re-create the fun of catching a ring from a wooden armlike feature stretched out near the circling carousel. Donald Coombe, as a young employee of the park, remembers that in the early days at Lakewood, riders used to vie for the horses closest to the outside. From this position, the lucky patron could grab a ring. If it was brass, the ride was free. Coombe also loaded the rings and was the only who knew where the brass one was.

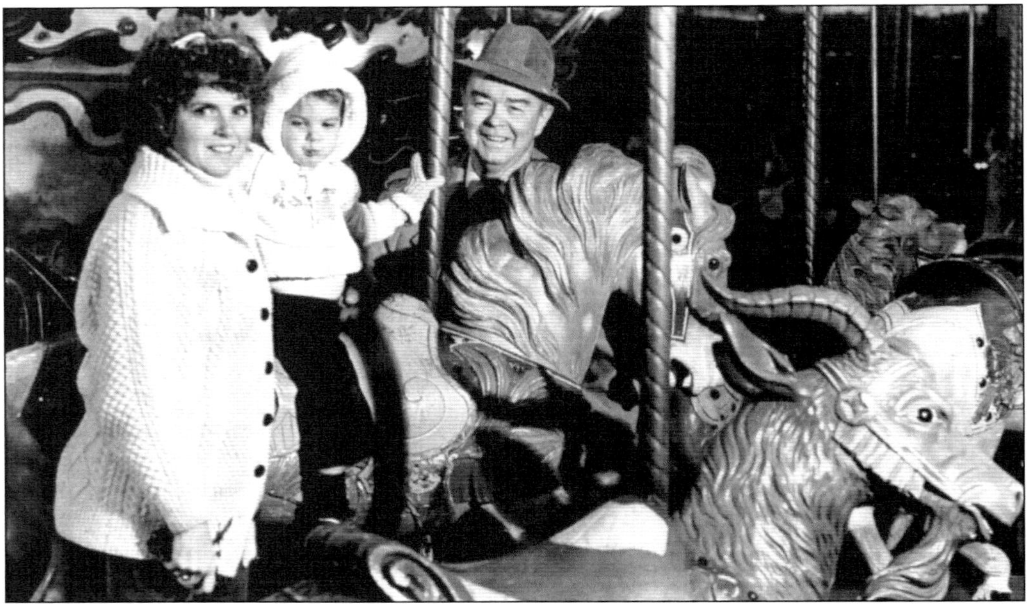

THE LAST RIDE, 1984. On the day the caravan from the Van Andel Museum arrived at Lakewood Park to disassemble and transport the flying horses to its new home, the Guinan family took one last ride. Pictured is owner Frank Guinan (right) with his daughter Janet Cunningham and granddaughter Beth Cunningham. Beth holds on to the brass pole and eyes the magnificently carved goat in the foreground.

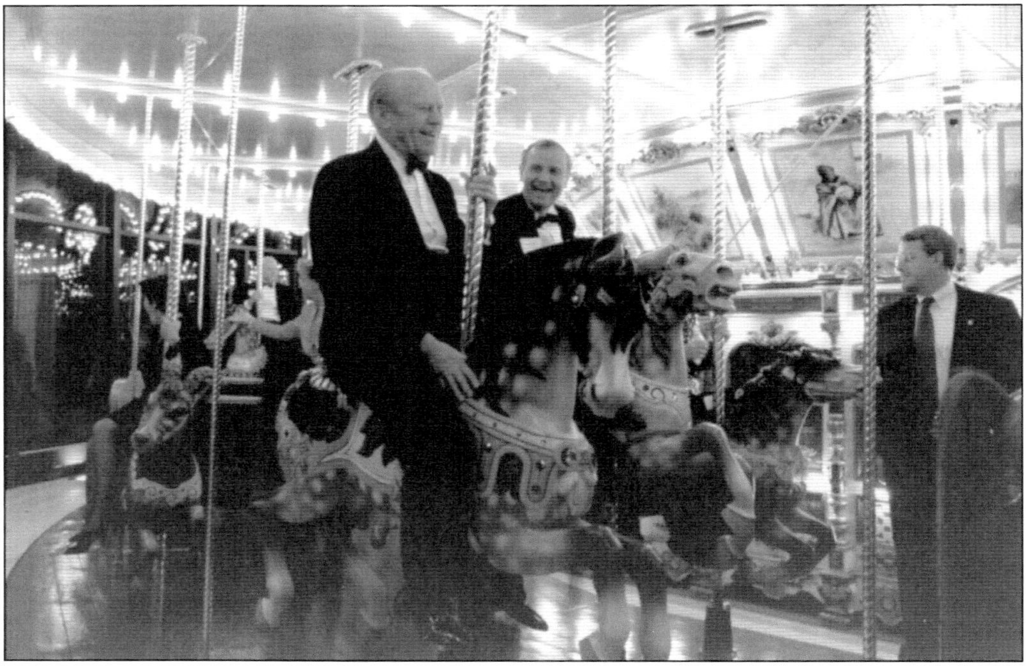

PRESIDENT FORD RIDES THE FLYING HORSES. At the gala unveiling of the restored Lakewood Park carousel in Grand Rapids, Michigan, Pres. Gerald and Betty Ford joined friends on a magical ride. (Courtesy of the Van Andel Museum.)

THE BELOVED GIRAFFE. On a 2003 trip to the Van Andel Museum in Grand Rapids, Michigan, George and Janet Cunningham visited the beautifully restored Lakewood Park carousel. The beloved giraffe was more than willing to give a big smile as he also poses for the photographer. Some of the other hand-carved animals, as well as their new glass-encased home, are pictured in the background.

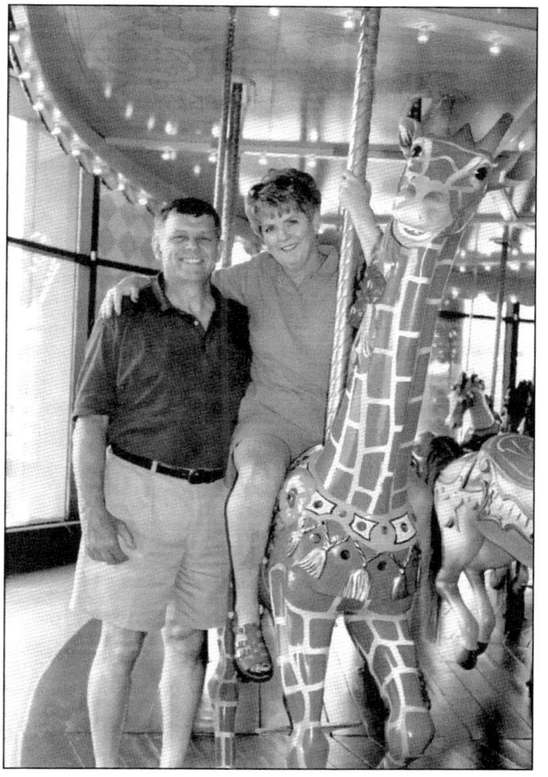

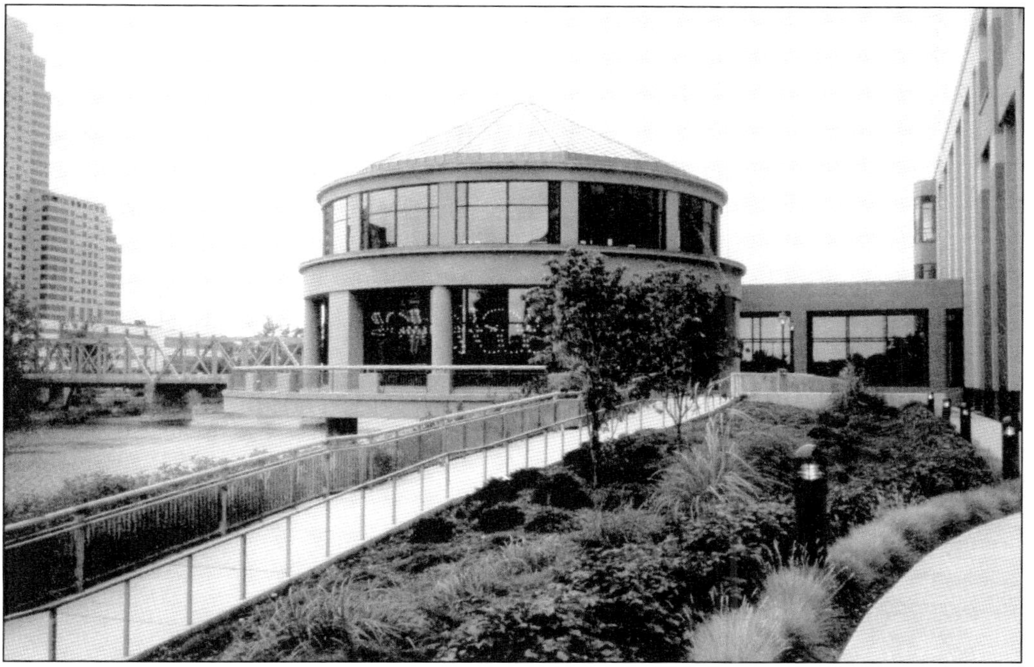

A NEW HOME. Today the Spillman carousel and its original ticket booth are housed in a custom-built glass-and-granite rotunda overlooking the Grand Rapids River.

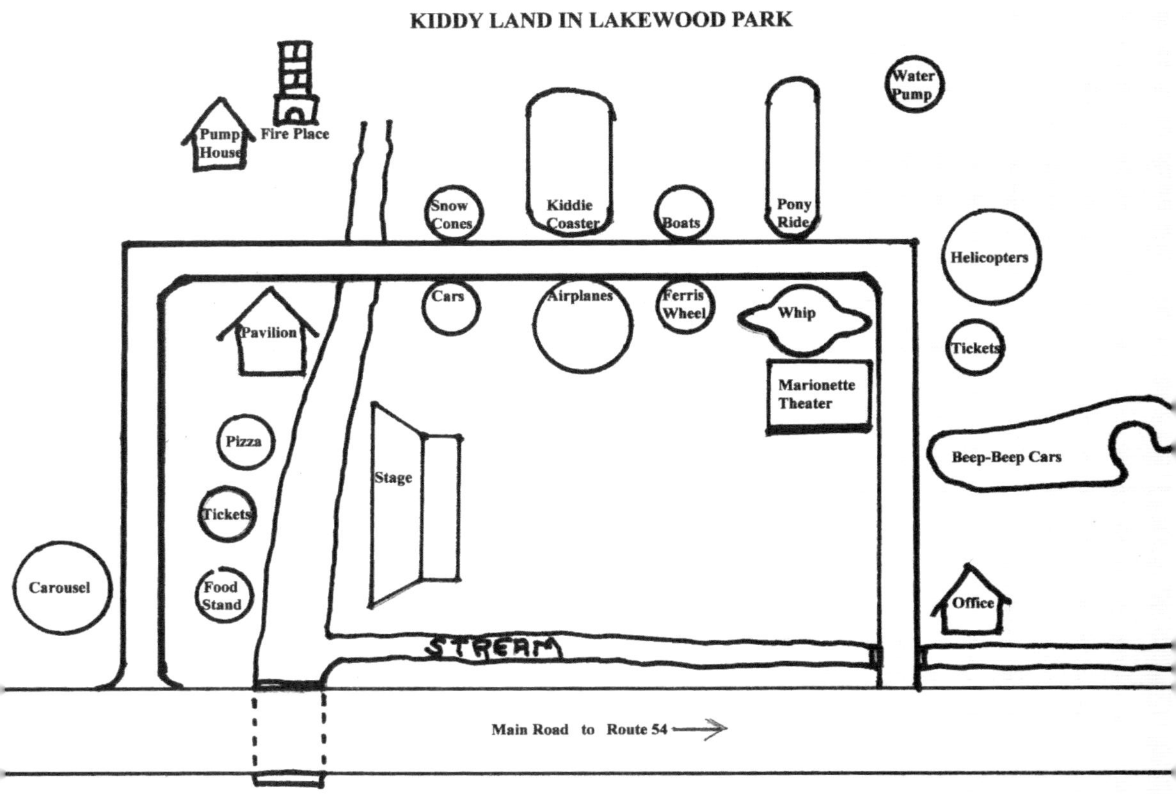

KIDDIELAND MAP. This hand-drawn map details the layout of Lakewood Park's Kiddieland area from the years 1940 to 1984. It was located across the road from the swimming pool and extended to the entrance road. Bordered by the stream on all sides, Kiddieland was shaded with mature trees and lush with green grass.

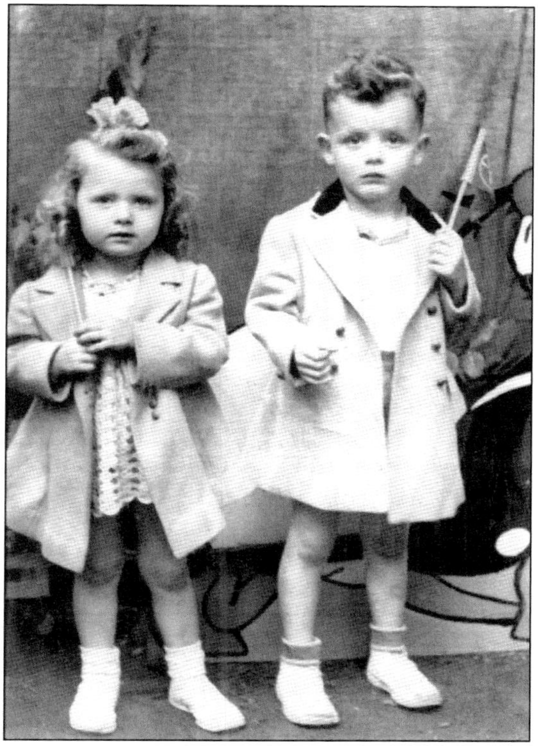

PARK VISITORS. A day's outing at Lakewood Park in the 1940s was cause for dressing up and commemorating the event with a photograph. Pictured are Paul J. Ryan and his younger sister Mary Ann, who resided in Mahanoy City, just a few miles from the park. (Courtesy of Paul J. Ryan and Shirley Thomas Ryan.)

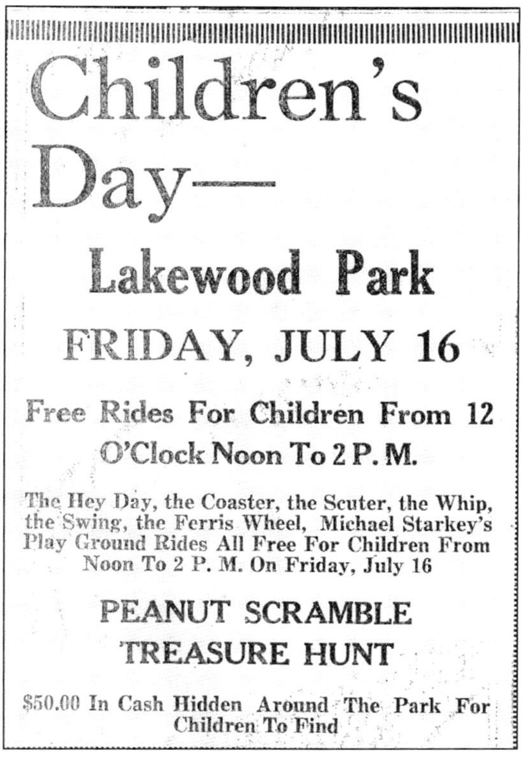

CHILDREN'S DAY. This advertisement from the *Record American* newspaper describes the type of fun that children could have at Lakewood Park.

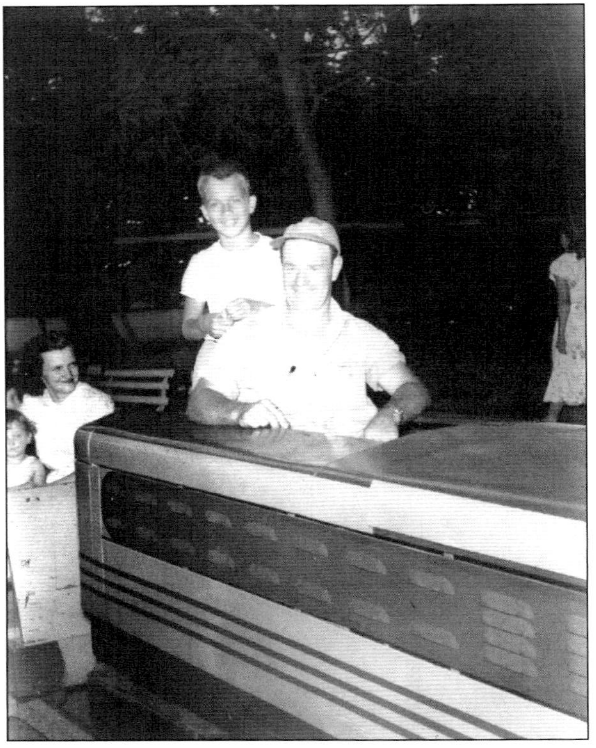

Train Rides, 1950s–1970s. Throughout the history of Lakewood Park there were three trains, which guests rode through the park grounds. The first, called the miniature train, traveled through the picnic groves beginning in the 1920s. No photograph of this train exists. Pictured here is the second train, a sleek model with three passenger cars. The train's engineer for more than 30 years was John Fogarty (right), seen here with Richie Guinan.

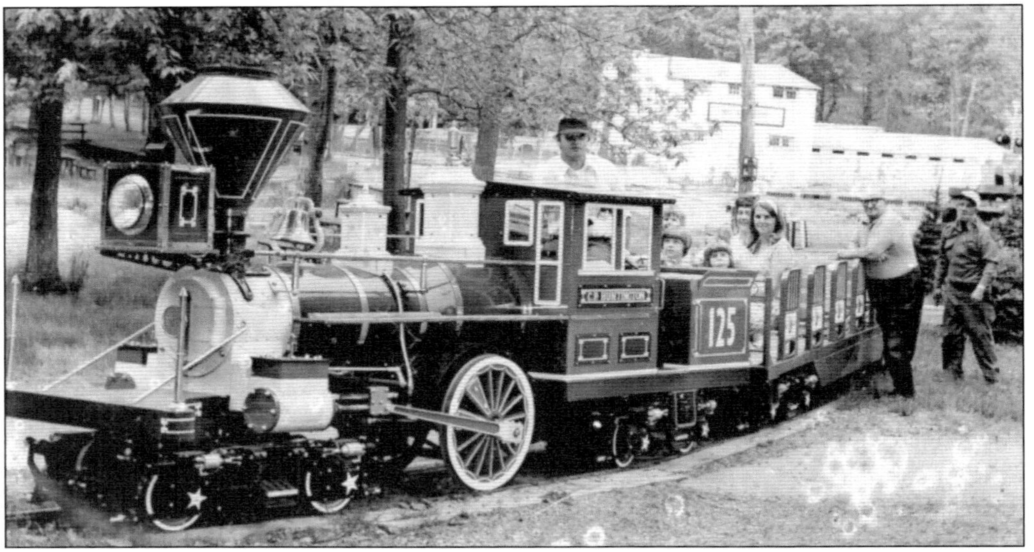

Riding the Rails, 1975. A train ride through the Lakewood Park tunnel, over the stream, and through the picnic grove was always a park fixture. This train, featuring the name *C.P. Huntingdon*, was made in 1973 by Chance Manufacturing. Pictured are engineer E. J. Lucyk and passengers, from left to right, (first row) Mark and Lisa Cunningham; (second row) Meg and Michael Grigalonis Jr. and Janet Cunningham; (third row) Peggy Grigalonis. Standing alongside the train are an unidentified delivery truck driver and Edward Bradbury, a longtime park maintenance man.

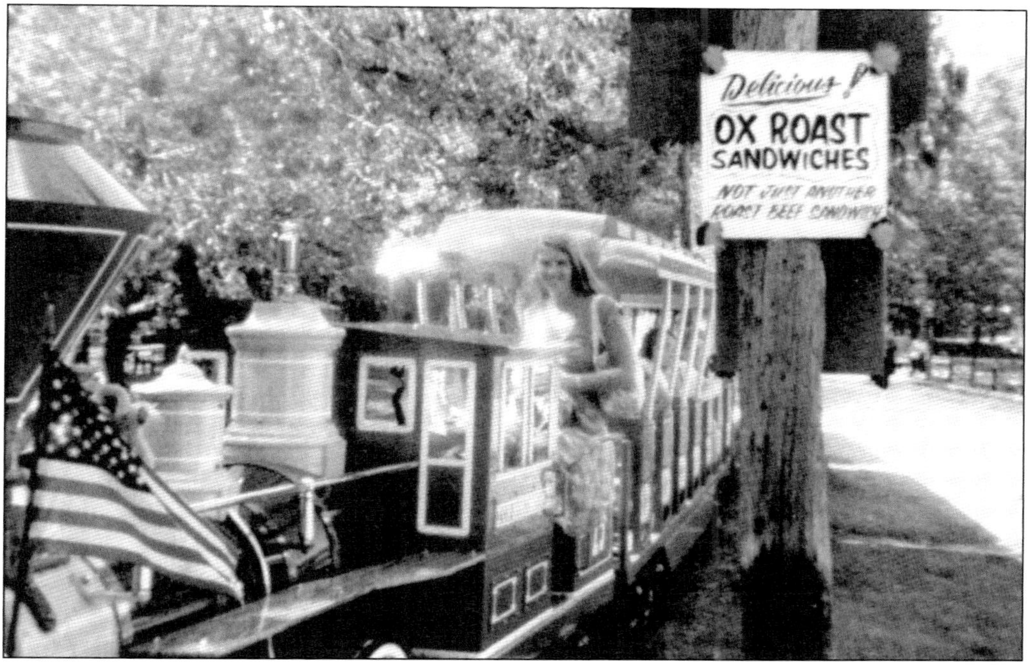

Nancy Guinan. Nancy Guinan, Frank Guinan's youngest daughter, sits in the driver's seat waiting for the arrival of engineer John Fogarty.

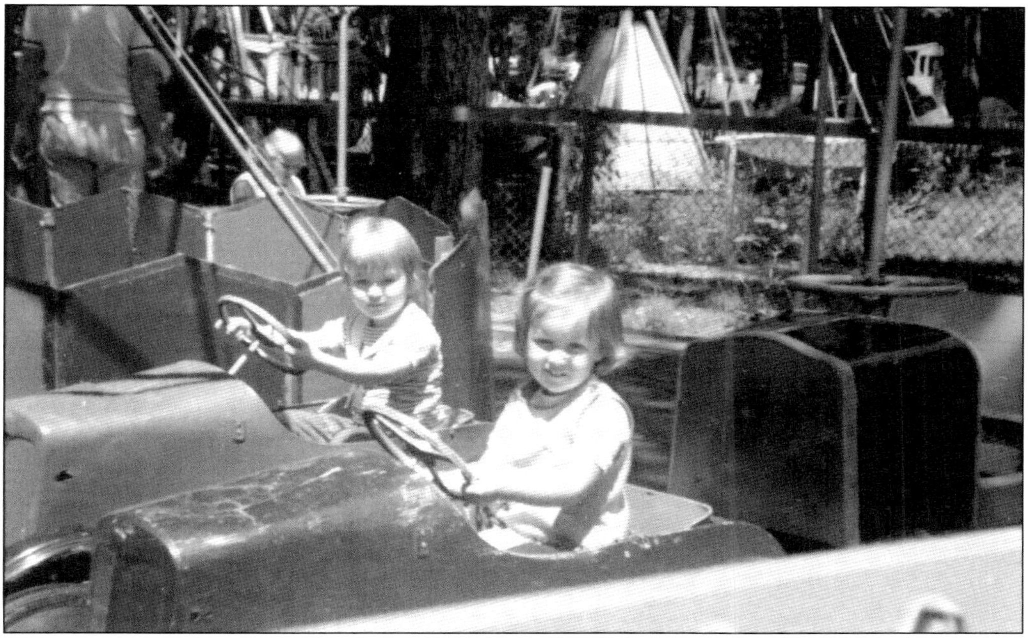

The Original Kiddie Car Ride. This photograph captures the park's first kiddie car ride located across from the Kiddieland roller coaster. The cars moved together in a circle while the rider pretended to steer. In the background are the airplane ride and Ferris wheel. Pictured during a Ukrainian Day outing are Paula Duda Holoviak (seated left) and an unidentified visitor. (Courtesy of Paula Duda Holoviak.)

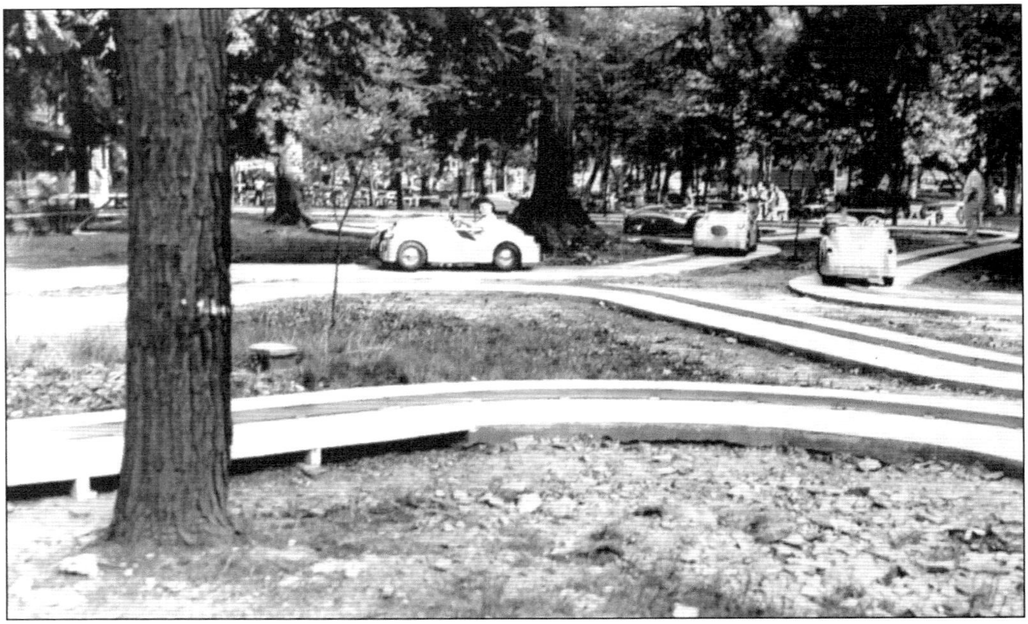

KIDDIE CARS, C. 1960. Affectionately known as the "beep-beep cars," this ride was added to Kiddieland in the late 1950s. Children pretended to drive their cars as the mechanism transported them through the cooling shade of the park's lush trees and past forest creatures like squirrels and rabbits. It was great fun for every little boy and girl.

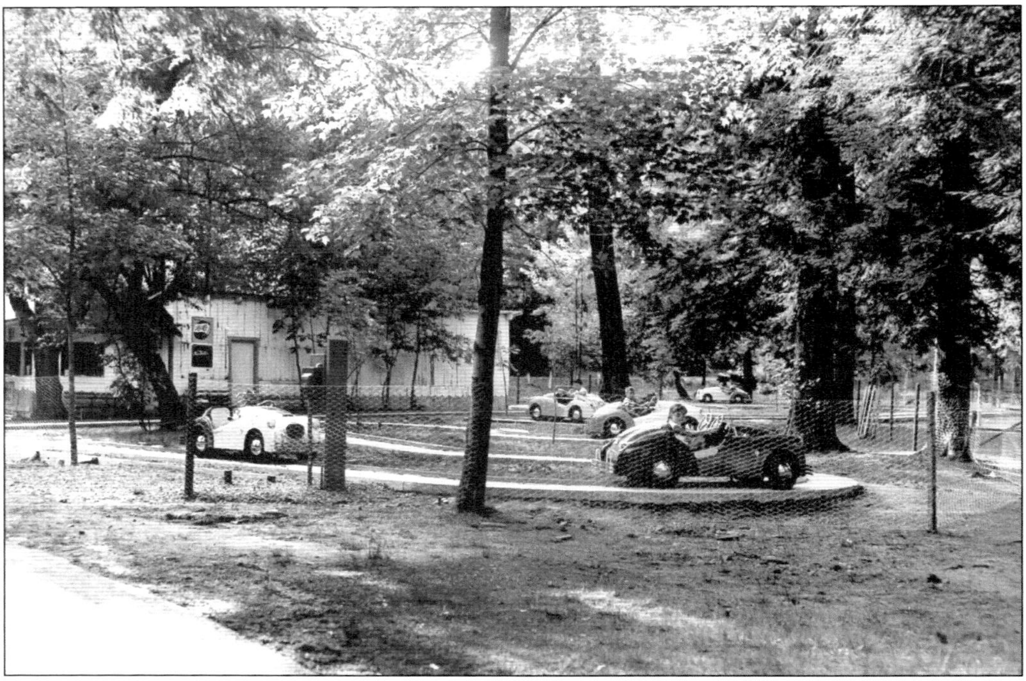

BEEP-BEEP CARS, 1960. In this view of the drivers and their cars, the shady track through the grove is visible. In the background are combination food stand/cabins where concessionaires lived and worked during the season.

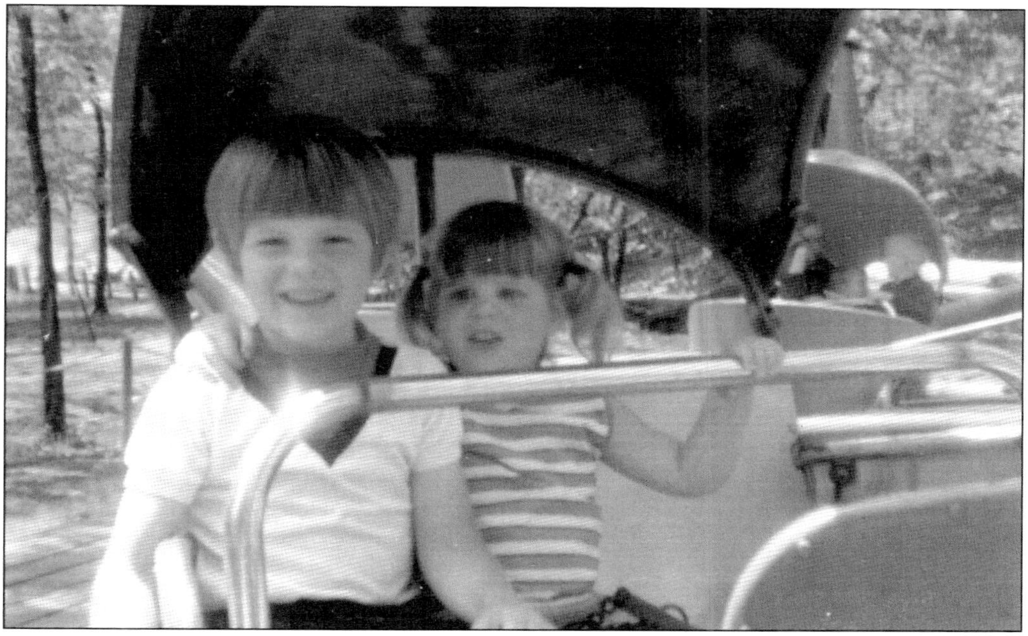

THE HELICOPTERS, 1972. Added to Kiddieland in the late 1950s, the flying helicopters were a favorite of Lakewood Park visitors. The helicopters "flew" up and down when passengers pulled or pushed the control bar. Pictured as they take turns piloting are Mark Cunningham, age seven, and Lisa Cunningham, age four.

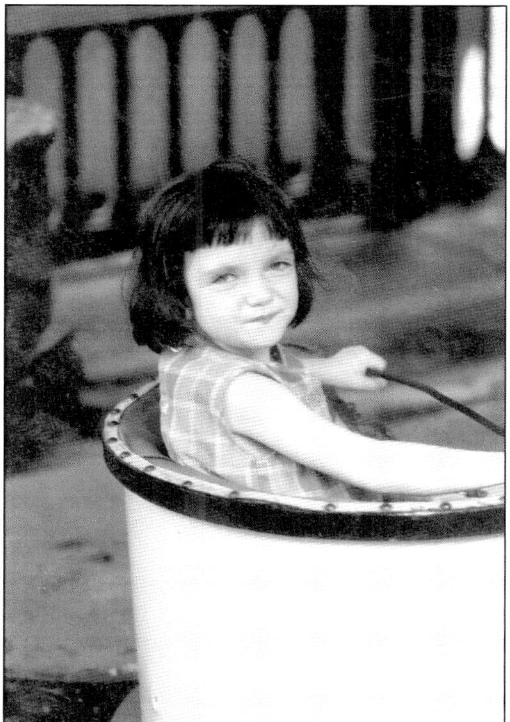

THE WHIP, 1968. One of the original Kiddieland rides was the Whip. Designed and built as an adult ride by W. F. Mangels Company, it was patented in 1914. The children's version at Lakewood Park consisted of eight cars attached to cables turned by a motor that moved the cars around an oval track. The thrill for children was when they were whipped around each end turn. Here Mary Beth Purcell readies for her ride. (Courtesy of Mark Purcell and Mickey DeCesare.)

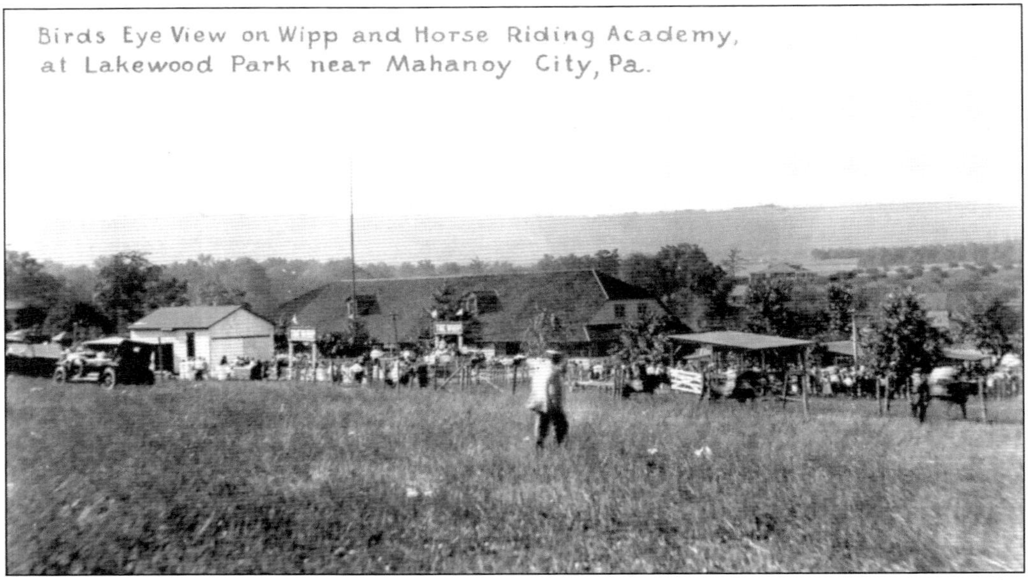

HORSE-RIDING ACADEMY, C. 1926. Horses were part of the Lakewood Park experience from the earliest days. This c. 1926 postcard shows the park grounds closest to the railroad tracks, which later became parking lots. A large fenced-in area was originally provided for patrons interesting in learning to ride a horse. In the center of the photograph is a small sign for the Whip, an early adult ride similar to the Kiddieland version that consisted of multiple cars whipping the rider around an oval metal track.

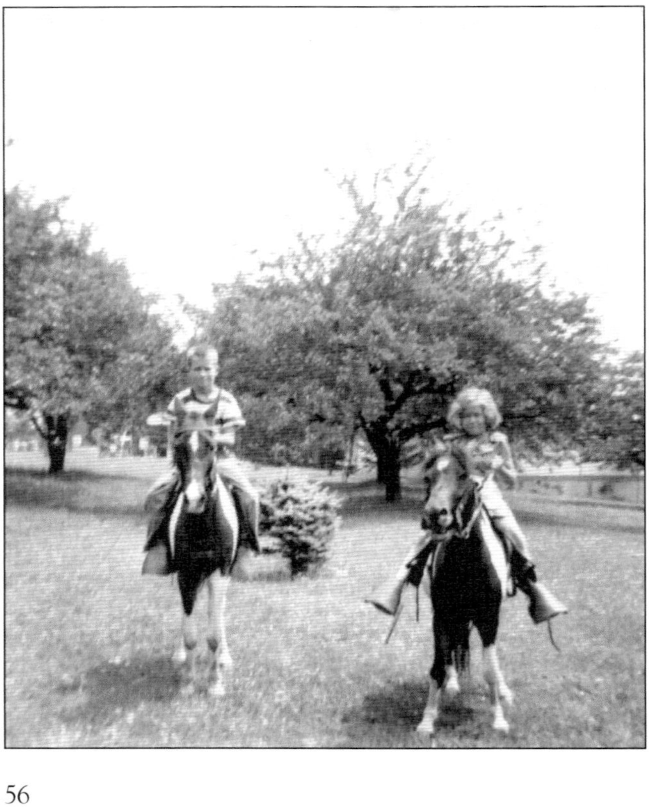

LIVE PONIES, 1952. In Kiddieland, stable boys guided ponies as young children rode around a fenced-in path. Pictured are Richie and Peggy Guinan enjoying the ponies during a short exercise run.

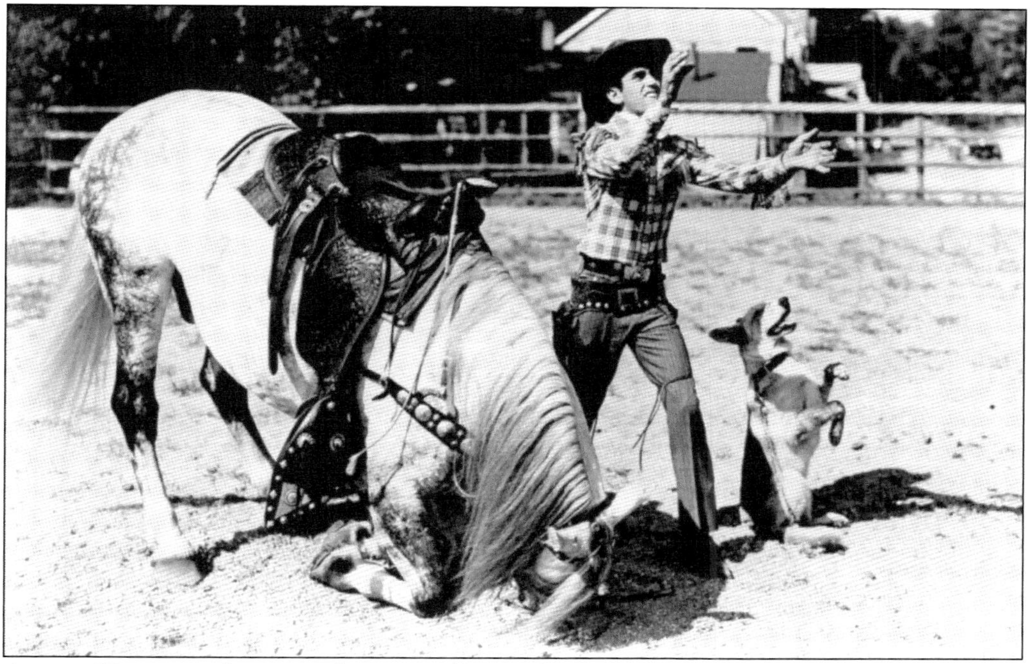

ACTION HEROES. Park visitors often enjoyed live performances featuring horses. Pictured are cowboy Joe Phillips and Smokey the Wonder Horse performing tricks. Children and adults were entertained by these acts, especially when cowboy movies were popular in theaters and on television.

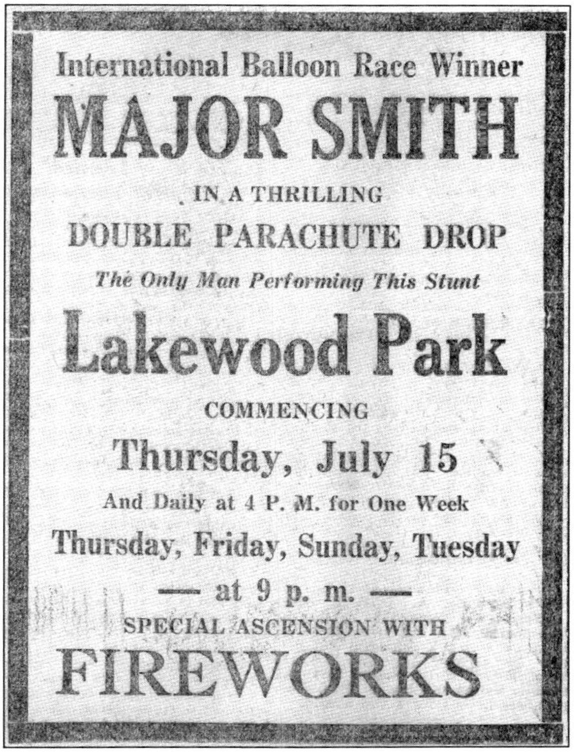

International Balloon Race Winner

MAJOR SMITH

IN A THRILLING

DOUBLE PARACHUTE DROP

The Only Man Performing This Stunt

Lakewood Park

COMMENCING

Thursday, July 15

And Daily at 4 P. M. for One Week

Thursday, Friday, Sunday, Tuesday

— at 9 p. m. —

SPECIAL ASCENSION WITH

FIREWORKS

THE PARACHUTE DROP. From the earliest days, Lakewood's management promoted the park by featuring live performances to increase attendance. Usually with a lot of hype, men who walked on wires or were buried beneath the ground were booked. This 1926 newspaper advertisement from the *Record American* boasts a performance that includes death-defying tricks with a balloon and parachute. Puck Sullivan, 100 years old, wrote this exciting account as an eye witness in the *Evening Herald* newspaper. The first feature attraction the park presented for the public, absolutely free, was the death-defying balloon ascension. The balloonist went up from the island at startling speed hanging from a trapeze and opened a parachute that floated him to a landing a long distance from the park. Despite all the bruises, he was back the next Sunday to do it all over again.

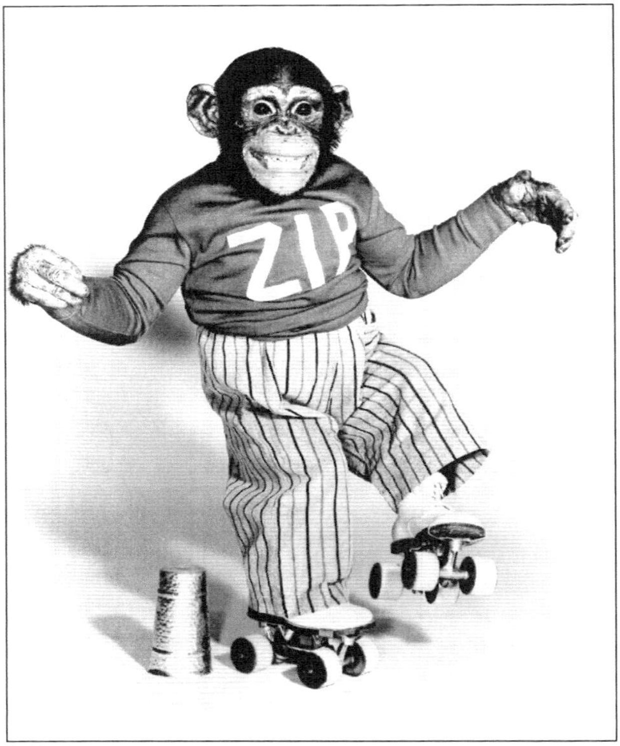

ZIPPY THE CHIMPANZEE. Zippy the chimpanzee was a television star popular with children of the 1950s. Zippy performed tricks and shook hands with children at the Lakewood Park Kiddieland stage, which featured weekly entertainment during the 1950s and 1960s. Television stars and local talent including family polka bands, dancing school performers, and politicians graced the stage. Near the Kiddieland stage were picnic tables, a stream, concessions, rides, large brick fireplaces, and water pumps for drinking and cooking.

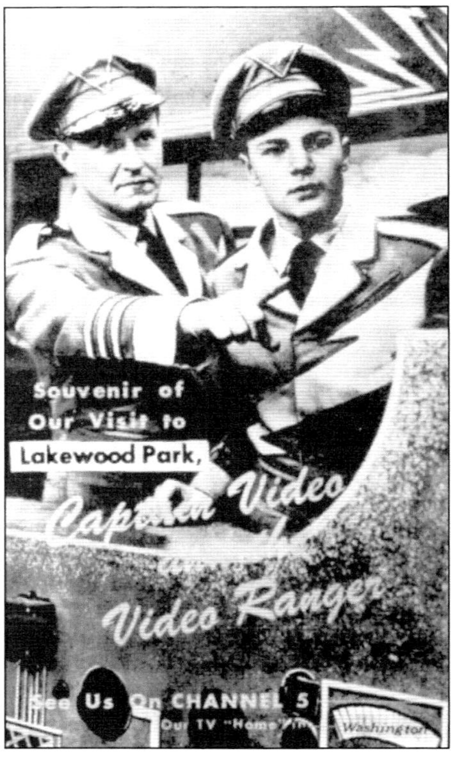

CAPTAIN VIDEO COMES TO LAKEWOOD. Captain Video, another popular television personality of the 1950s, appeared at Lakewood Park. His show was one of the first science fiction television series. It was filmed live and enjoyed by a devoted audience of children who occasionally influenced the story line.

SALLY STARR, 1950S. Almost every child in northeastern Pennsylvania during the 1950s loved Sally Starr, so of course she was an attraction at Lakewood Park. Host of a children's program for Philadelphia station WFIL-TV, Starr always dressed as a cowgirl with a hat, gun, and holster. Her program *Popeye Theater* presented Popeye cartoons and Three Stooges shorts. She was also the hostess of *Starr Theater*, featuring cowboy movies. Both programs ran from the 1950s through 1971. Linda Petosa, owner of this original photograph, tells the story of her dad, a musician, who had a mad crush on Starr and received an autographed picture from her when they were performing in the same New Jersey club. (Courtesy of Linda Petosa.)

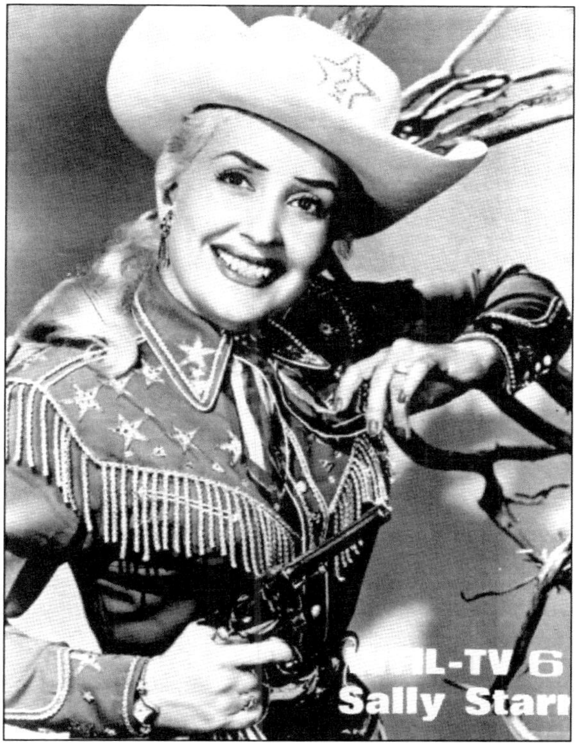

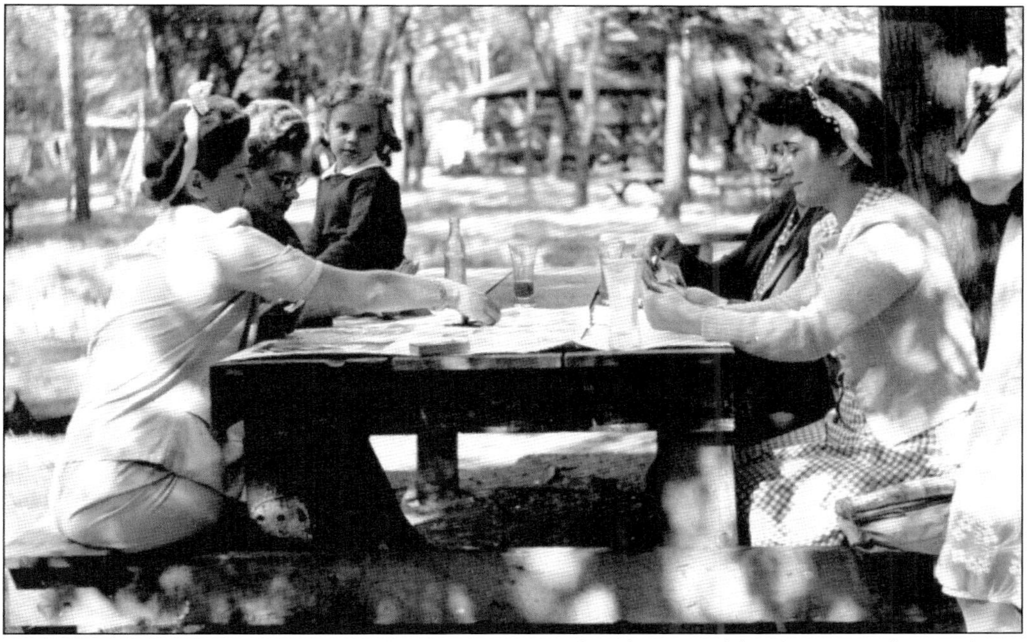

BRIDGE IN THE GROVE. Although most visitors played games like fingers and tug-of-war, these ladies practice their bridge skills on a picnic table in the grove. From left to right are Margaret Guinan, Josephine Guinan, Richard Jr. and Josephine's daughter Kathy, Ruth Ford, and unidentified.

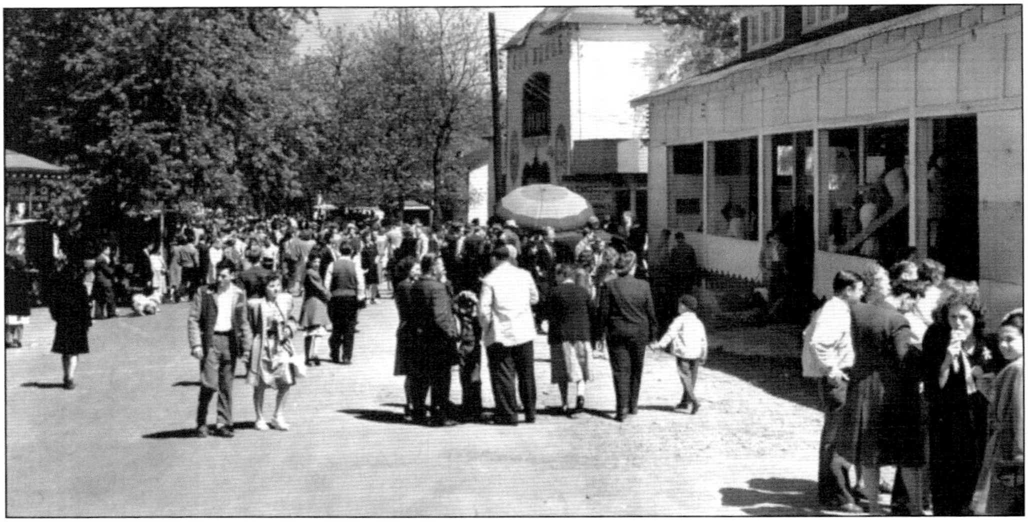

WALKWAY, LATE 1940S. The park's walkway at the top of the hill led down toward the right past the Hey Dey, a whip-type ride, and the fun house, which later became Laugh in the Dark. In the early days of the park, the fun house was an almost fully darkened walk-through attraction with obstacles, mirrors, and scary thrills. Continuing along the path were the Dodgems bumper cars and the Wild Mouse. To the left in the photograph are a full-service restaurant, the Althoff waffle and candy apple stand, the large skating rink, the bingo stand, and the wooden roller coaster. Since the park was open only during warm-weather months, May to September, it is surprising to see men in suits.

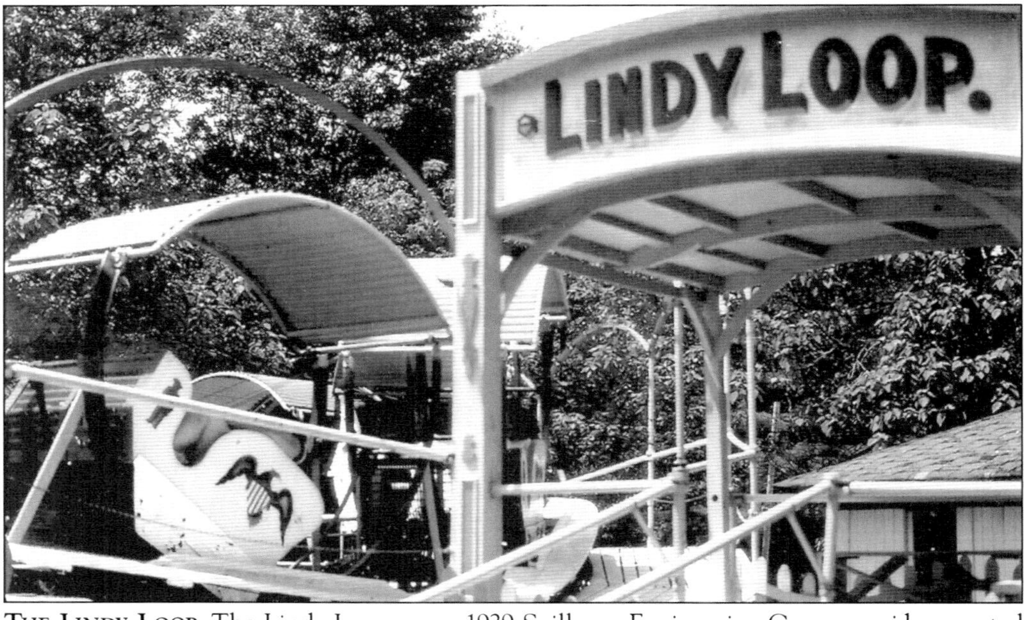

THE LINDY LOOP. The Lindy Loop was a 1929 Spillman Engineering Company ride operated at Lakewood Park by the Saullo family. The canopy-topped ride featured cars resembling old-fashioned sleighs mounted on crescent-style rails. Located directly across from the dance hall, the Lindy Loop, along with the Hey Dey and the Octopus, was a popular ride during dance intermissions. (Courtesy of Marie Ellen Koval-Steeves.)

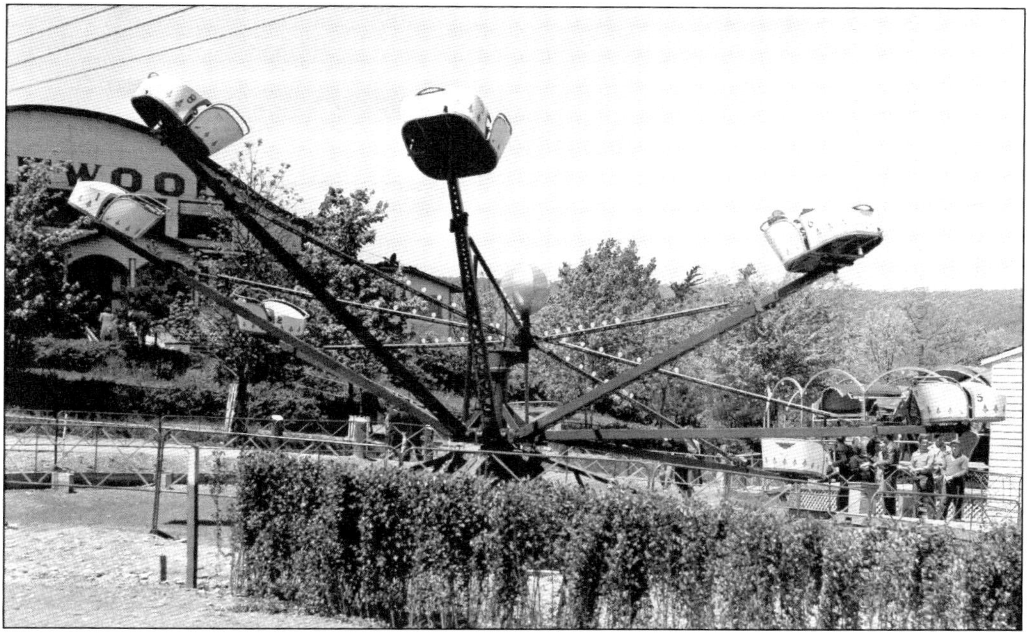

THE OCTOPUS. Owned and operated by the Saullo family, the Octopus came to Lakewood in the 1950s shortly after it was first manufactured. The ride consisted of a set of arms with cars on the end. As the arms raised and lowered from the ride's hub, and the cars spun clockwise and counter-clockwise, leaving riders a bit dizzy.

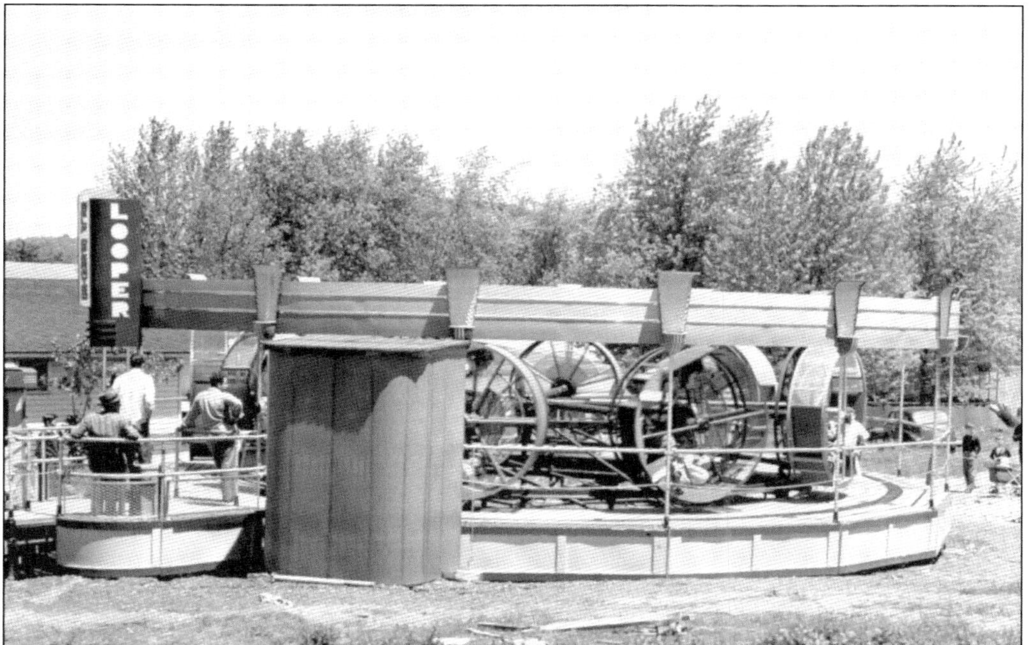

THE LOOPER, 1950S. Another of the Saullo brothers' rides, the Looper transported riders on a full forward or backward somersault. The Looper was located in back of the fun house, approximately where the old Whip and riding academy were housed.

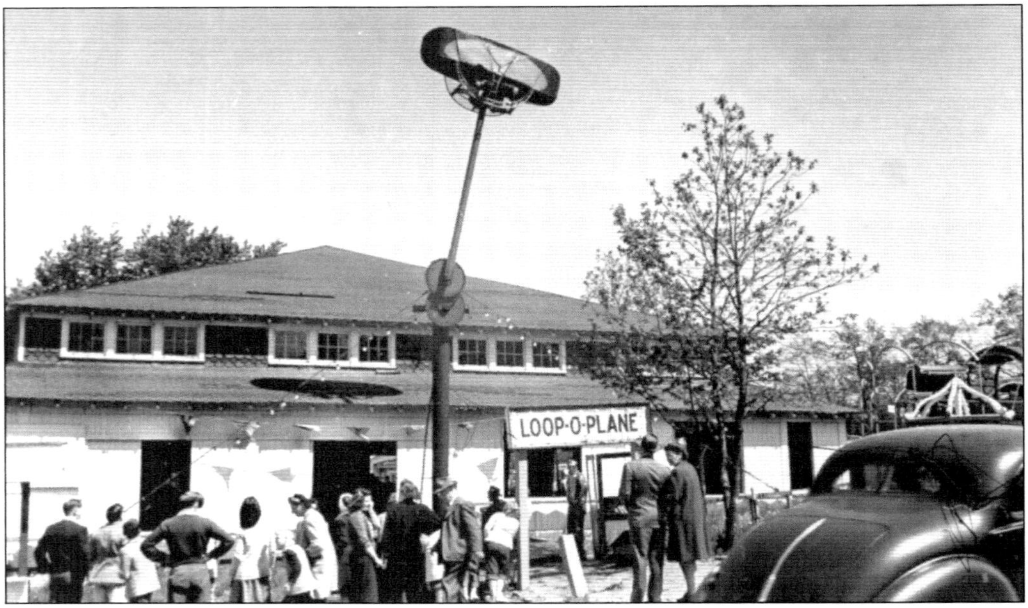

Loop-O-Plane, 1940s. The Loop-O-Plane, located across from the dance hall and near the Lindy Loop, was considered by many to be the most dangerous in the park. Two riders were strapped in with a lap belt and then propelled in a complete loop, sometimes stopping at the top as seen in the photograph above. There always seemed to be more Loop-O-Plane spectators than there were passengers.

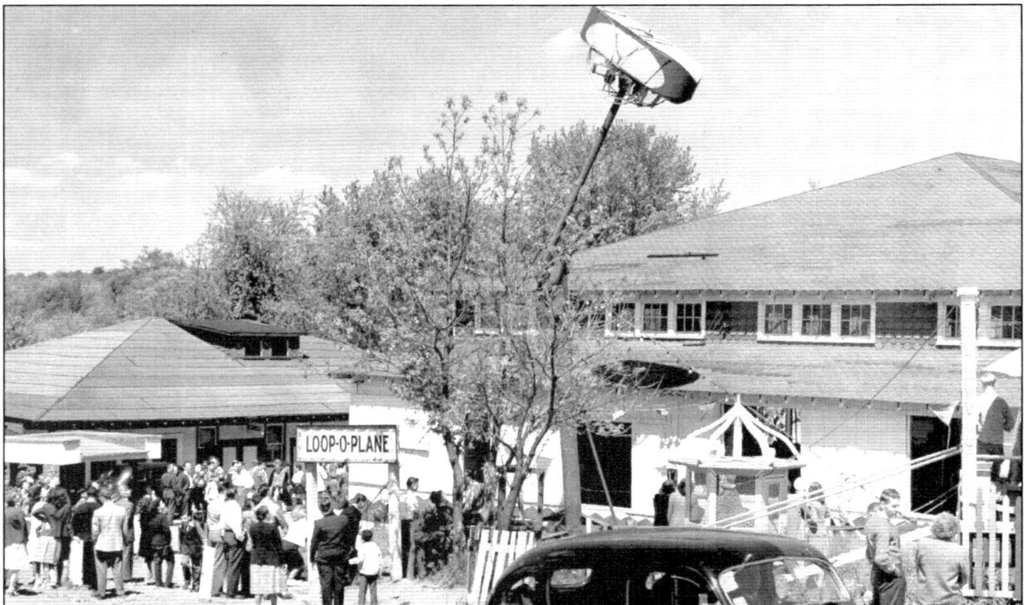

Hitch a Ride to Lakewood. In this photograph, one of the attractive, custom-made ticket booths can be seen along with a 1940s automobile. It was rare that a solo driver made the trip to Lakewood Park. In surrounding towns, if residents did not know a friend with a car, men and women alike hitched a ride by standing on the highway going to the park.

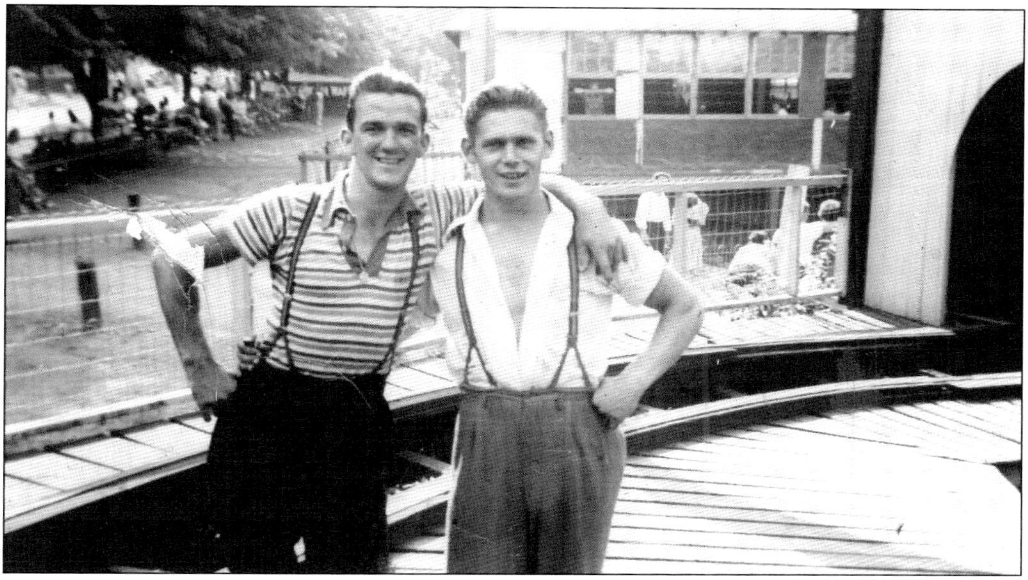

THE ROLLER COASTER. Standing in front of Lakewood's large wooden roller coaster are longtime park employee Emilio "Mal" Pedriani (left) and friend Eddie Costa. Carpenter, mechanic, ride operator, and bartender, Pedriani enjoyed his work at the park so much he relocated his family to Lakewood each summer for many years. Pedriani also owned and operated the park's Kiddieland roller coaster, eventually transferring it to his brother Daniel Pedriani, who hired Mal's son Francis and their relative Charlie Mogish to work it. (Courtesy of Francis and Barbara Pedriani.)

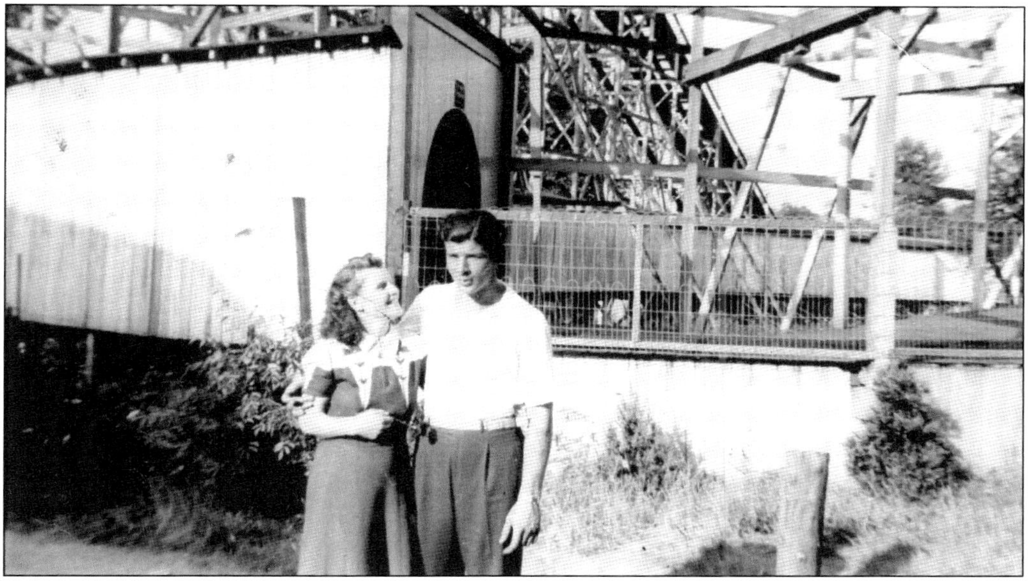

THROUGH THE COASTER TUNNEL. Pictured in front of Lakewood's roller coaster are Anna (Flaim) Pedriani and an unidentified person. The coaster was located at the end of the path of adult rides. A coaster ride began with passage through a long, dark tunnel, the entrance to which is visible in the background of this photograph. Lois Althoff Musser, whose family operated a Lakewood Park concession, remembers enjoying her first kiss in the coaster tunnel. (Courtesy of Francis and Barbara Pedriani.)

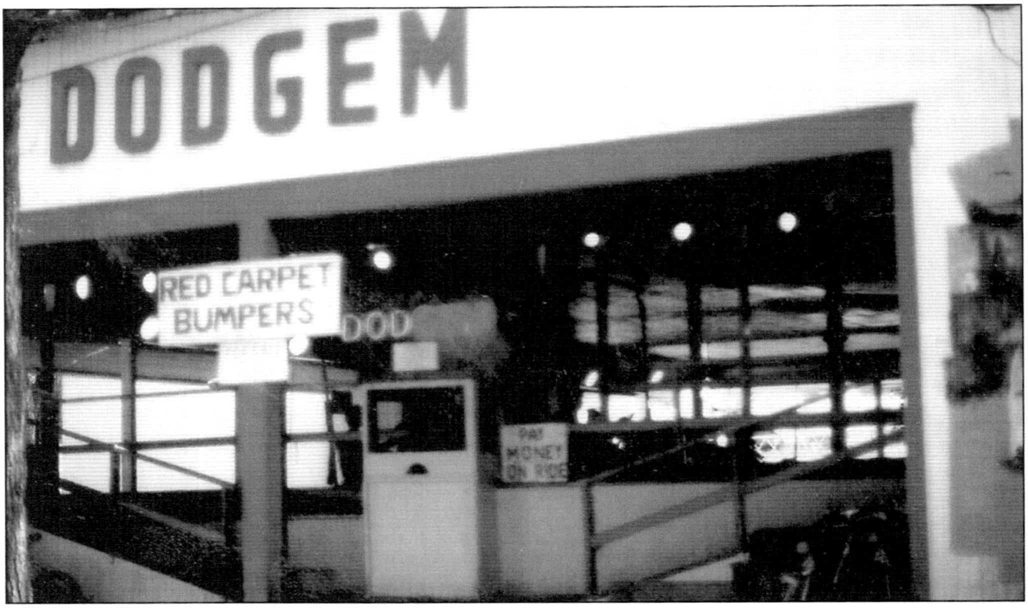

The Dodgems. The Dodgems were one of the older rides in the park and were originally located within a structure known as the skating rink or beer hall and craft hall. Local entrepreneur Charlie Bair purchased the cars, which ran on electricity and had rubber around their bases. They were designed to bump into one another and took their name from their manufacturer, Dodgem. The Dodgems were so popular that soon Bair constructed a large building along the major ride walkway that included a special floor and ceiling just for the cars. The ride continued in operation until the park's closing. (Courtesy of Marie Ellen Koval-Steeves.)

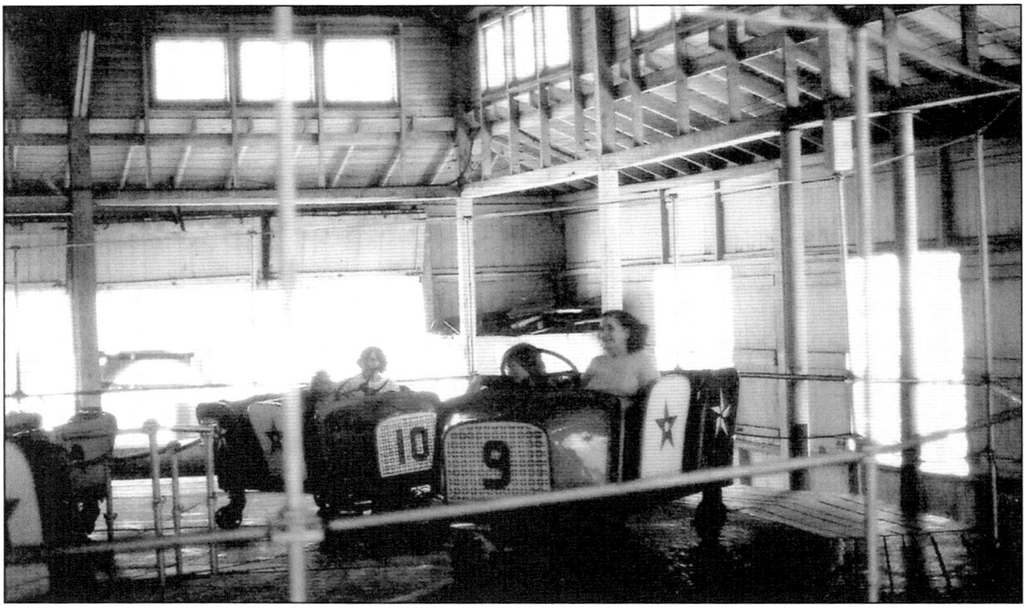

The Hey Dey. Housed across from the restaurant and down from the dance hall, the Hey Dey was one of the oldest rides in the park. Joseph "Red" Burke was the only person who ever operated this ride. (Courtesy of Marie Ellen Koval-Steeves.)

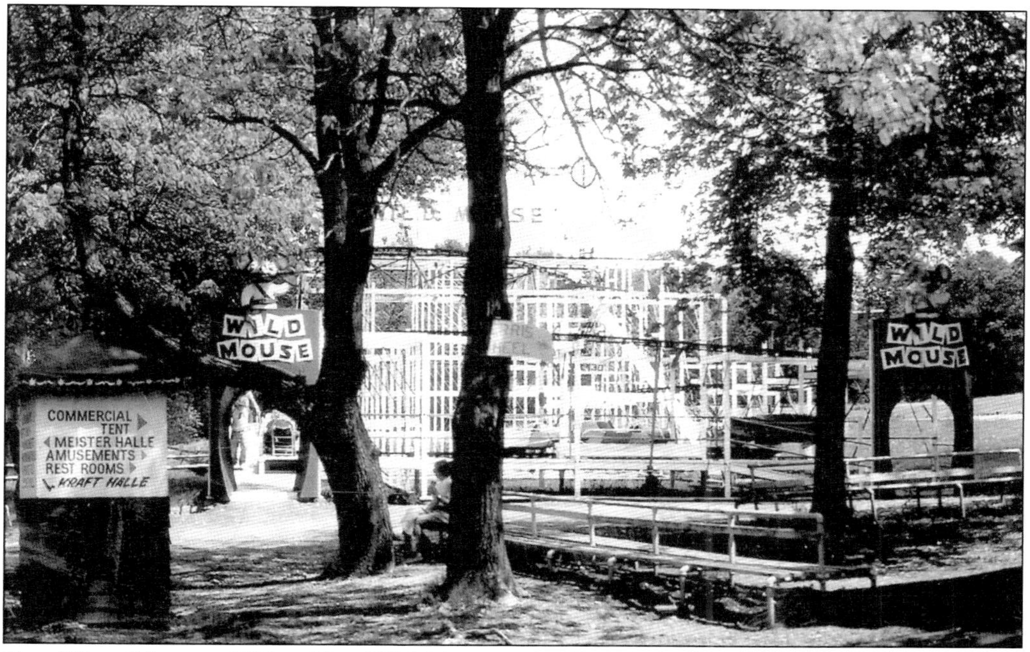

THE WILD MOUSE, 1970S. The Wild Mouse, erected in 1959, located at the end of the adult ride path and across from the roller coaster, was a favorite attraction of those who loved fast coaster-type rides. (Courtesy of Marie Ellen Koval-Steeves.)

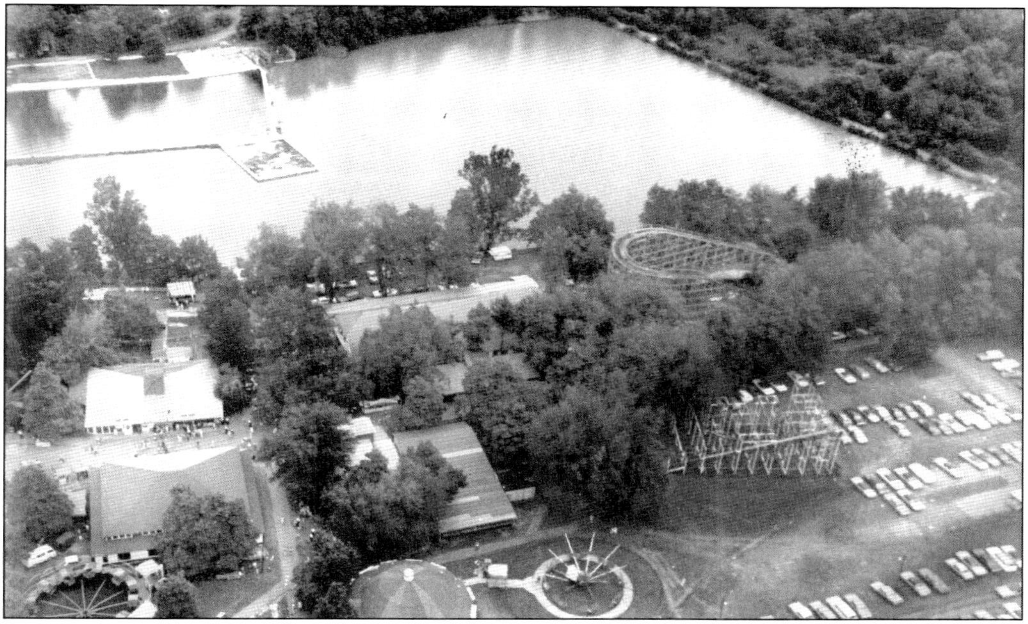

AERIAL PHOTOGRAPH, 1970S. This bird's-eye view of Lakewood Park shows the Octopus (bottom left) and the Lindy Loop and Hey Dey (directly above). The center group of rides includes the Looper, Flying Scooters, Laugh in the Dark, and Dodgems. On the far right is the Wild Mouse. Along the park's walkway are, from left to right, the restaurant, the Althoff waffle stand, the skating rink (beer hall), the bingo stand, and the roller coaster.

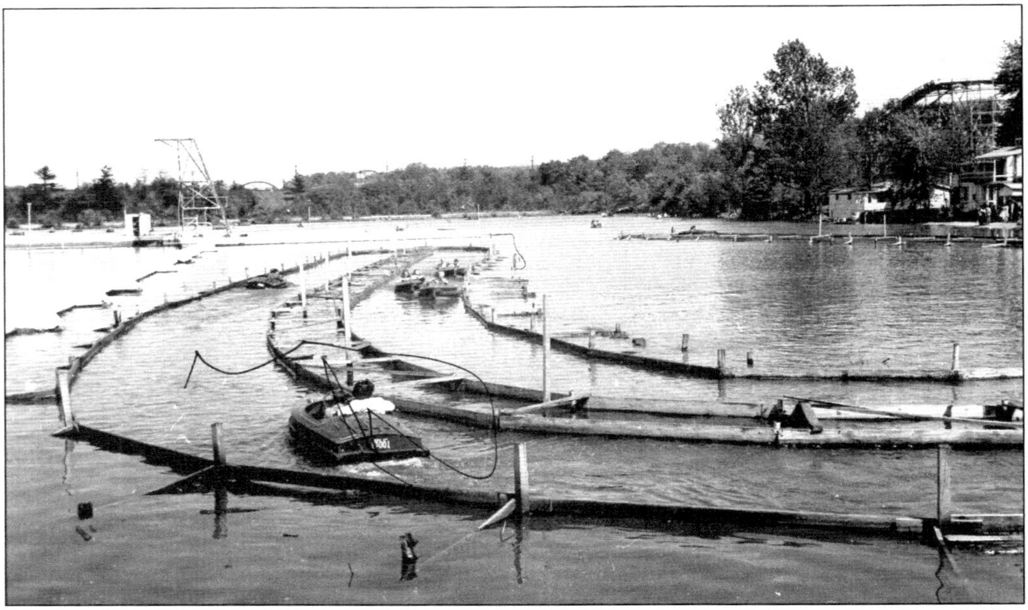

Motorboats, 1940s. As engines became more common, the demand for motorized rides at Lakewood Park increased. The motorboats supplemented the park's original rowboats and quickly surpassed them in popularity. Riders controlled each boat's steering and gas within a defined wooden track that toured the park's scenic lake.

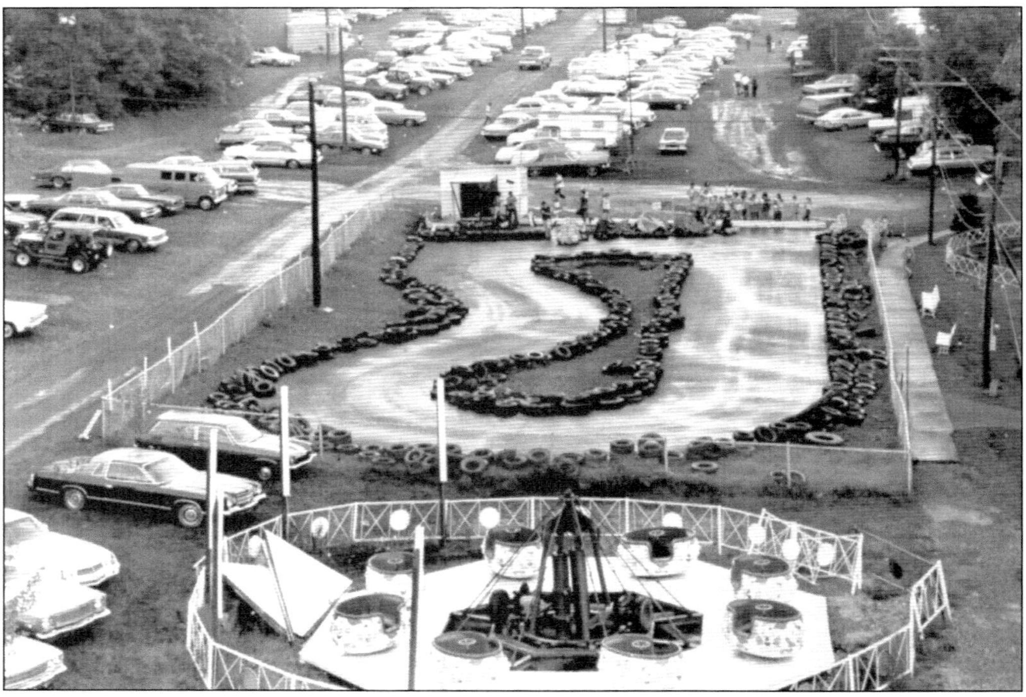

Go-Karts, 1970s. One of the last rides added to the park was small gasoline engine cars totally controlled by the driver on an open macadam track. This ride was located across from the dance hall, adjacent to a parking lot.

Three

THE DANCE HALL

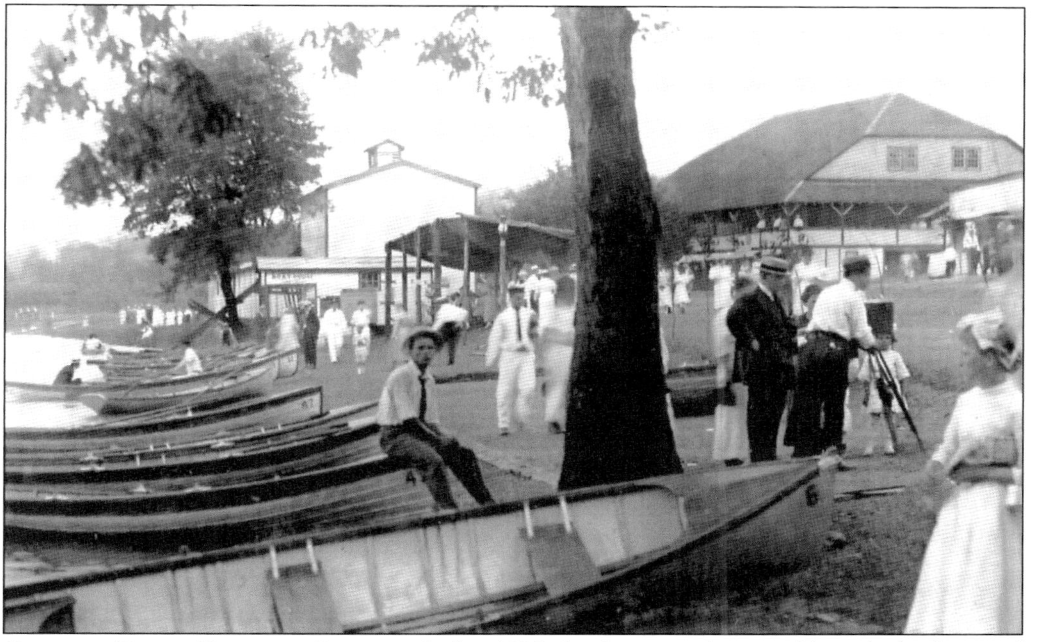

ORIGINAL DANCE PAVILION. Sometime before 1920, the dance pavilion, visible in the background (right) of this photograph, was built. Its interior was used for music and dancing, while its porch was a popular spot for promenading and enjoying the lake view. (Courtesy of Joseph Moore.)

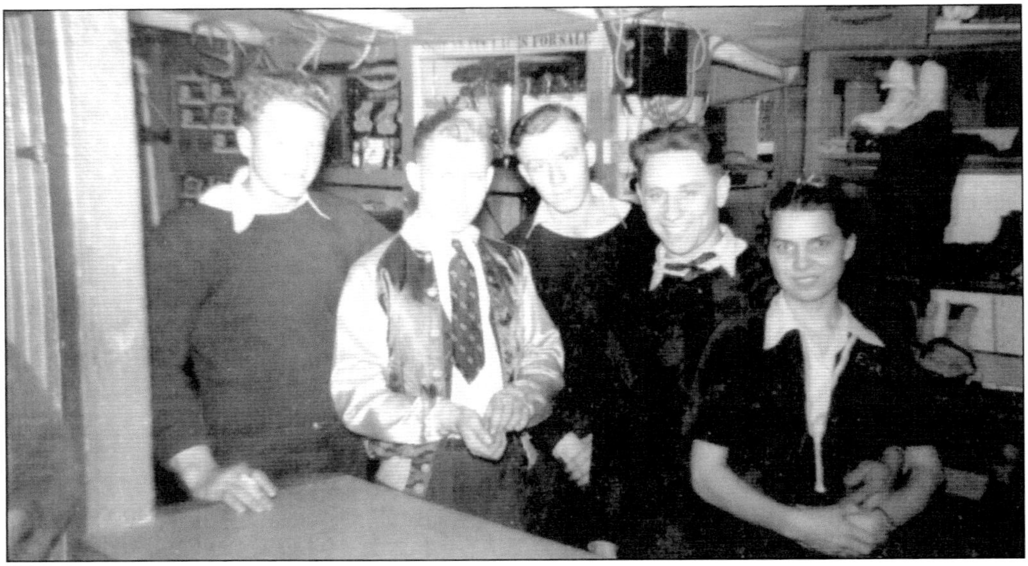

SKATING RINK OFFICE. When the new dance hall, known as the Lakewood Ballroom, was built in 1925, the old dance pavilion became available for entrepreneurs. First Charlie Bair operated the Dodgems ride here and offered skating in the building. Later Joe Mayesky bought the skating business from Bair upon returning home after serving in the navy. Pictured in the office of the rink are its operators and friends, from left to right, Joseph "Red" Burke, Charlie Mayesky, Bill Hudson, and concession owners Joe and Evelyn Mayesky. Joe's brother, Charlie, dates the picture: "I don't remember who took the picture, but it was a Thursday night, July 1941. I had on a white shirt and tie. Normally I did not wear a shirt and tie, but Thursday nights after we closed the rink I would go up to the Lakewood Ballroom to dance. Every Thursday they had the top bands: Glenn Miller, Kay Keiser, Guy Lombardo, Benny Goodman, and others played there." (Courtesy of the Mayesky family.)

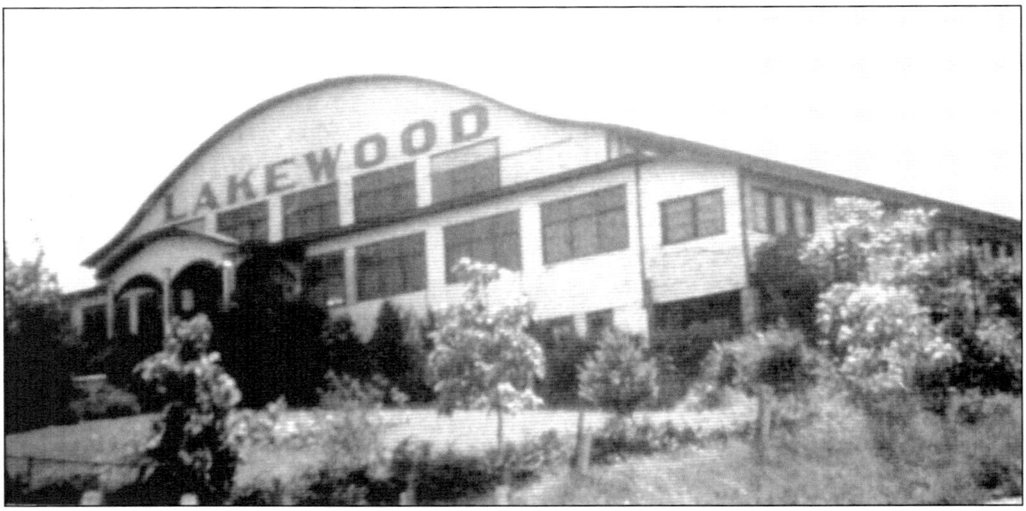

LAKEWOOD BALLROOM. Completed in 1925, the Lakewood Ballroom became one of America's dance capitals during the era of the big bands. The ballroom provided a magical escape, and people came by the thousands every Monday and Thursday night to celebrate the age of swing in the magnificent venue.

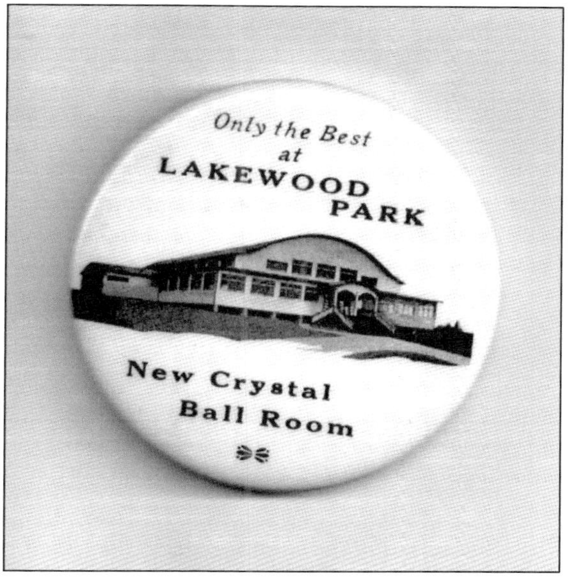

THE CRYSTAL BALLROOM. This pin was manufactured in 1925 to announce the opening of the new dance hall. The facility boasted a 168-foot-long-by-104-foot-wide floor, which was built in such a manner that the dancing space was totally unobstructed. Its floor was made of maple and walnut imported from South America. The roof was supported by columns of wooden arches, creating a very high vaulted ceiling. A 12-foot promenade surrounded the dance floor with rocking chairs separating dancers from bystanders.

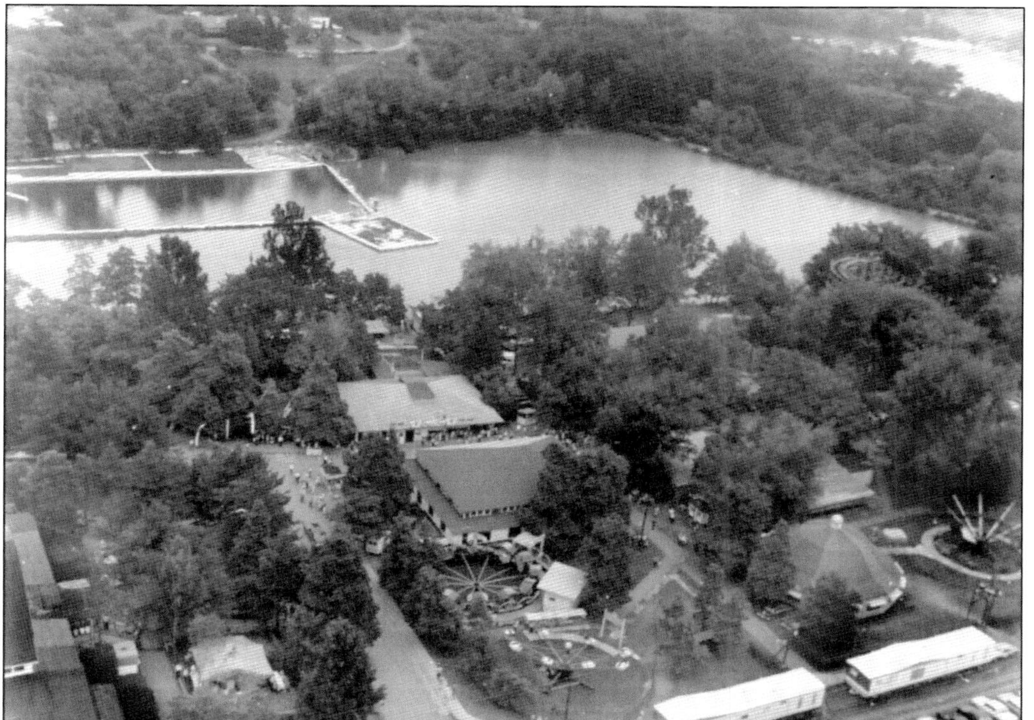

LAKEWOOD AND LAKESIDE PARK. This aerial photograph of Lakewood Park shows how closely located it was to Lakeside Park, which is the body of water visible at the far top right. Always ingenious at stretching a dollar, each park's patrons would purchase tickets for its respective dance, plan to meet friends along the path between parks during intermission, and switch tickets so each group could also enjoy the band at the other park. Management eventually caught on and began stamping hands with ink visible only under ultraviolet light.

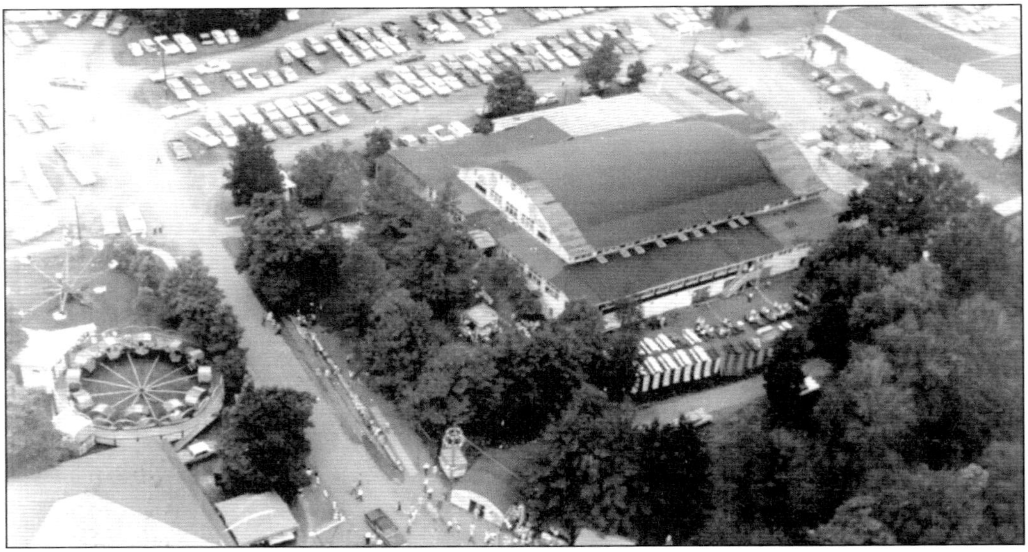

AERIAL VIEW OF THE DANCE HALL. This aerial photograph provides a southward view of the top of the hill in Lakewood Park. In the center of the photograph is the dance hall. The Lakewood Theater is visible at the far right. Ballroom dances always ran from 8:30 to 12:30 p.m. It was a very proper ballroom where men were expected to wear jackets and ties. Sometimes a properly suited fellow would pay his admission, have his hand stamped, and find an open window through which to pass his tie out to a buddy, so he could also be admitted. During dance intermissions, the park's rides were open, and nothing compared to the thrill of a roller coaster ride in the dark of night.

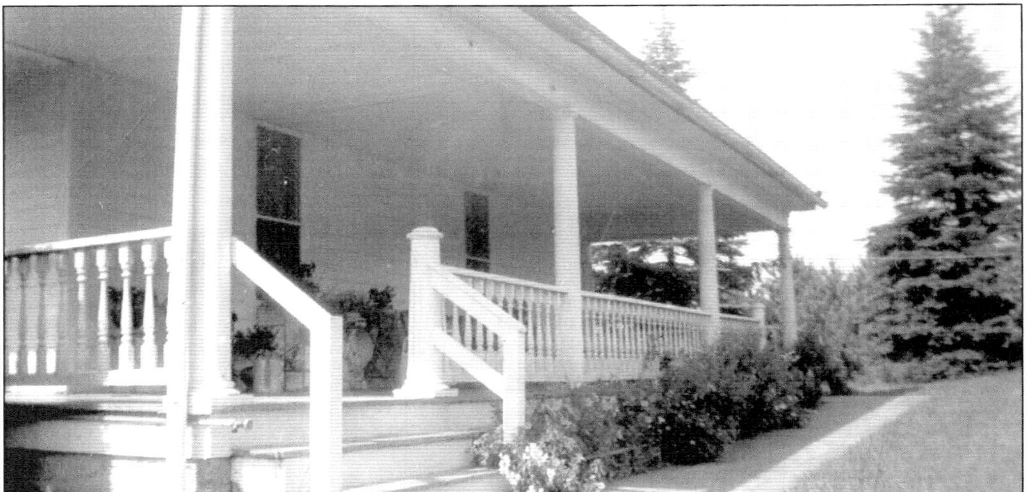

BUNGALOW OF RICHARD AND JULIA GUINAN. The distinction of creating the most celebrity chaos at Lakewood Park goes to Rudy Vallée. Vallée had booked two events for one night, a radio broadcast and an appearance at Lakewood. Richard Guinan Sr. insisted that the radio broadcast be recorded at the Guinan bungalow at Lakewood after which Vallée could easily make the short trip to the ballroom for his performance. Not surprisingly, the news leaked and the Guinan bungalow was overrun with fans eager for a close-up peek at the star. So many people crowded onto the bungalow porch that night, the entire structure collapsed.

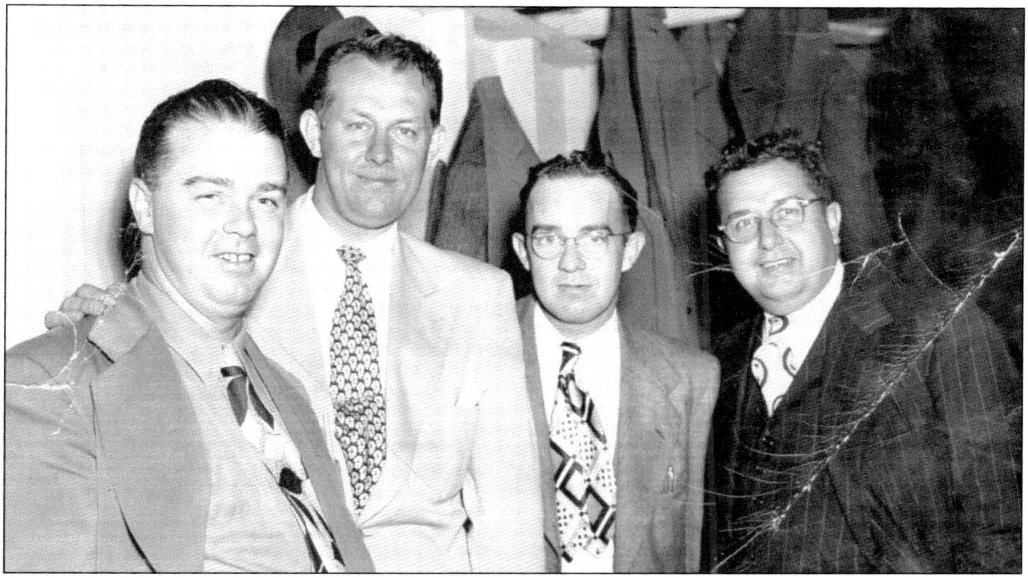

VAUGHN MONROE. The performer who drew the biggest crowd to Lakewood was Vaughn Monroe, whose first appearance broke the all-time attendance record with over 6,000 persons in the ballroom. Monroe was one of the most popular male vocalists of the 1940s and 1950s, with a rich baritone voice; he also played trumpet and trombone and led his orchestra. On June 12, 1948, Vaughn Monroe's coast-to-coast radio show was broadcast from the Lakewood bandstand. The announcer was Bert Parks. Seen here from left to right are Frank Guinan, Monroe, Richard Guinan Jr., and Daniel Guinan II.

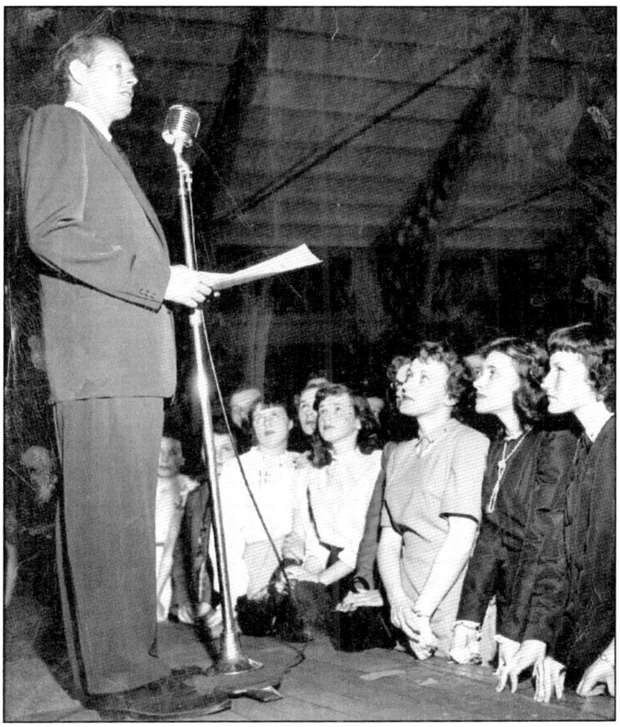

MONROE WITH CROWDED BANDSTAND. There were always admirers who gathered in front of the Lakewood stage and stayed there, never dancing. They came to hear the horns blow and the reeds sing. Prominent band members played solo parts lasting several minutes, accompanied by loud clapping. In those days, bands did not have powerful amplifiers and speakers. At Lakewood there was only a single microphone that served as a public address system where the leader introduced songs. The band's vocalist also used the microphone. If the guys in the band could blow and the dance hall and stage were designed properly, as Lakewood's were, then the music could be heard anywhere.

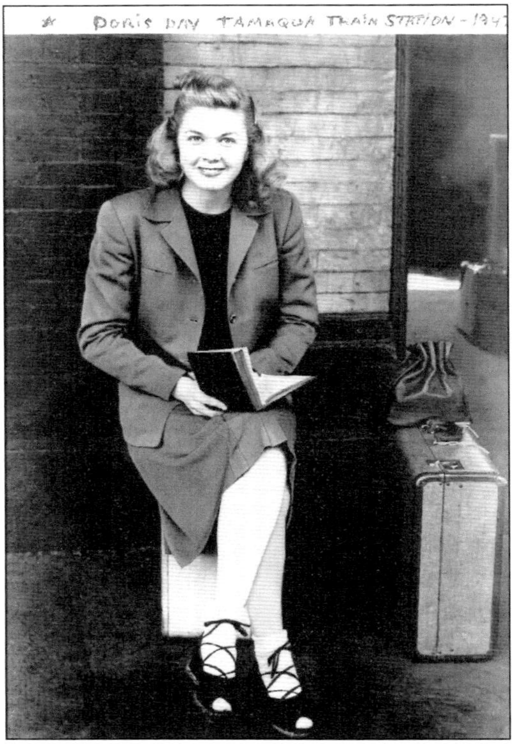

DORIS DAY. Most big bands and their vocalists traveled by bus, but Doris Day came by train. Before her movie stardom, Day sang with the Les Brown and His Band of Renown. Day is pictured here in 1947, posing for an admirer while she waits to be picked up at the Tamaqua Reading Railroad station on her way to the Lakewood Ballroom for a Thursday night gig. (Courtesy of Save Our Station.)

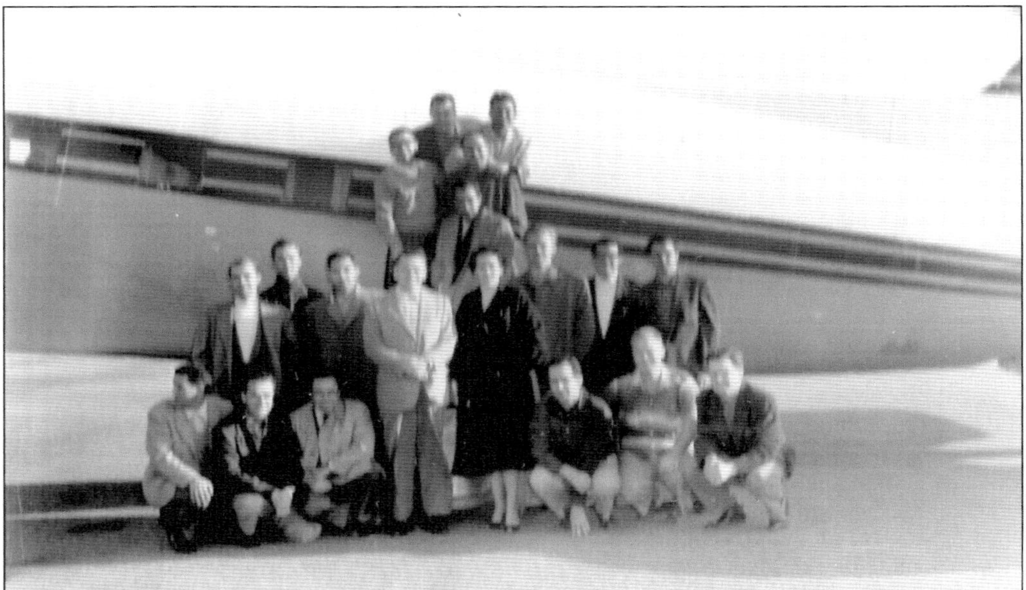

CHRISTMAS GREETING FROM LES BROWN AND HIS BAND. This photograph is from a Christmas card that Les Brown, a Schuylkill County native, sent to the Daniel Guinan II family. Born and raised in Reinerton near Tower City, Schuylkill County, Brown became a national sensation and traveled by small plane to his orchestra's many gigs. Les Brown and His Band of Renown were fronted by many vocalists, the most famous of whom was Doris Day.

DUKE ELLINGTON. One of the most influential figures in jazz, Duke Ellington gave American music its own sound for the first time. Ellington played over 20,000 performances in Europe, Latin America, the Middle East, and Asia and thrilled audiences at Lakewood Park, returning annually.

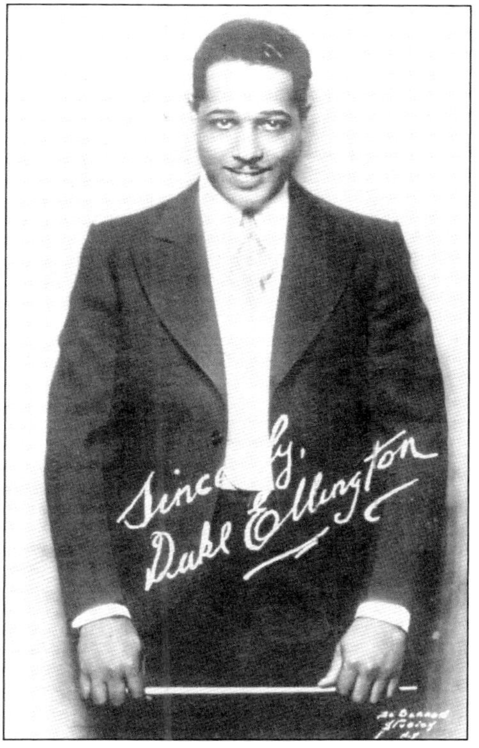

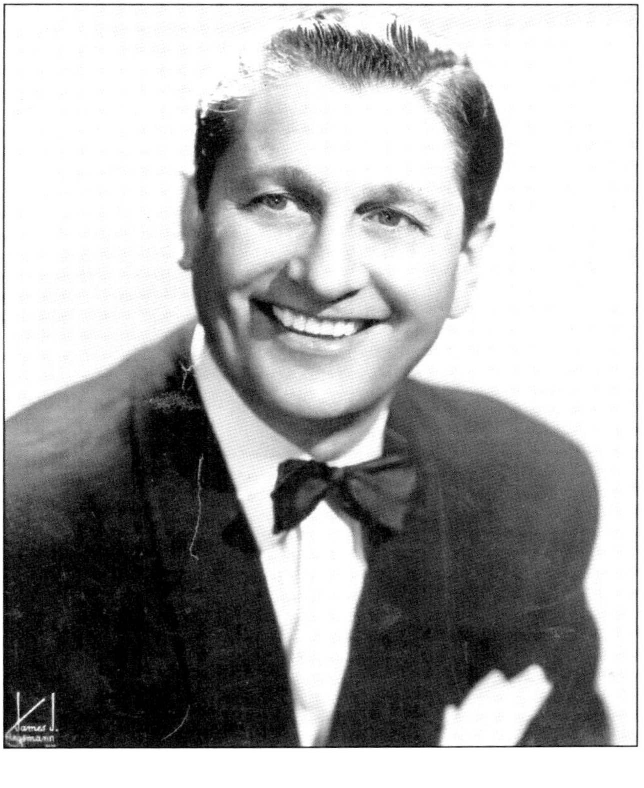

LAWRENCE WELK. A musician, accordionist, bandleader, and television impresario, Lawrence Welk hosted *The Lawrence Welk Show* from 1951 to 1982. Welk enjoyed "hot jazz," but his show always featured his champagne music of polkas and novelty songs. Lakewood fans supported him enthusiastically.

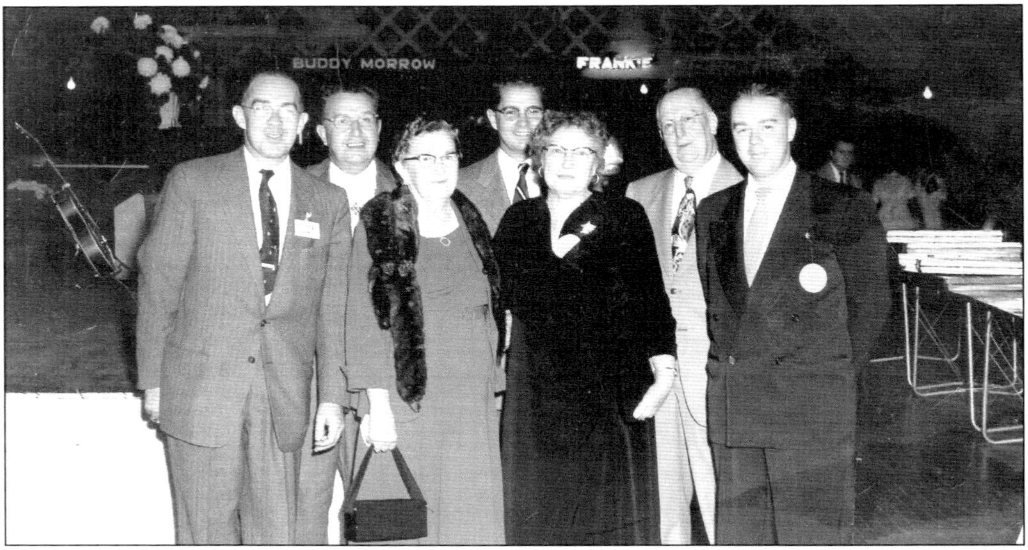

GUINAN FAMILY CELEBRATION. Pictured in the 1950s in the Lakewood Ballroom are the four Guinan brothers, with their mother, Julia, and congressman Dr. Ivor Fenton and wife Margaret. In addition, Guinan's Department Store employees are also present. This picture was a special find for their children, because only a few were taken that captured all four brothers with their mother. Pictured are, from left to right, (first row) Richard Guinan Jr., Julia Guinan, Margaret (Lewis) Fenton, and Frank Guinan; (second row) Daniel Guinan II, Larry Guinan, and Dr. Ivor Fenton.

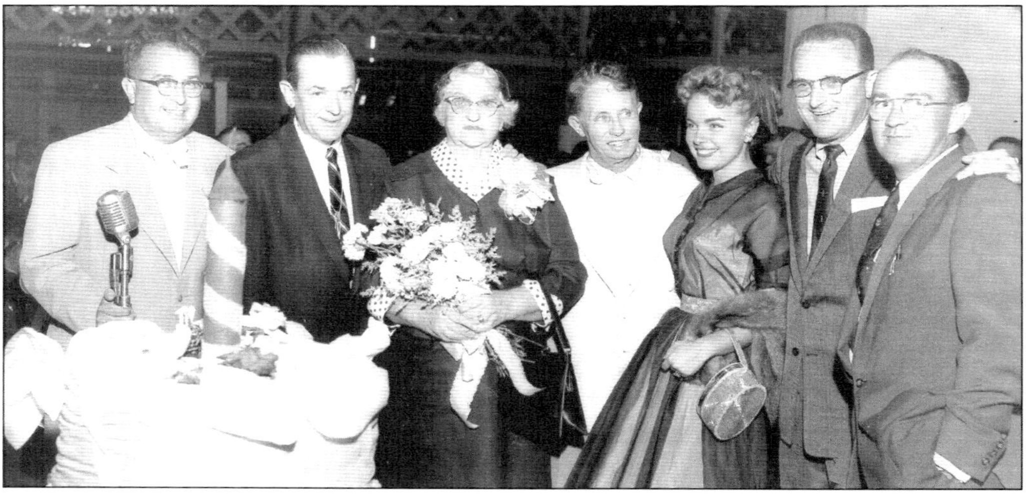

MOM DORSEY'S 80TH BIRTHDAY PARTY. Tommy and Jimmy Dorsey formed the Dorsey Brothers Orchestra in 1934 but within a year split to form their own bands. Both bands played Lakewood Park frequently. Tommy with his lead vocalist, Frank Sinatra, recorded many of the top hits of the swing era. A special treat was in store for fans when Tommy and Jimmy came "home" to play for their mother's 80th birthday party. Pictured at the celebration on Thursday, August 26, 1954, are, from left to right, Daniel Guinan II; Jimmy Dorsey; Theresa "Mom" Dorsey, mother of famous sons; Bert Wheeler, who was appearing the next week at the Lakewood Theater, Terry Moore, a vivacious movie star performing at the Lakewood Theater who came to congratulate Mom Dorsey after the show; Tommy Dorsey; and Richard Guinan Jr.

BINGO AT THE LAKE. According to Donald Coombe, former park employee, this 1931 token recalls the biggest regularly scheduled event during the immediate postwar years (aside from the Thursday night dances)—the famous Pat's bingo party. Around 1946, Pat Gallagher of the Barnsville area began running free bus service on Tuesday nights from a variety of locations in the region. The ballroom was filled wall to wall with tables, chairs, and 5,000 patrons. Just setting the tables up and taking them down was a major effort requiring a team of part-time employees.

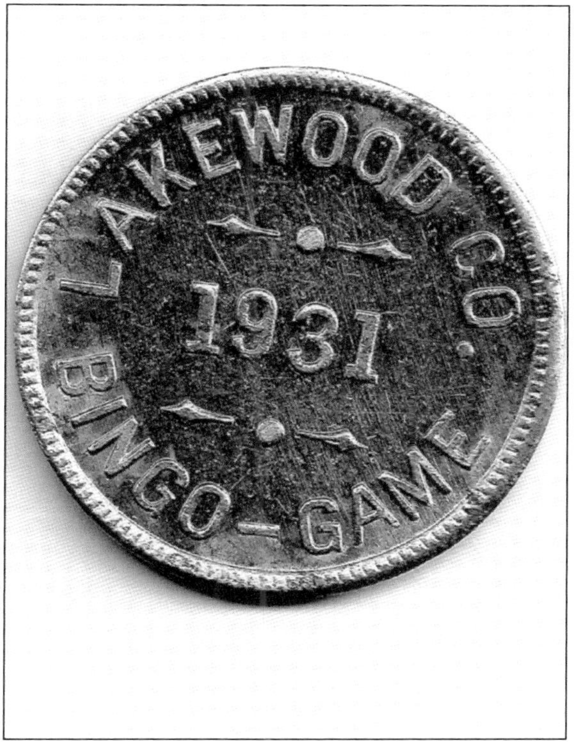

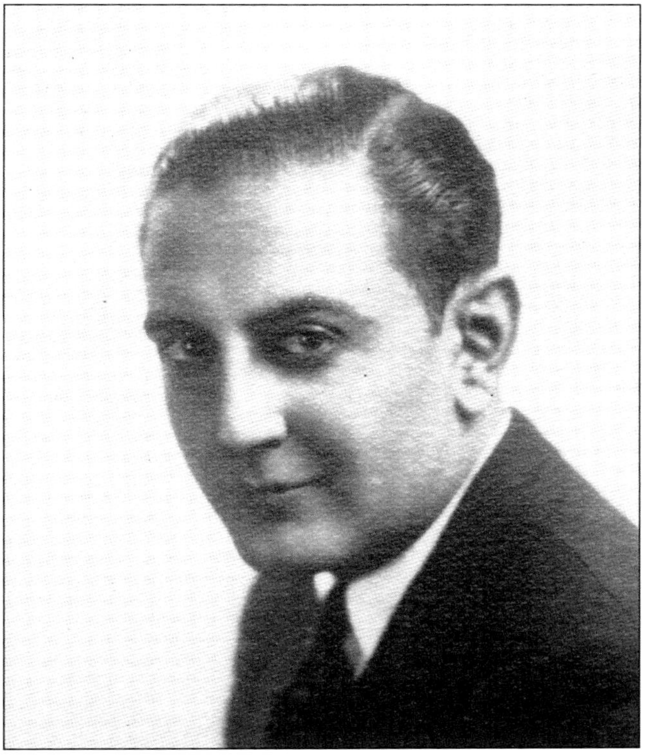

GUY LOMBARDO AND HIS ROYAL CANADIANS. Guy Lombardo played at Lakewood Park for 27 consecutive years. His band was billed as "the sweetest music this side of heaven" and sold more than 300 million phonograph albums. The Royal Canadians were noted for playing the traditional "Auld Lang Syne" as part of the New Year's Eve celebrations in Times Square.

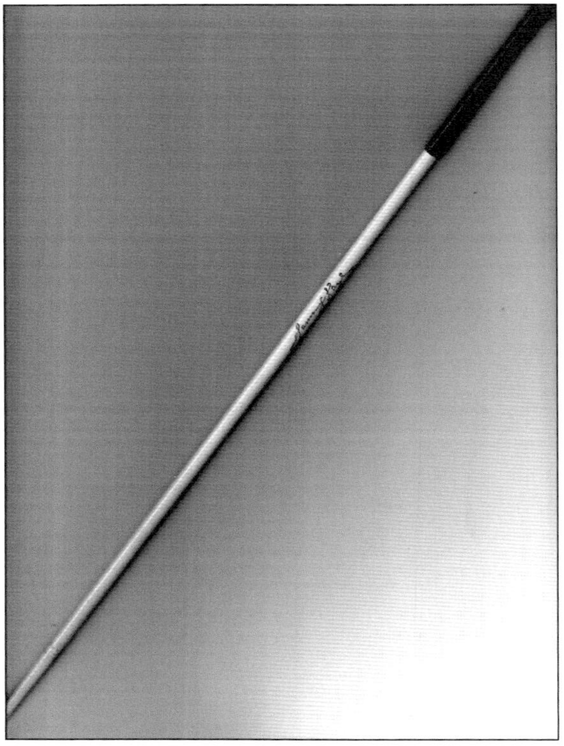

SAMMY KAYE. A great act of the Sammy Kaye Orchestra and an early audience participation favorite was "Do You Want to Lead the Band?" At every appearance, Kaye would invite several people from the audience to come onstage to use his baton to "conduct" the big band. At the end of the act, the crowd would vote with loud applause for its favorite. During Kaye's 1959 Lakewood Park appearance, Michael Grigalonis of Mahanoy City won Kaye's baton along with bragging rights for the next year.

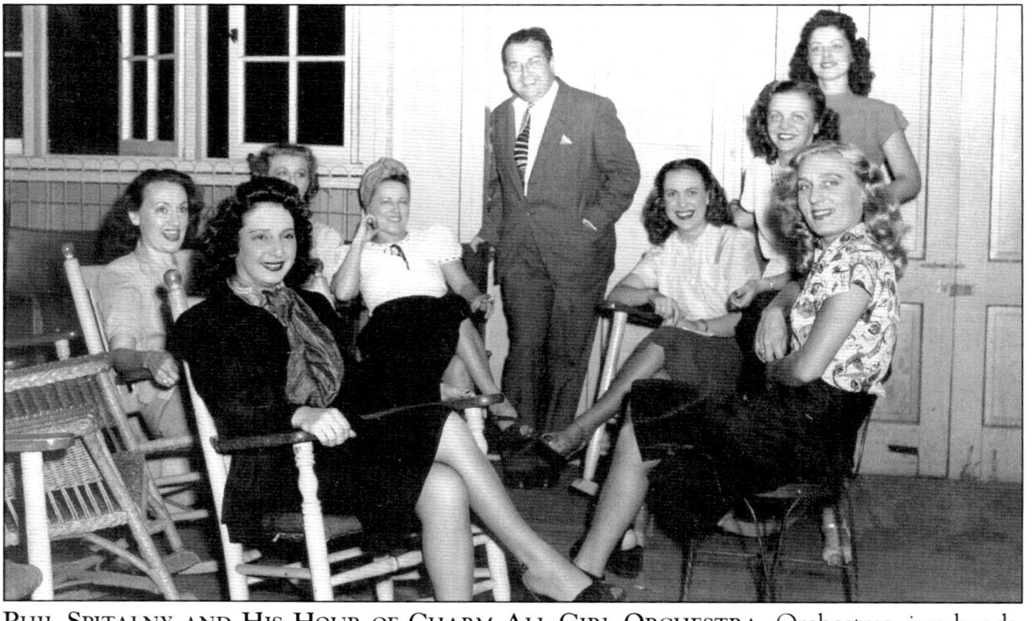

PHIL SPITALNY AND HIS HOUR OF CHARM ALL-GIRL ORCHESTRA. Orchestras, jazz bands, and marimba bands composed entirely of women were not uncommon in the 1930s, but with the coming of World War II, all-girl orchestras became the rage. Pictured here are Daniel Guinan II and the violinists from Phil Spitalny's all-girl orchestra on the familiar rocking chairs of the ballroom.

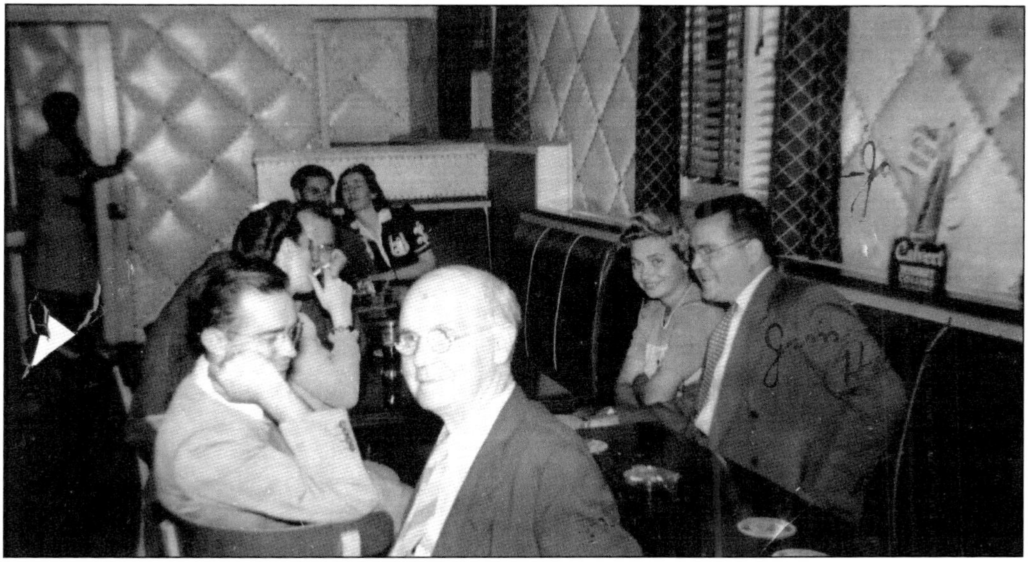

AMERICAN ROOM. Resembling a swank New York City grill, the American Room in the Lakewood Ballroom was decorated in blue, white, and a touch of red. The room featured padded leather walls trimmed with upholstery tacks, leather booths, a 30-foot-long padded bar, and a raised platform for piano and vocals. Enjoying a break from dancing are, from left front, Richard Guinan Jr., Richard Guinan Sr. (cofounder), Josephine Guinan (wife of Richard Jr.), and Jim Haughney.

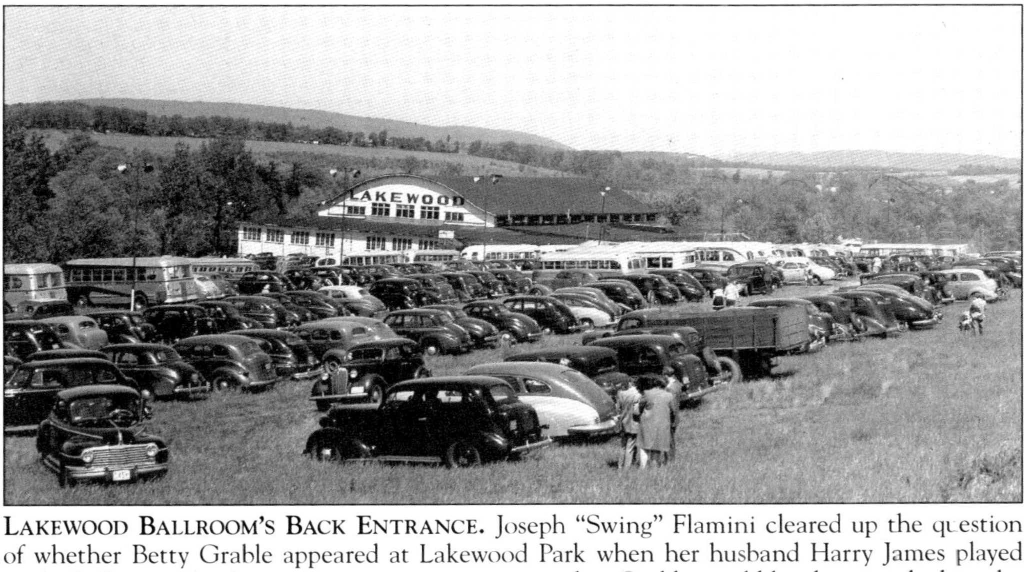

LAKEWOOD BALLROOM'S BACK ENTRANCE. Joseph "Swing" Flamini cleared up the question of whether Betty Grable appeared at Lakewood Park when her husband Harry James played at the ballroom. At the time, rumors were rampant that Grable would be there, and when she did not show, most people thought the rumor may have been a publicity stunt. Flamini swears that Grable was there—but only at the back door and only for a moment. Flamini had a chance meeting with Joe Matthews of the Matthews Detective Agency, who was charged with guarding Grable that evening. "Come to the back door at 9:00, Swing, and I'll introduce you to Betty," Matthews told Flamini. "And there she was," according to Flamini, "briefly and not feeling well." Grable never did come into the ballroom, but Flamini met her that night at Lakewood.

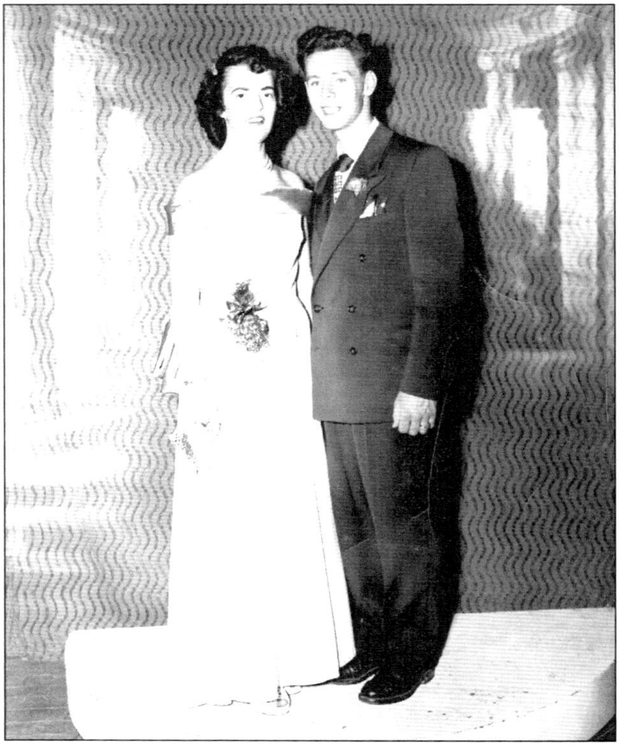

High School Proms. Puck Sullivan, 100 years old, recalls that his graduation in 1926 was celebrated at a dance and dinner at Lakewood Park. More than 20 years after Sullivan's graduation, the Mahanoy City High School class of 1949 held its prom there too. Pictured are Donald Coombe and his date, Joan Benedict. They, like their classmates before and after them, danced to a local live band and rode the amusements at intermission in their prom attire. (Courtesy of Donald Coombe.)

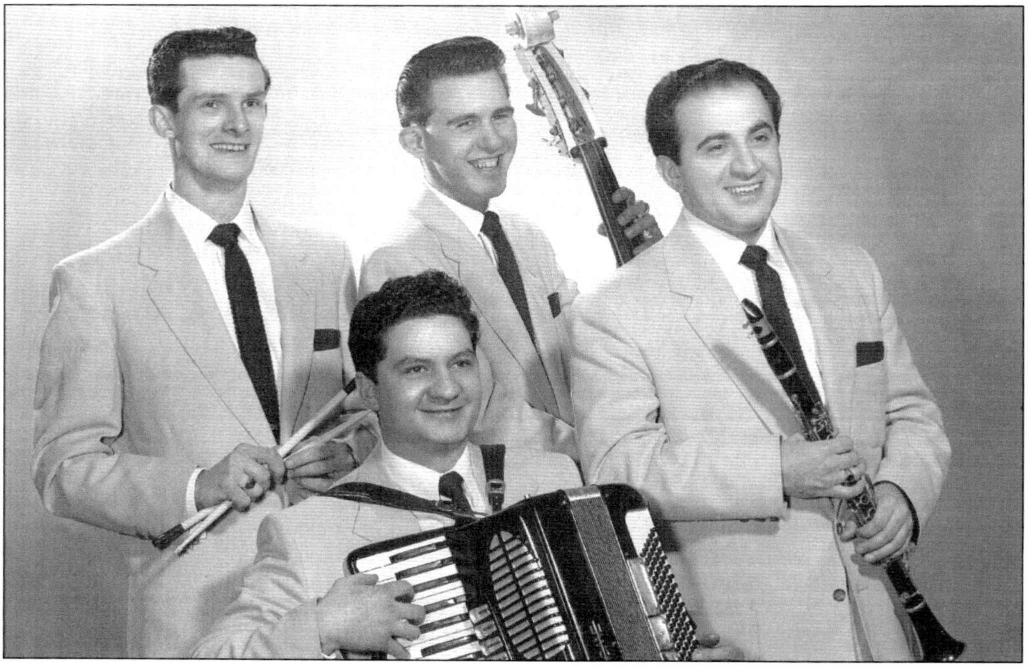

The Million Aires. Pictured here is one of the local bands that played at Lakewood Park for high school dances. Pictured are Joseph "Swing" Flamini (clarinet), Jack Brady (drums), Jerry Hyland (bass), and Lou Jordan (accordion). (Courtesy of Joseph "Swing" Flamini.)

HIGH SCHOOL PROM, 1958. Through the 1950s and 1960s, graduates continued to celebrate with a dance in the grand old hall. Here Michael Grigalonis and Marie Mokol Marlow pose for their formal portrait. (Courtesy of Marie Mokol Marlow.)

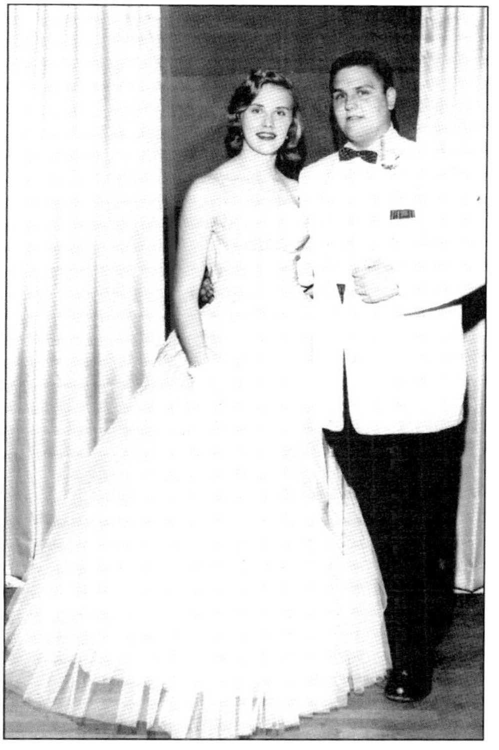

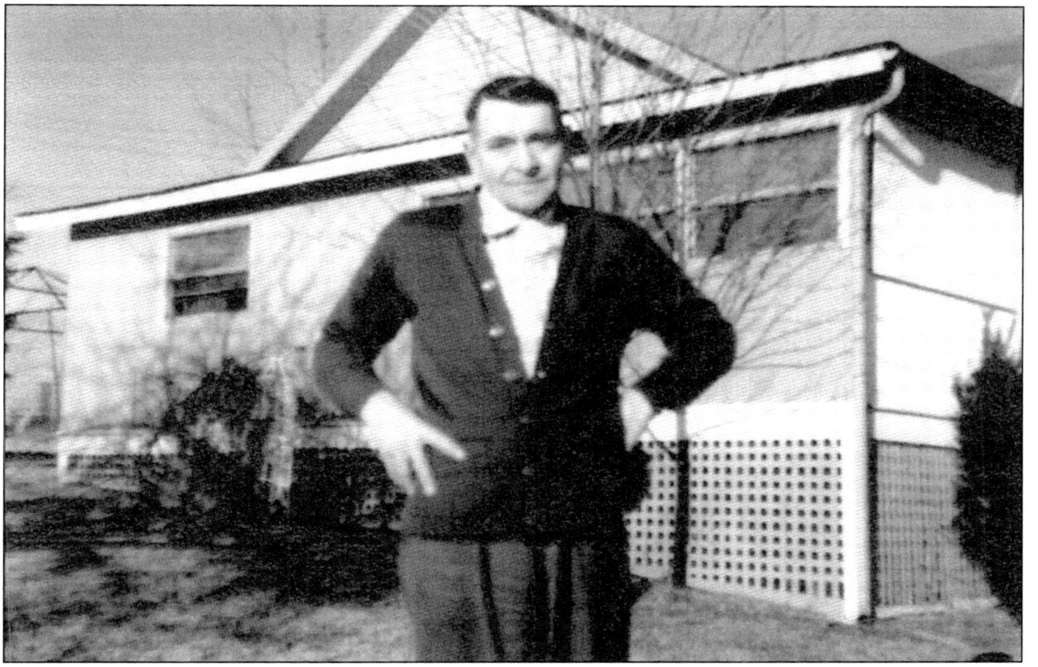

LEON ECKERT, 1950S. Caretaker, gardener, and lifelong friend of the Guinan family, Leon Eckert lived in the Guinan summer bungalow year-round. Eckert oversaw the dance hall in particular but assumed caretaker duties for the entire park 365 days a year.

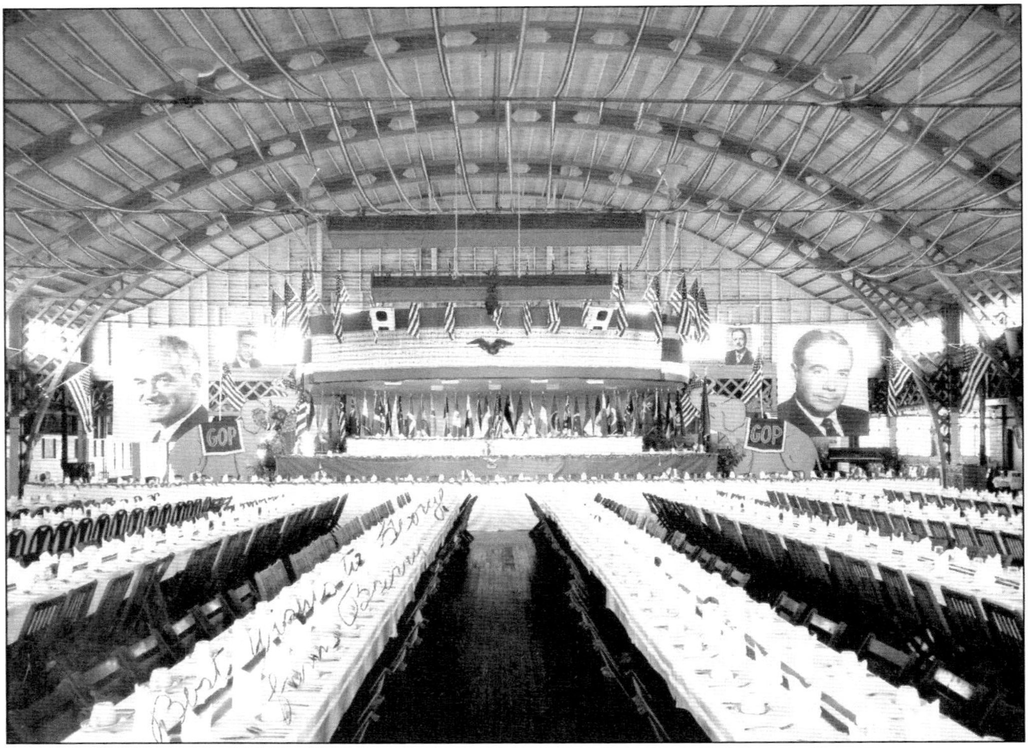

POLITICAL EVENTS AT THE LAKEWOOD BALLROOM. Politics were always important to people in the coal region, and ballrooms served as great venues for events and rallies. Seated in the large open area, one could see and hear his or her party's favorite candidate. Many noteworthy politicians rocked the Lakewood Ballroom as much as any dance band could. This picture is from the Republican banquet for candidate William Scranton for governor and candidate Barry Goldwater for president.

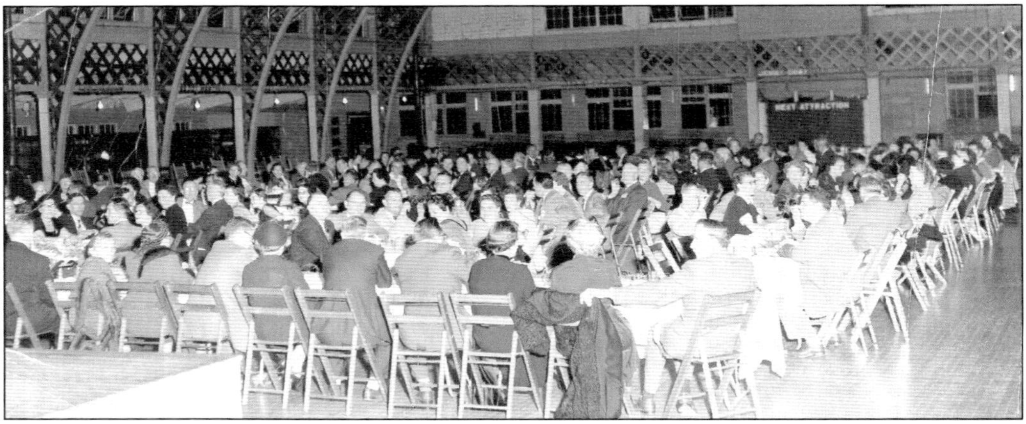

EMPLOYEE DINNER. Employees of Mahanoy City, Mount Carmel, Shamokin, and Berwick and their families celebrated the 50th anniversary of Kate Bier's employment with the Guinan family. Bier was housekeeper, nursemaid, and friend to the Guinan family beginning in her teenage years. Bier cooked for the best-known people in the entertainment industry while they were guests in the Guinan home.

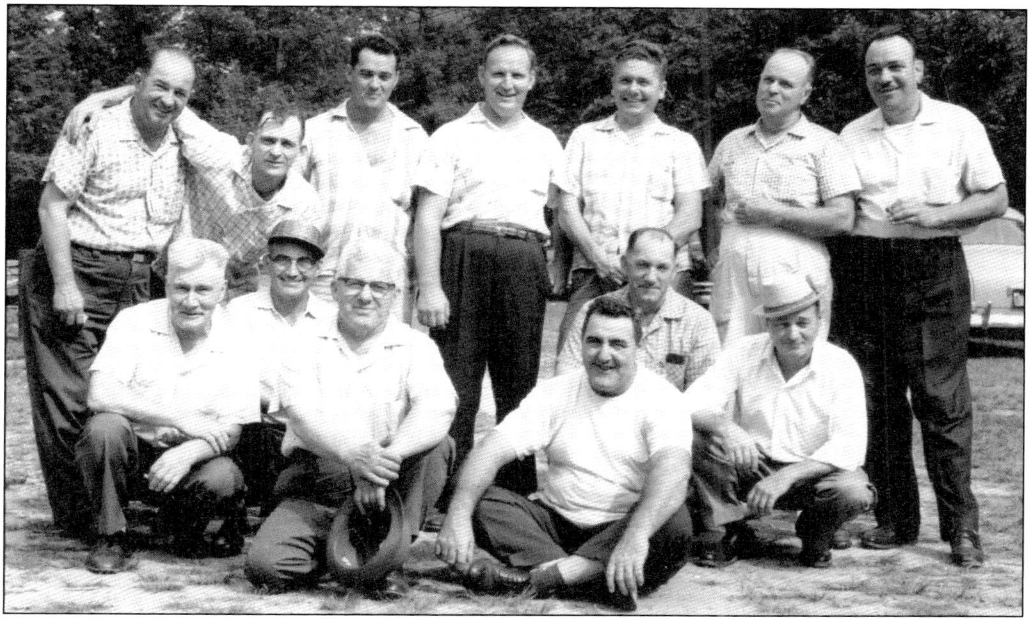

First Aid Team, St. Nicholas Colliery, c. 1950s. Safety was vitally important to miners. Beginning in the early 1900s and continuing to the 1950s, teams from collieries took safety courses and competed in first aid meets to hone their skills. Large meets of at least 40 teams were held at the Lakewood Ballroom. Pictured is the St. Nicholas breaker team. The man wearing the straw hat is Shirley Ryan's uncle, Marshall Phillips, from Suffolk Patch. (Courtesy of Shirley Thomas Ryan.)

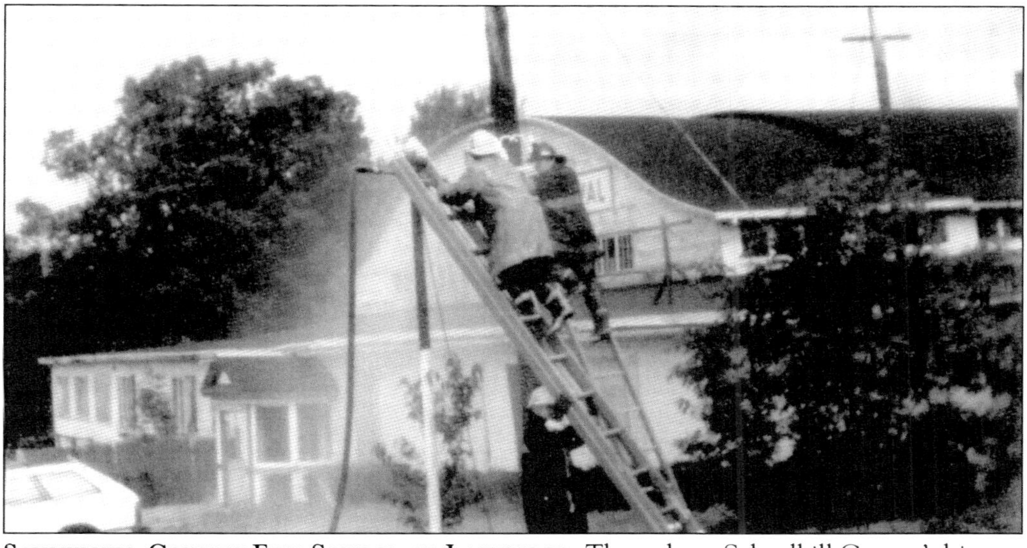

Schuylkill County Fire School at Lakewood. Throughout Schuylkill County's history, the job of firefighting was carried out by volunteer fire companies formed in each community. Until it bought its own training grounds outside Frackville, the Schuylkill County Fire School was located at Lakewood Park. This photograph was taken outside the rear entrance to the dance hall as the men were being trained. Ironically, the ballroom was later destroyed by fire of suspicious origin, as there was no electricity or heat in the building. (Courtesy of the Schuylkill County Firemen Historical Society.)

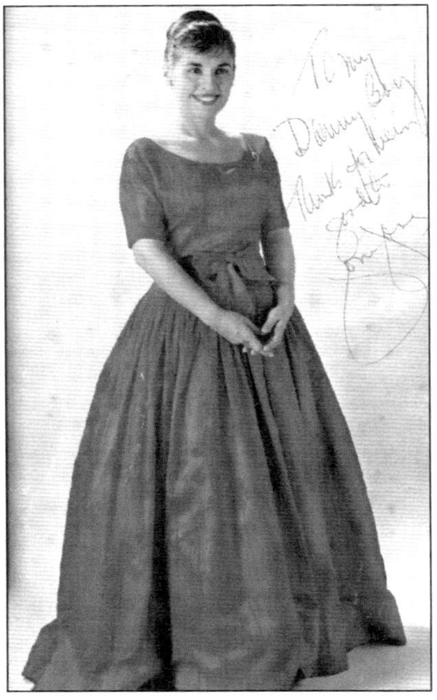

JONI JAMES. Every orchestra had a featured singer who occasionally had more star power than the band. Joni James was one of those incredible talents. Whenever she took the stage at Lakewood Park, she packed the house. Reviews note that she had an unusual sound and style, described as tender, confidential, and urgent. No wonder so many patrons tried to push close to the bandstand to watch this star sing "Why Don't You Believe Me." Popular in the 1950s, she still performs today. This photograph was autographed for Danny Guinan.

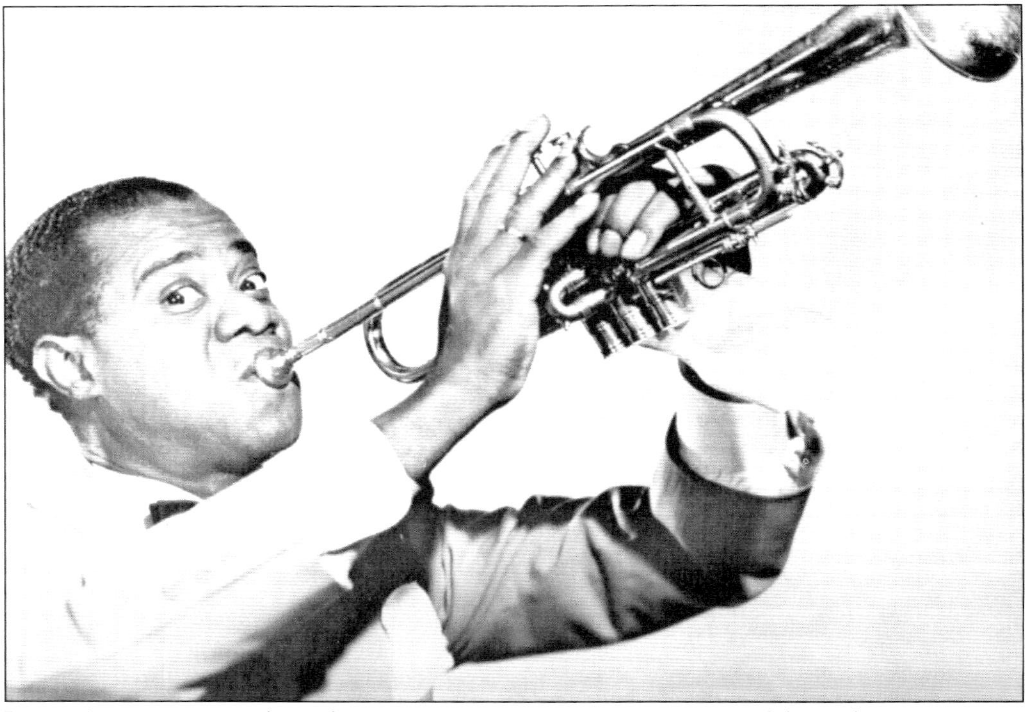

LOUIS ARMSTRONG. Perhaps the most important American musician of the 20th century, Louis Armstrong had an influence that extended beyond jazz and into popular music as well. His voice, described as gravelly, could blend lyrics and melody. He was also skilled at scat singing or wordless vocalizing. Armstrong is an American cultural icon. Frank Guinan's daughter Janet remembers her dad being embarrassed when he could not find a room for him to stay at because of his color.

JAYE P. MORGAN. One of the most dynamic personalities in show business, Jaye P. Morgan was the lead singer with the Frank DeVol Orchestra. Morgan appeared on many television shows, had a recording contract with RCA, and headlined the most famous ballrooms in the country. A crowd was always guaranteed at Lakewood with her appearance.

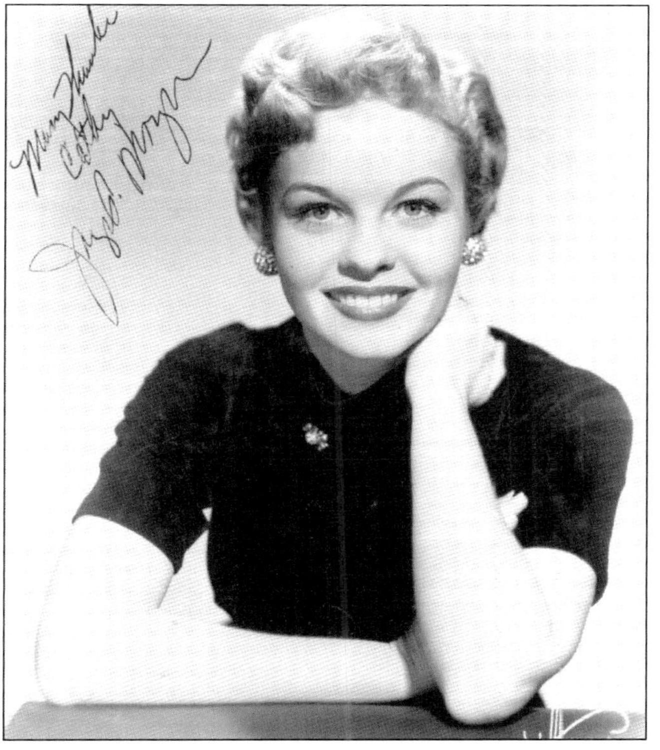

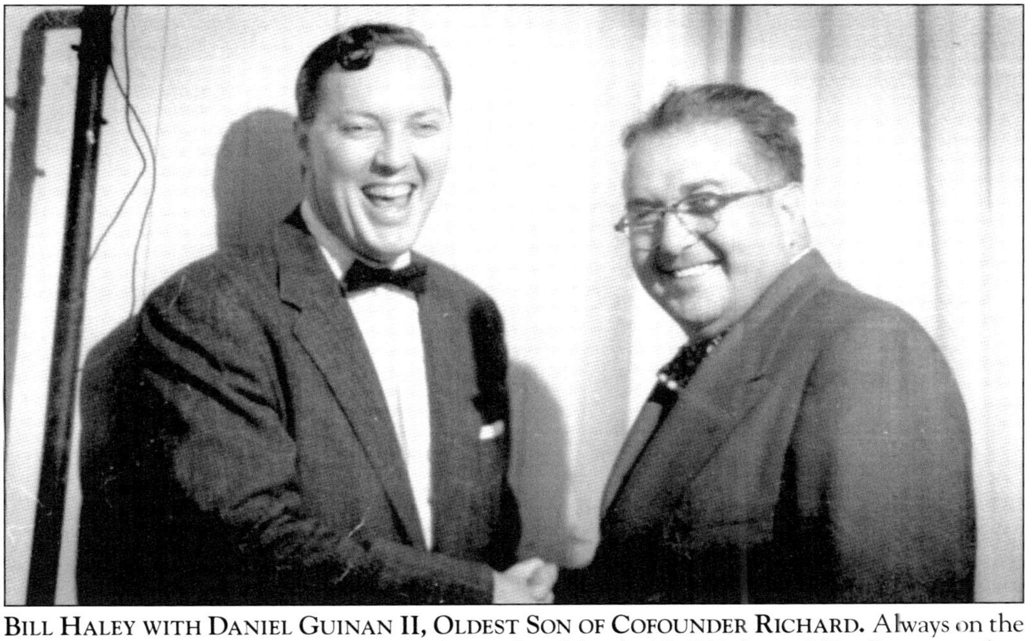

BILL HALEY WITH DANIEL GUINAN II, OLDEST SON OF COFOUNDER RICHARD. Always on the cutting edge of what was hot in music, Lakewood Park booked Bill Haley and His Comets as they released an early rock-and-roll favorite, "Rock around the Clock." A native son of Philadelphia, Haley won acclaim on Dick Clark's *American Bandstand*. His split curl and energetic stage behavior was later compared to Elvis Presley's revolutionary style.

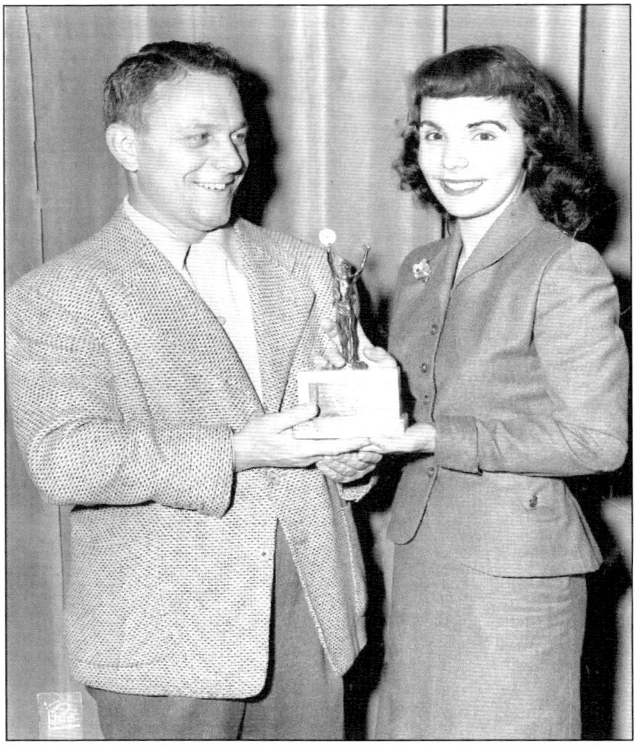

TERESA BREWER. Teresa Brewer was one of the most popular female singers of the 1950s. She started performing at age two, but her career really took off with her signature song "Music, Music, Music." Brewer only made one appearance at Lakewood Park.

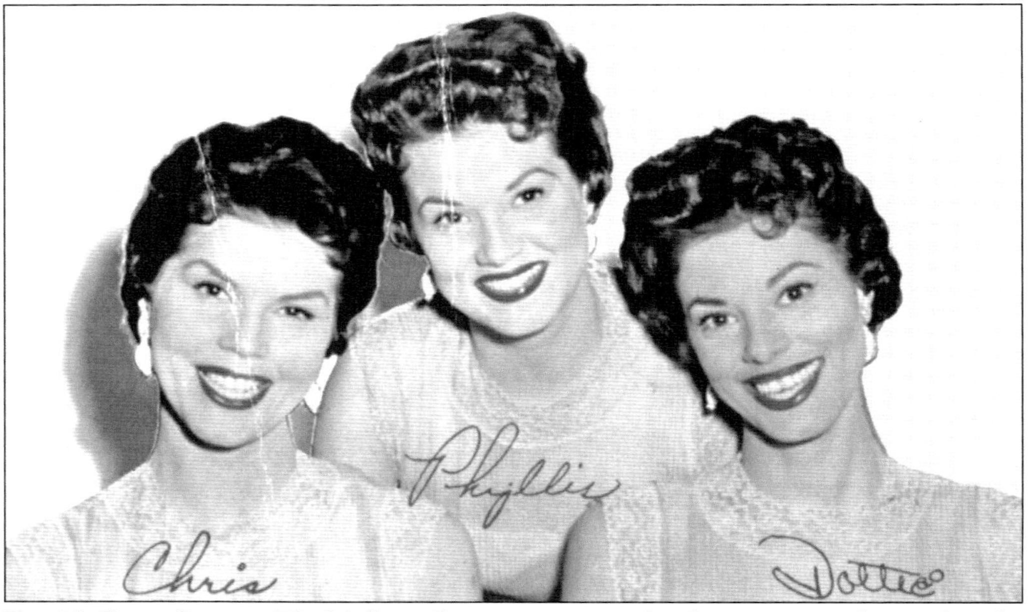

THE MCGUIRE SISTERS. The McGuire Sisters were so popular they were invited to perform for five presidents of the United States as well as Queen Elizabeth. They appeared in 1952 on *Arthur Godfrey's Talent Scouts* and regularly headlined at the ballroom in Lakewood. Marilyn Evans of Mahanoy City remembers collecting $5 admission and supervising the coats available for men who came without jackets.

THE FOUR LADS. The Four Lads launched their career in 1950 and continue to provide many wonderful moments to remember. A Canadian singing group, they have been entertaining for 59 years. Peggy Guinan got this autograph behind the stage at a performance in Barnesville.

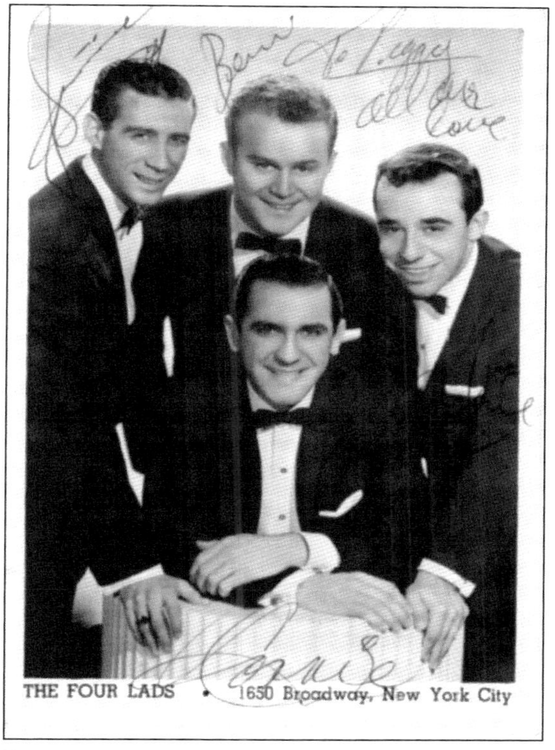

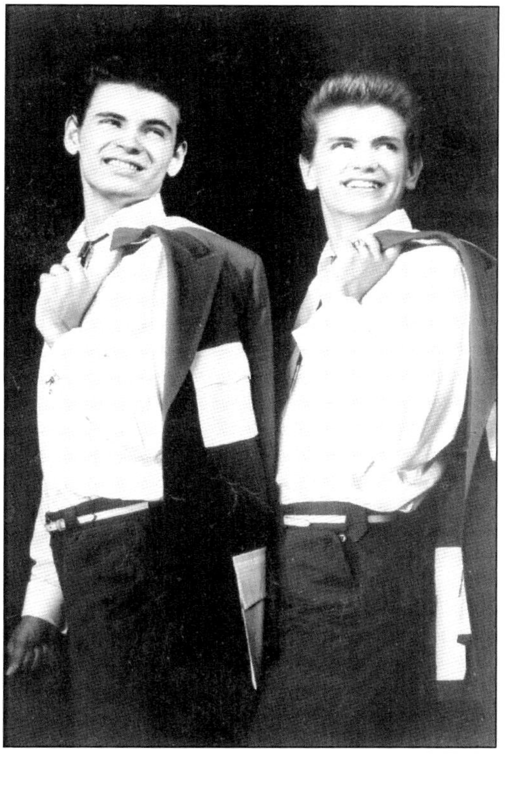

THE EVERLY BROTHERS. Don and Phil Everly were guitar-playing performers with a country music influence that intertwined with rock and roll. They hold the record for the most top 100 singles by any duo (26). Mary Guinan remembers answering a telephone call from Phil Everly and nearly fainting. He was calling her father, Richard Jr., who booked them.

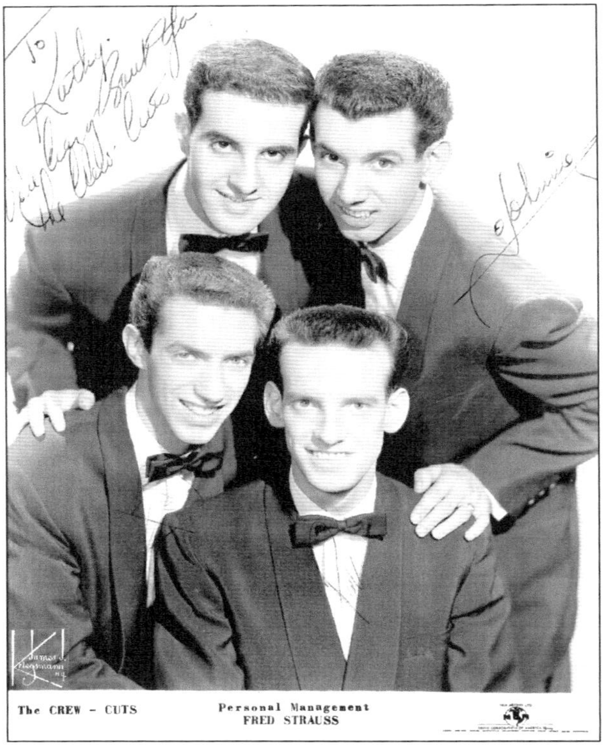

THE CREW CUTS. The Crew Cuts were another Canadian vocal quartet that charted in the United States and worldwide. They named themselves after the popular crew cut hairstyle. Their biggest hit was "Sh-Boom."

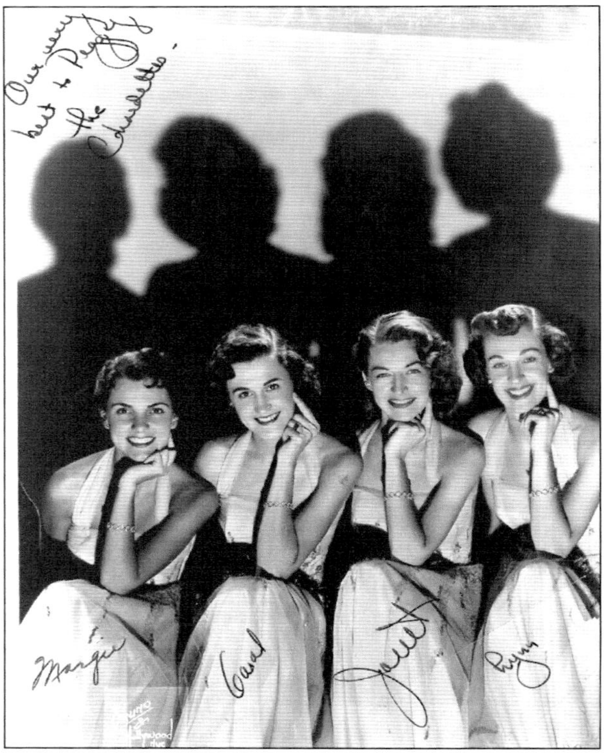

THE CHORDETTES. Singing four-part harmony, the Chordettes won *Arthur Godfrey's Talent Scouts* and appeared on *American Bandstand* for its first national broadcast in 1957, singing their biggest hit, "Mr. Sandman." That same year they performed at Lakewood Park.

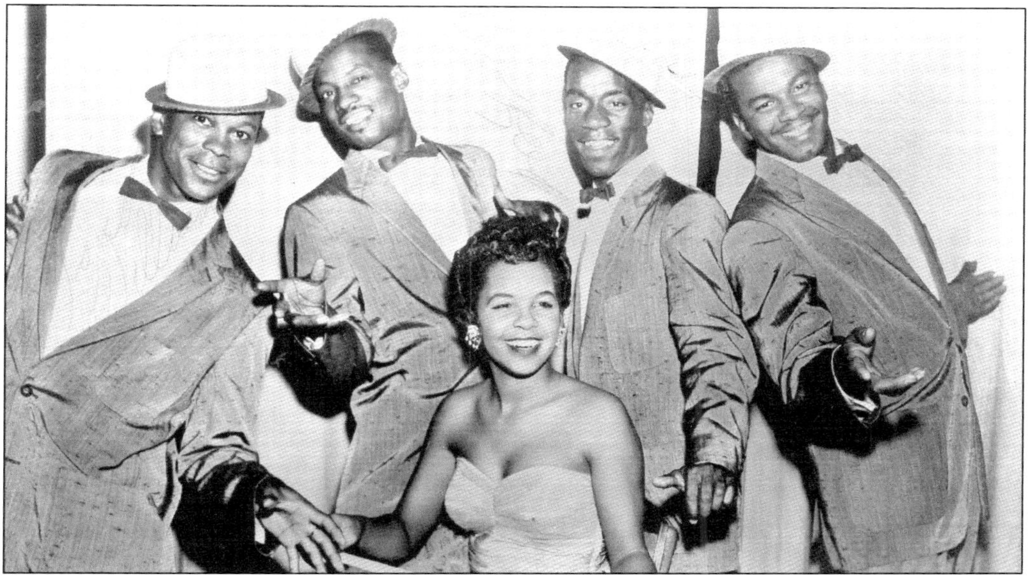

THE PLATTERS. The Platters were a successful vocal group of the early rock-and-roll era, and their first top 10 hit was "Only You" on the Mercury label. The follow-up single, "The Great Pretender," was their first national No. 1 hit, topping the chart for 11 weeks. In 1956, the Platters appeared in the first major motion picture based around rock and roll, *Rock around the Clock*, performing both "Only You" and "The Great Pretender." The Platters appeared at Lakewood at the height of their popularity.

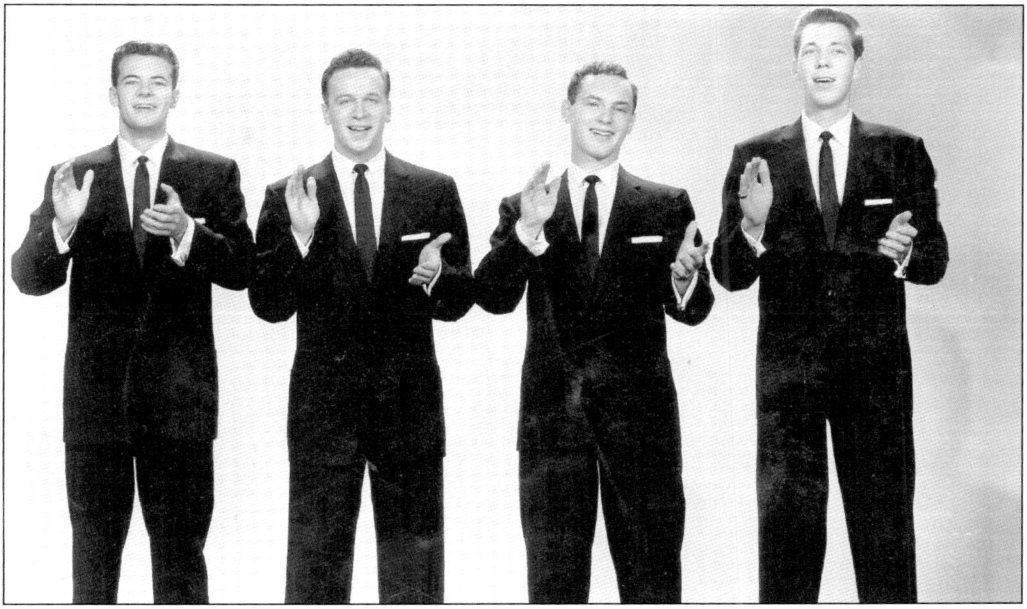

THE DIAMONDS. Starting in Canada as college friends who liked to sing, the Diamonds gained recognition on *Arthur Godfrey's Talent Scouts*. The Diamonds' first recording for Mercury was "Why Do Fools Fall in Love," a cover of Frankie Lymon and the Teenagers' version, which reached No. 12 in the United States. The Diamonds' biggest hits were 1957's "Little Darlin'" and 1958's "The Stroll."

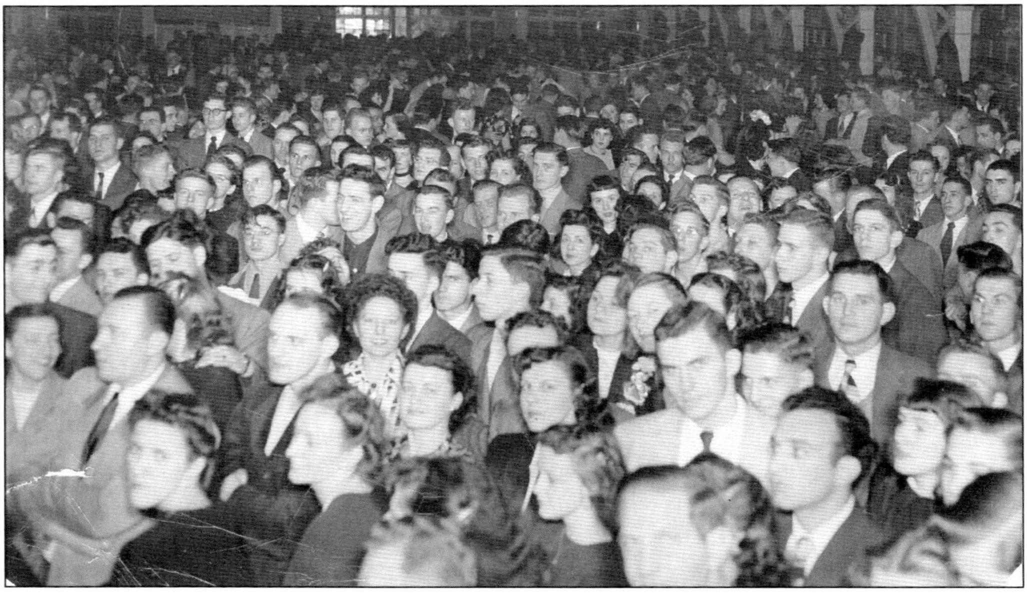

CAPACITY CROWD AT LAKEWOOD. From its beginnings in 1925 until its closing in 1984, the Lakewood Ballroom brought the nation's musical legends to northeast Pennsylvania. No crowd topped the one pictured here, thought to be the record-breaking crowd when Vaughn Monroe appeared at Lakewood in the 1940s.

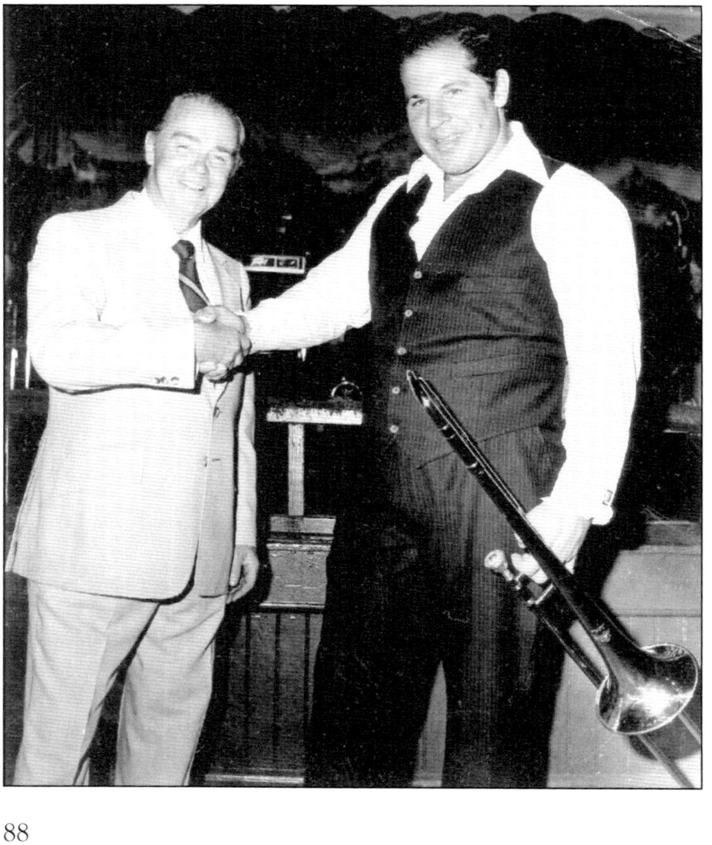

JACK MORGAN, 1970S. Jack Morgan (shown here with Frank Guinan at Lakewood Park) began playing trombone at age 13 and joined the orchestra of his father, Russ Morgan, at 17. The Russ Morgan Orchestra was heard on radio broadcast from the Biltmore Hotel in New York City and from the stage at Lakewood. Head of his own group for years, Jack Morgan appeared at Lakewood in the 1970s and was inducted into the Big Band Hall of Fame in 1997.

Four

ETHNIC CELEBRATIONS

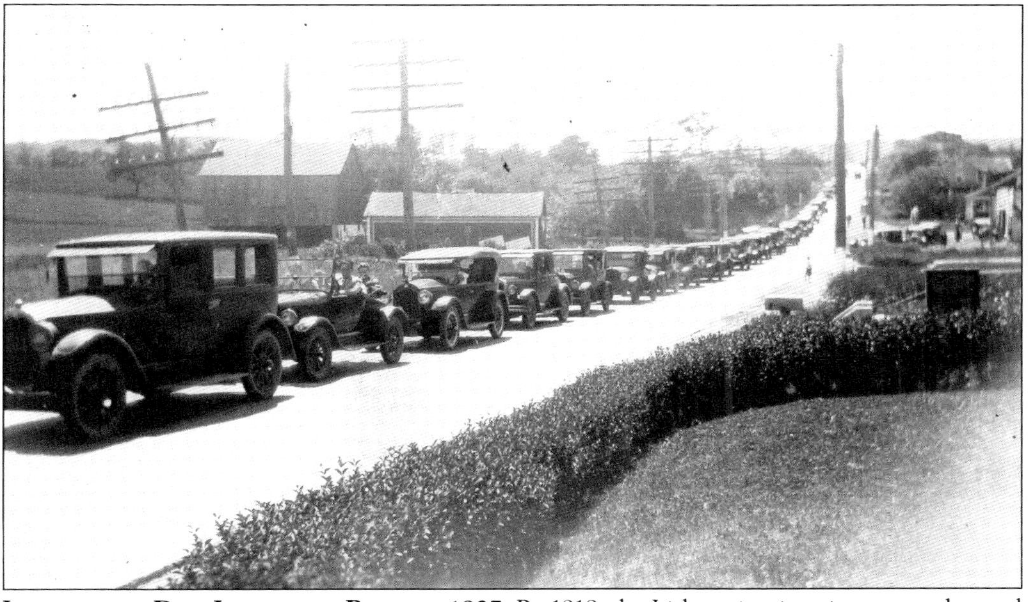

LITHUANIAN DAY, LAKEWOOD PARK, C. 1927. By 1919, the Lithuanian immigrants to the coal region were so numerous that Mahanoy City, Schuylkill County, was chosen as the site for a national Lithuanian convention. Even earlier in 1914, the Lithuanian community, through its churches, joined to hold the first recorded ethnic celebration in the United States—Lithuanian Day at Lakeside Park. No pictures exist of these outings, but in 1922, Lithuanian Day was moved to Lakewood Park, where it continued until the park's closing in 1984. Pictured here is traffic coming from the west and turning into Lakewood Park. (Courtesy of Carolyn Smith Maurey.)

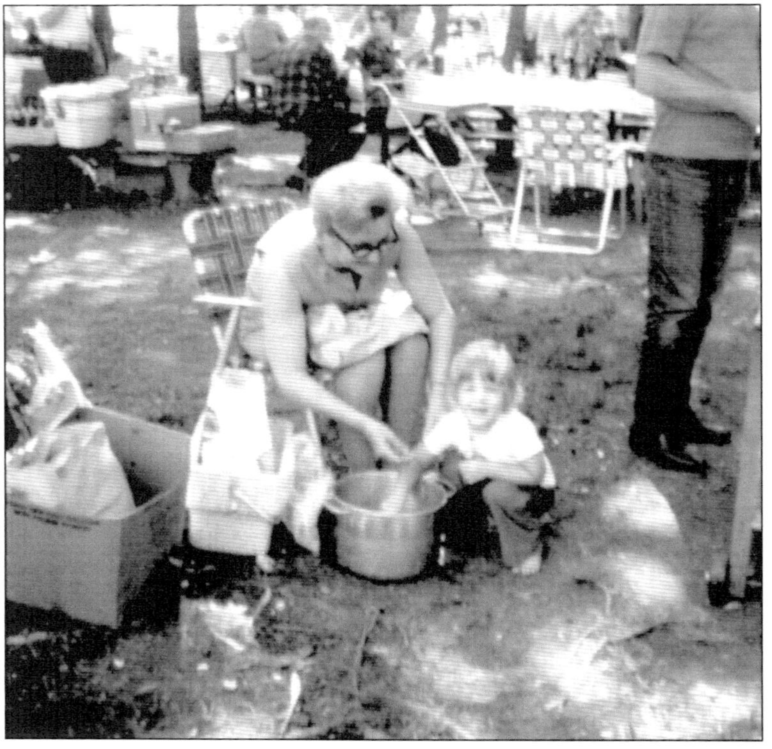

LITHUANIAN DAY, LAKEWOOD PARK, 1975. Lucy Lucyk teaches her granddaughter Tara how to make "Lakeside potatoes," a potato dish named for where it was made, rival Lakeside Park, at early Lithuanian Days.

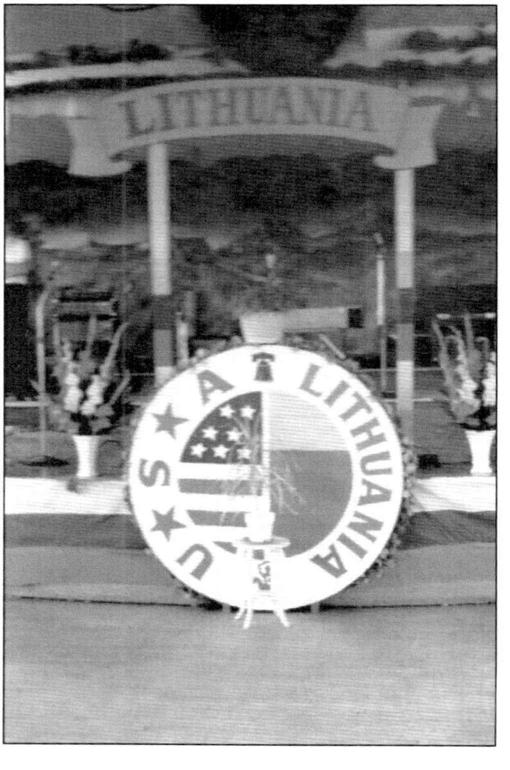

LITHUANIAN DAY AT LAKEWOOD BALLROOM. The stage at the Lakewood Ballroom is set for the Lithuanian Day ceremonies, beginning with a mass and singing in Lithuanian by invited dignitaries from throughout the Northeast, local faithful choirs, and the Junior Knights of Lithuania. (Courtesy of the Knights of Lithuania Museum.)

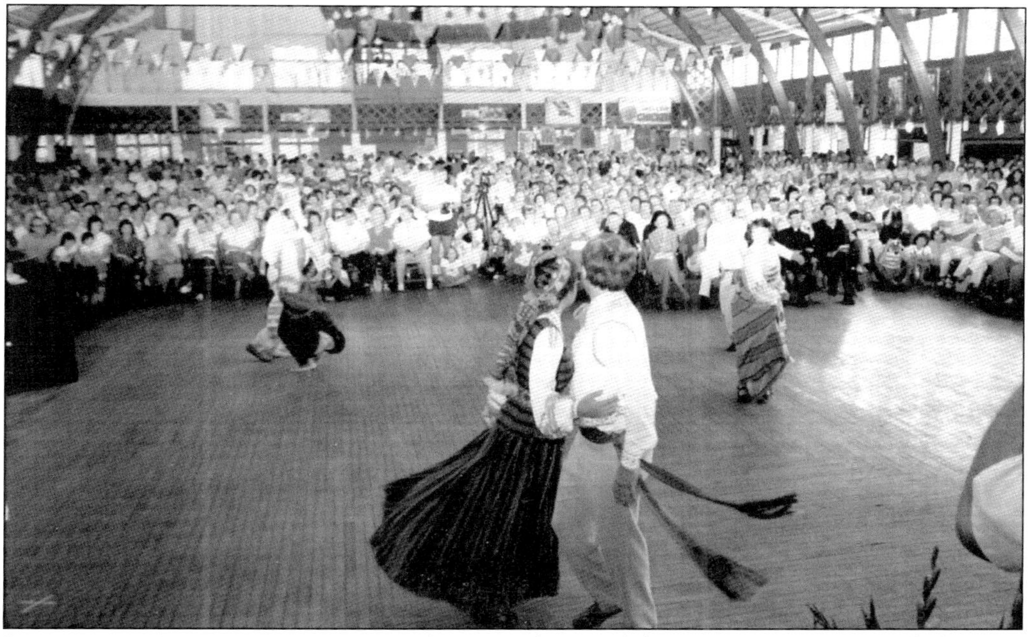

LITHUANIAN DAY DANCERS. Part of every ethnic celebration was singing and dancing. Committee members sought to bring in the best to perform at the dance hall. Pictured here are the Liepsna Dancers from New Jersey performing folk stories passed down through generations on the large ballroom floor. (Courtesy of the Knights of Lithuania Museum.)

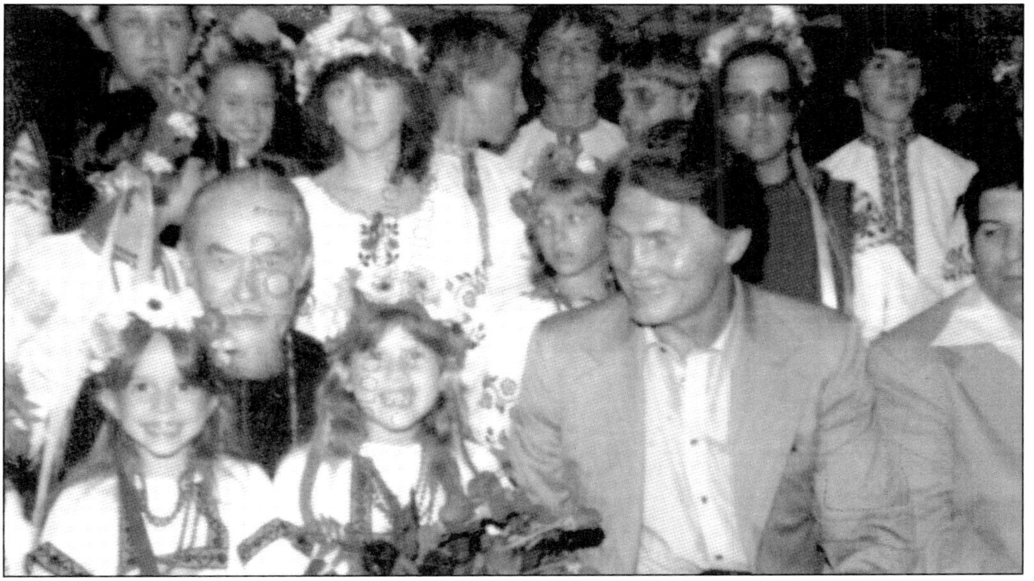

UKRAINIAN DAY, LAKEWOOD BALLROOM, 1980. Second in crowd size only to Lithuanian Day, Ukrainian Day at Lakewood began in 1934 and continued through its 50th anniversary held in July 1983. Pictured in this 1980 photograph are, from left to right, Deanne McBrearty, folk dancer; a Ukrainian priest; Helen McBrearty, folk dancer; and Jack Palance. Palance came home to Hazleton at least once a year, and this year he came to nearby Lakewood to celebrate his heritage. (Courtesy of Helen McBrearty.)

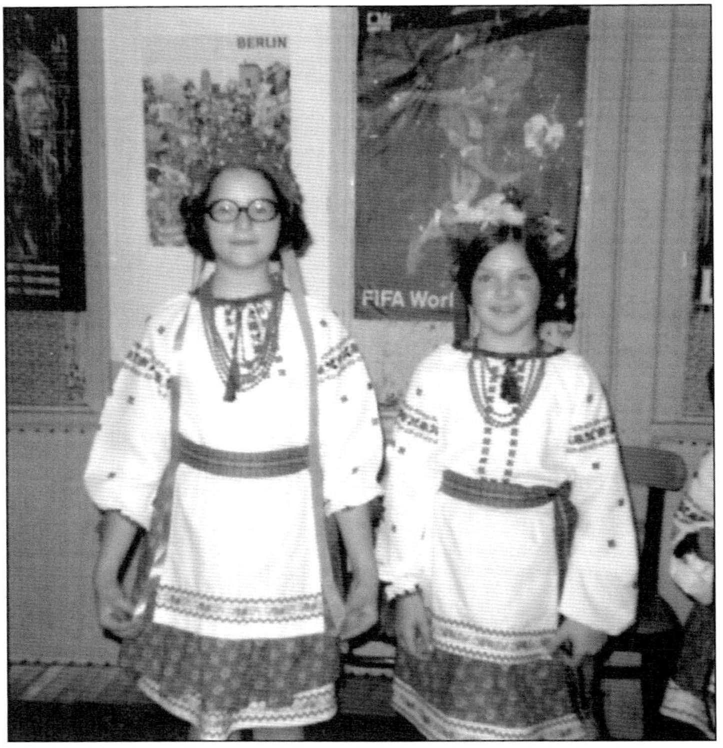

UKRAINIAN DAY, LAKEWOOD PARK. Ethnic day celebrations meant traditional mass, singing, and dancing in the ballroom. Children practiced folk dances taught by their elders throughout the whole year. Made the same way for generations, hand-embroidered costumes were handed down from mother to daughter, as is the one worn by Paula Duda Holoviak (left). (Courtesy of Paula Duda Holoviak.)

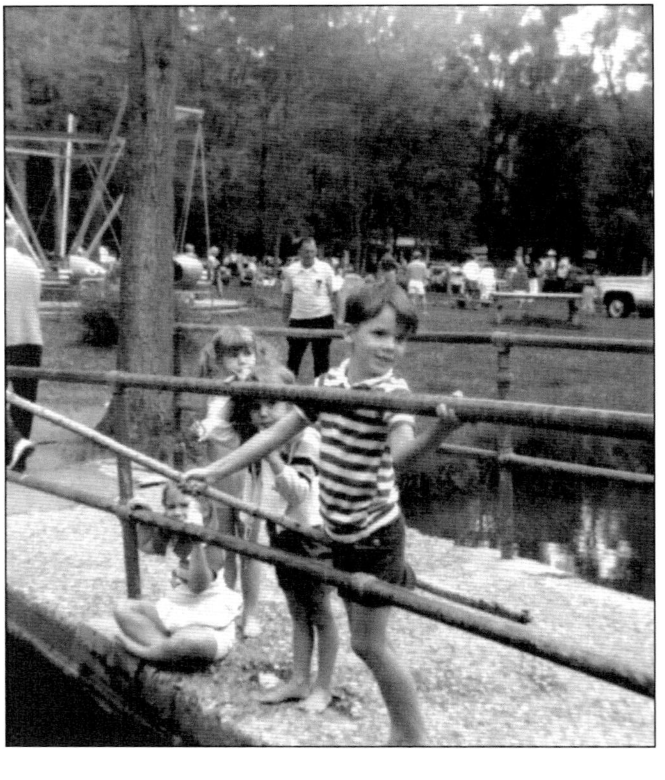

UKRAINIAN DAY, LAKEWOOD PARK KIDDIELAND, 1980. In the morning, ethnic devotion and cultural heritage was emphasized, but the afternoon was for the kids. At center, John McBrearty enjoys fishing with a stick on the bridge over the stream while his sisters watch. In the background to the left is one of the kiddie rides—the airplanes. (Courtesy of Helen McBrearty.)

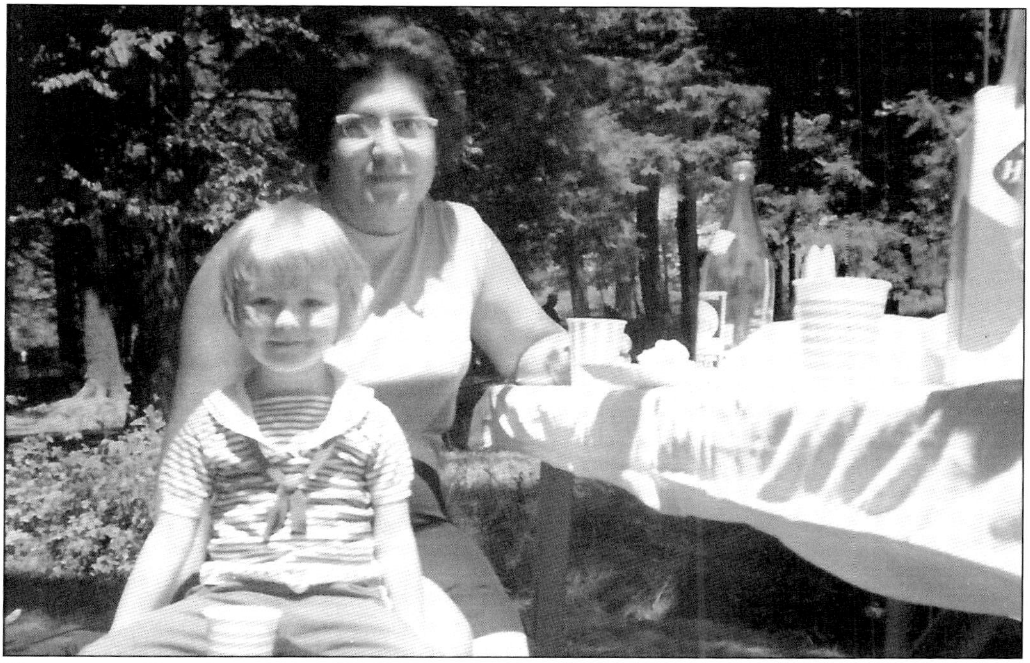

UKRAINIAN DAY, LAKEWOOD PARK KIDDIELAND. Tables decorated with flowers, ethnic food, and picnic staples were all part of the ethnic day celebrations. Paula Duda Holoviak and her aunt Dorothy Chevinski sit at their table in the Kiddieland grove near the rides and the stream. (Courtesy of Paula Duda Holoviak.)

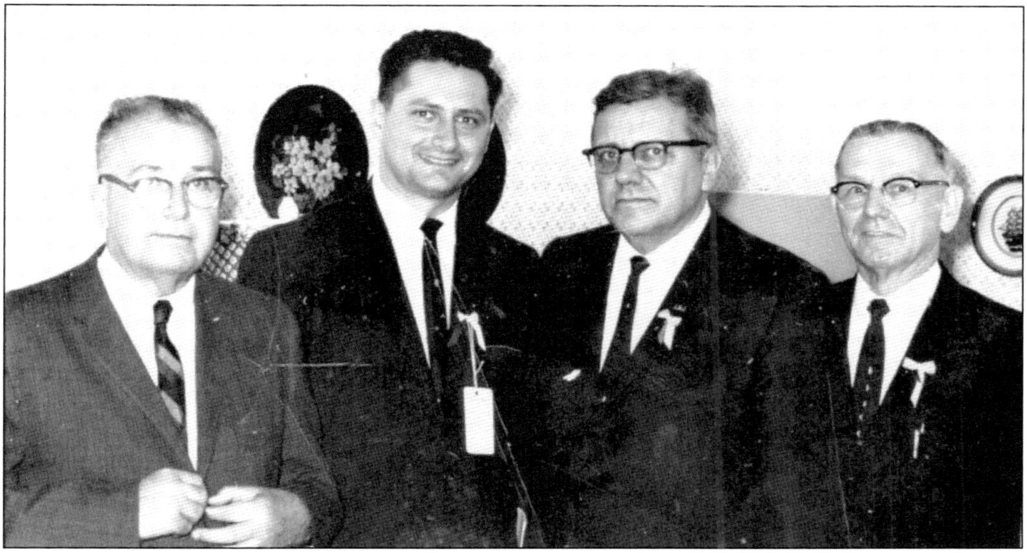

POLISH DAY, LAKEWOOD PARK, 1964. The Polish Day committee seized the opportunity to invite the then current United States postmaster general John A. Gronouski of Polish descent to be the speaker at its annual affair. Local political upstart James Goodman, who was running for his first term in the Pennsylvania House of Representatives, took the occasion to address the large crowd. Pictured are, from left to right, postmaster of Mahanoy City Daniel F. Guinan II, Goodman, Gronouski, and United States congressman George Rhoades.

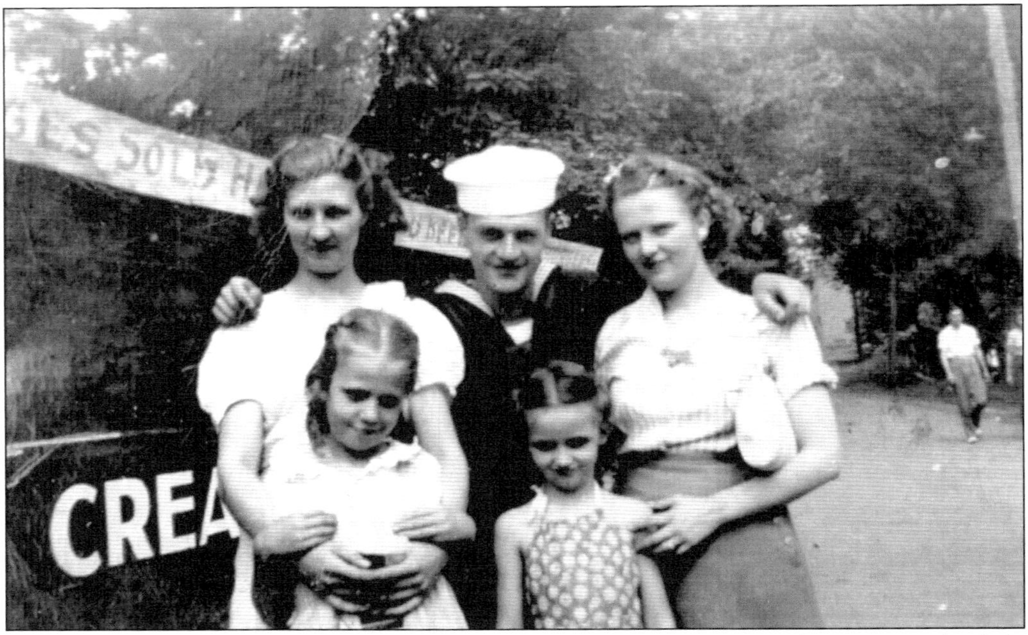

KRALICK STAND, LAKEWOOD PARK, 1942. Along with the Lithuanians, Ukrainians, and Polish, the Slovaks, Russians, and Italians had their days at Lakewood Park too. Time has erased which "big day" it was, but Carolyn Jenkins (front left) remembers celebrating at Lakewood when her brother (sailor Bob Jenkins) came home on leave. (Courtesy of Carolyn Jenkins.)

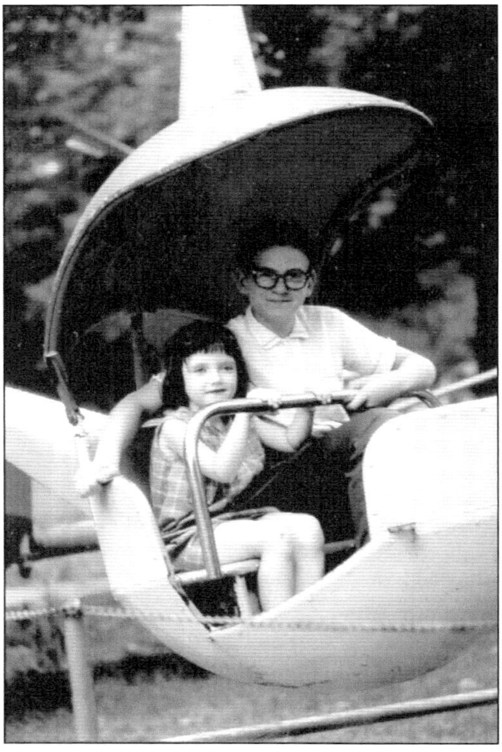

ITALIAN DAY, 1968. Mark Purcell (right), pictured at age 13, remembers spending every Italian Day of his youth at Lakewood. He has vivid memories of the mass said by Fathers Randazzo and Romano at the hall, an Italian band, all the rides, and lots of good food. With him in this picture is his sister, Mary Beth Purcell. While children were on the rides, men played a game in Italian called fingers. (Courtesy of Mark Purcell and Mickey DeCesare.)

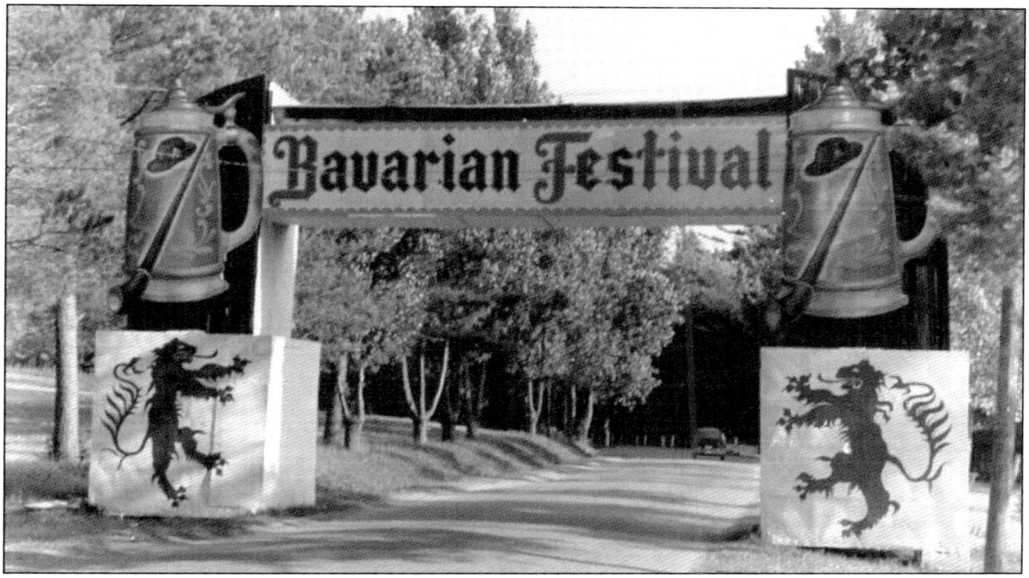

BAVARIAN FESTIVAL, ENTRANCE TO LAKEWOOD PARK, 1969–1984. The Bavarian Festival was founded in 1969 by Kermit Deitrich, who dreamed of having a beer festival with authentic German food, music, crafts, and atmosphere. He found the perfect spot for his dream when he happened upon Lakewood Park. The huge hall with its vaulted, sky-lit ceiling, the multipurpose buildings, the lake, and the shaded grounds met his needs perfectly. Pictured here is the entrance to Lakewood during the Bavarian Festival.

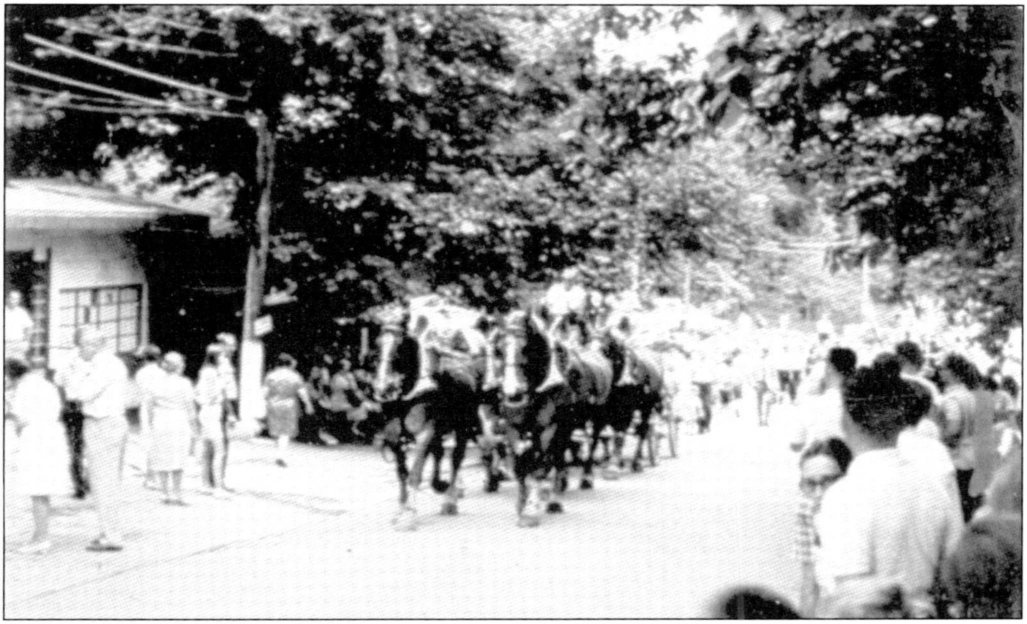

BAVARIAN FESTIVAL CLYDESDALES. A highlight of every Bavarian Festival was the wagon of beer pulled by six authentic Budweiser Clydesdale horses that lived at the park during the two-week festival. (Courtesy of Dale Freudenberger.)

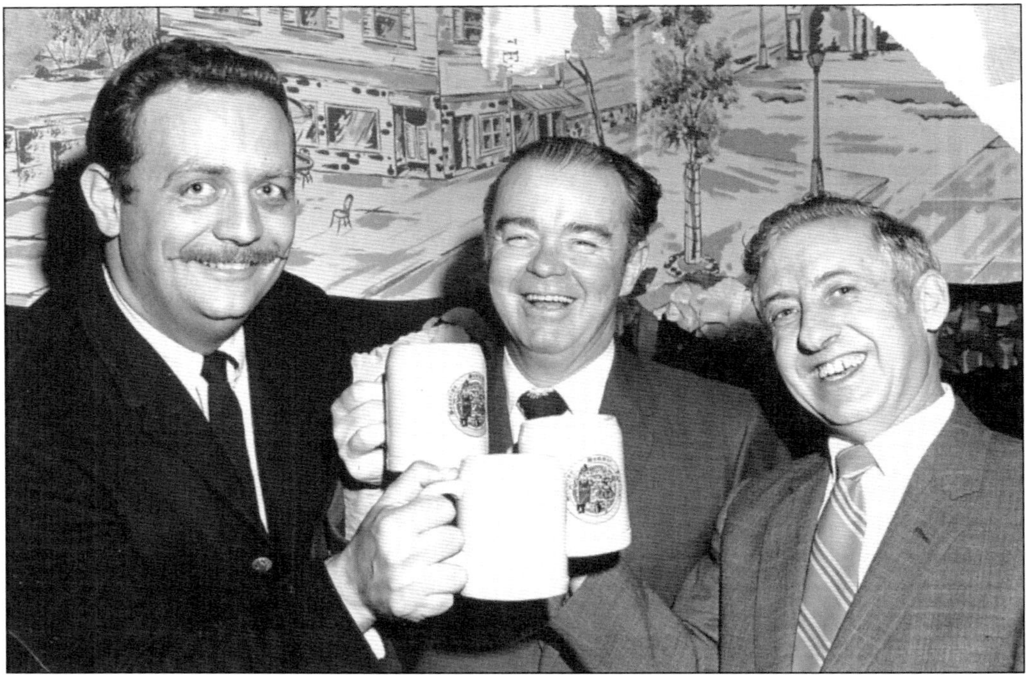

BAVARIAN FESTIVAL FOUNDER AND FRIENDS, 1970S. Kermit Deitrich, founder of the Bavarian Festival at Lakewood, enjoys a beer with Frank Guinan (center), co-owner of Lakewood Park, and George Althoff Jr. (right), longtime concessionaire at Lakewood. (Courtesy of Mary Althoff Koch.)

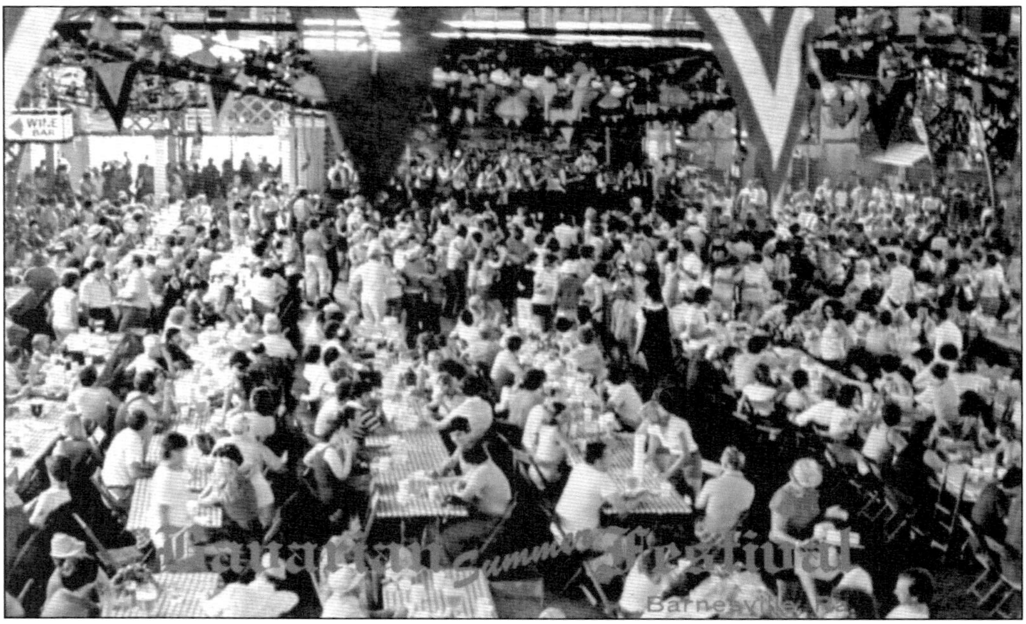

BEER HALL NO. 1. Pictured here is the dance hall filled with thousands enjoying German music by an oompah band. Festivalgoers were entertained by German folk dancers, a German restaurant with waitresses in dirndl skirts serving food, and a contagious atmosphere of crowds singing and dancing. (Courtesy of Dale Freudenberger.)

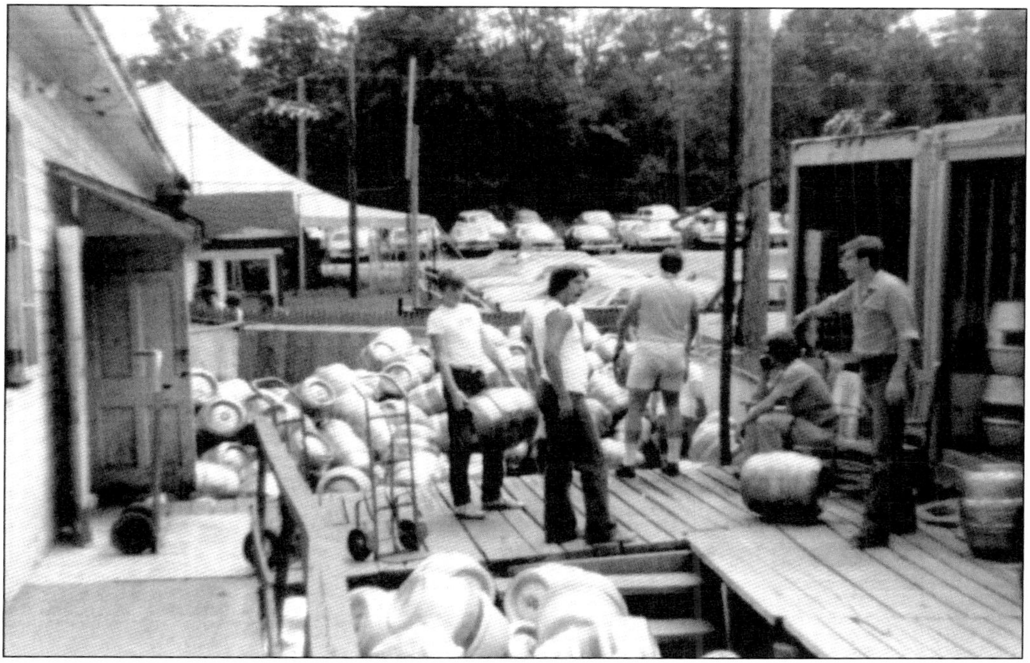

Rear Entrance to Beer Hall. The back of the hall was a beehive. Refrigerated trailers held tons of food and drink. Here workers are shuffling full and empty beer barrels into the hall. (Courtesy of Wally and Blanche Starkey.)

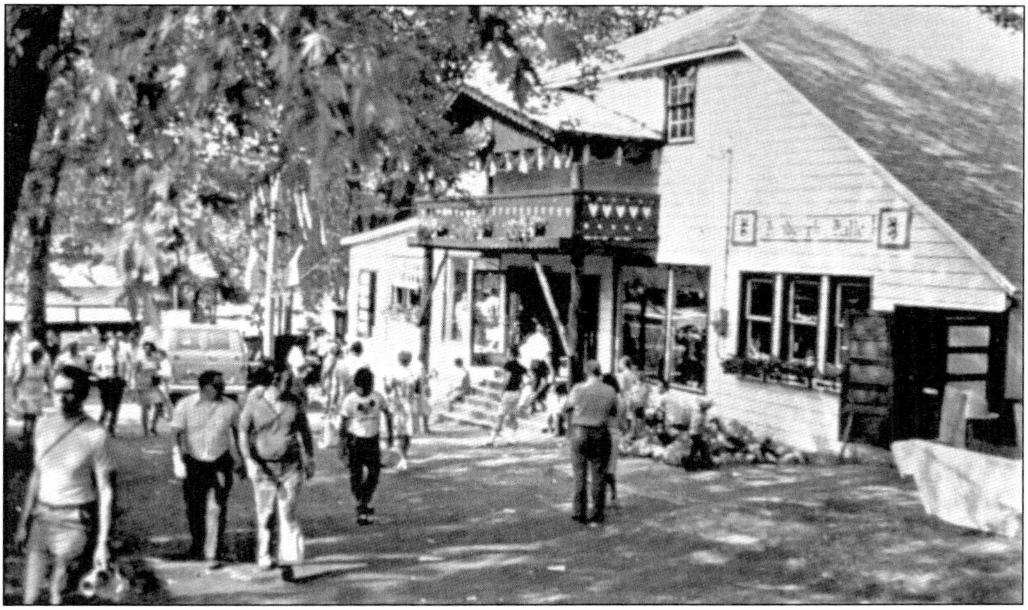

Bavarian Festival Craft Hall/Beer Hall No. 2. As more people wanted to join in the fun atmosphere of beer hall No. 1, the need for another venue became apparent. Down the hill from the large hall, the former skating rink at Lakewood was transformed into a Bavarian beer garden and hall No. 2. The same music, dancing, and food that filled hall No. 1 were found here in a smaller setting. (Courtesy of Dale Freudenberger.)

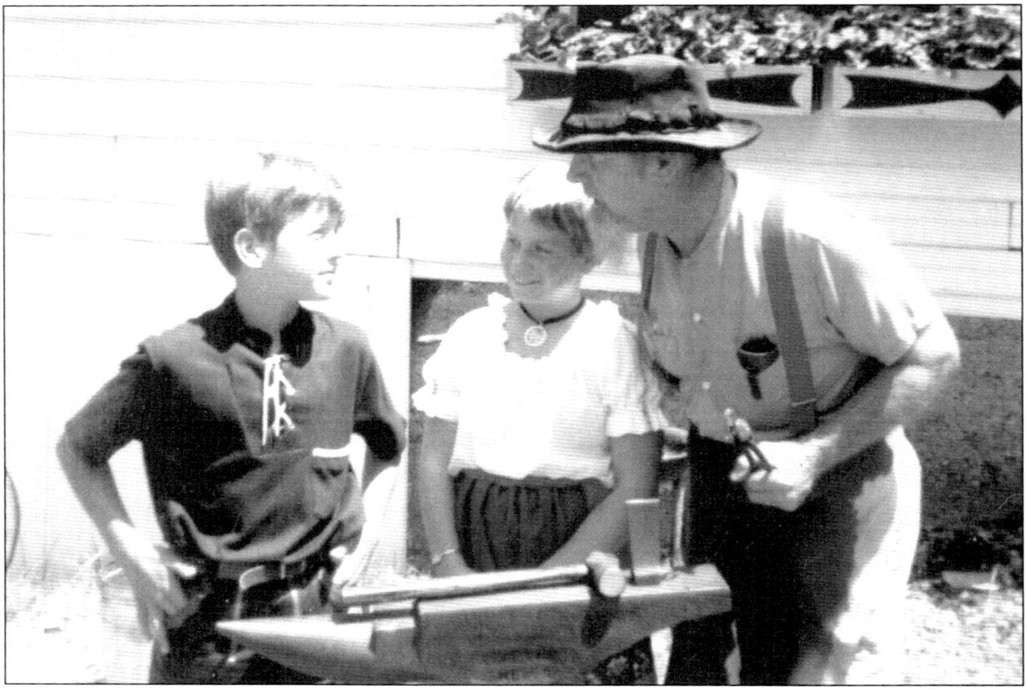

CRAFT DEMONSTRATIONS. Outside of the craft hall, P. J. Guinan interacts with the wrought iron maker who crafted useful and decorative items available for purchase.

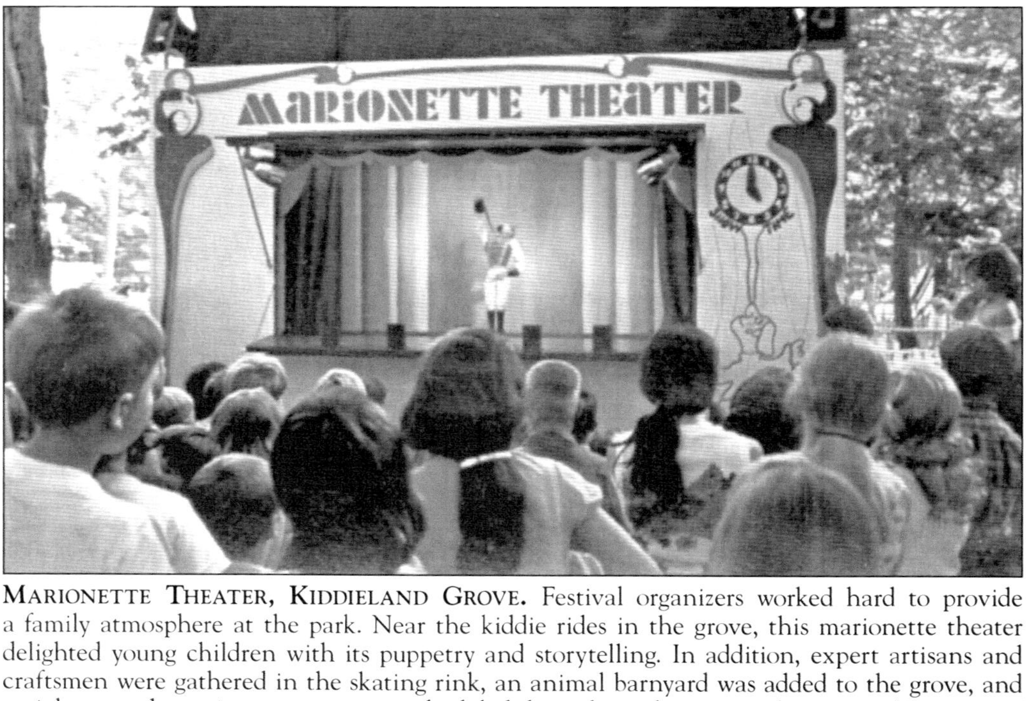

MARIONETTE THEATER, KIDDIELAND GROVE. Festival organizers worked hard to provide a family atmosphere at the park. Near the kiddie rides in the grove, this marionette theater delighted young children with its puppetry and storytelling. In addition, expert artisans and craftsmen were gathered in the skating rink, an animal barnyard was added to the grove, and aerial acts and sporting contests were scheduled throughout the surrounding areas. (Courtesy of Dale Freudenberger.)

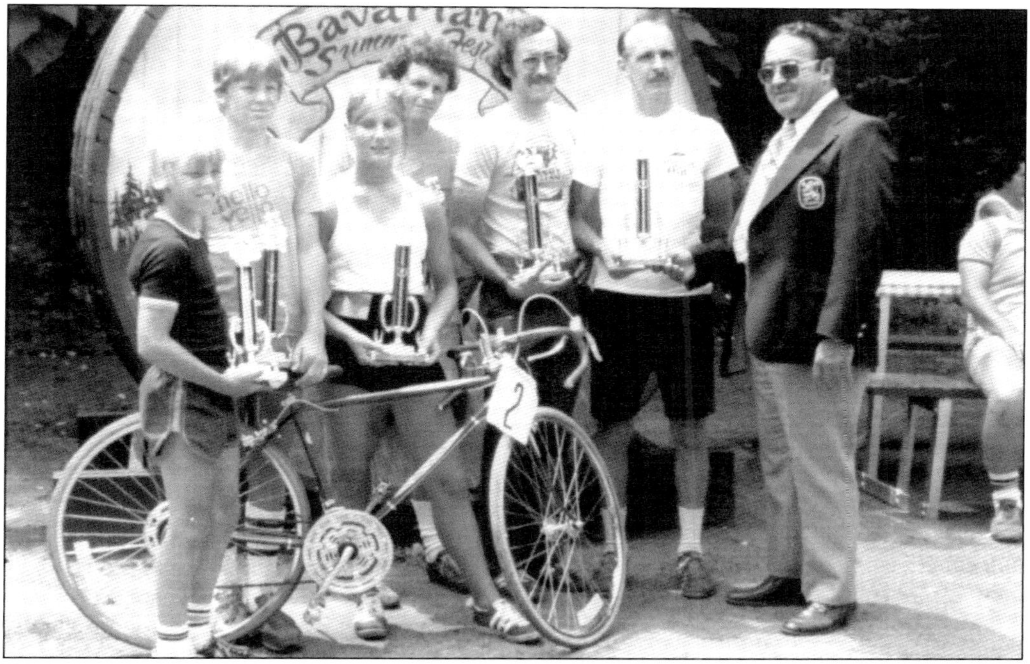

BAVARIAN FESTIVAL, LAKEWOOD PARK, 1978. On the festival schedule of sporting events was the annual bike race. The winners, including Matthew Lucyk (far left), pose for this picture in front of the familiar Bavarian beer keg.

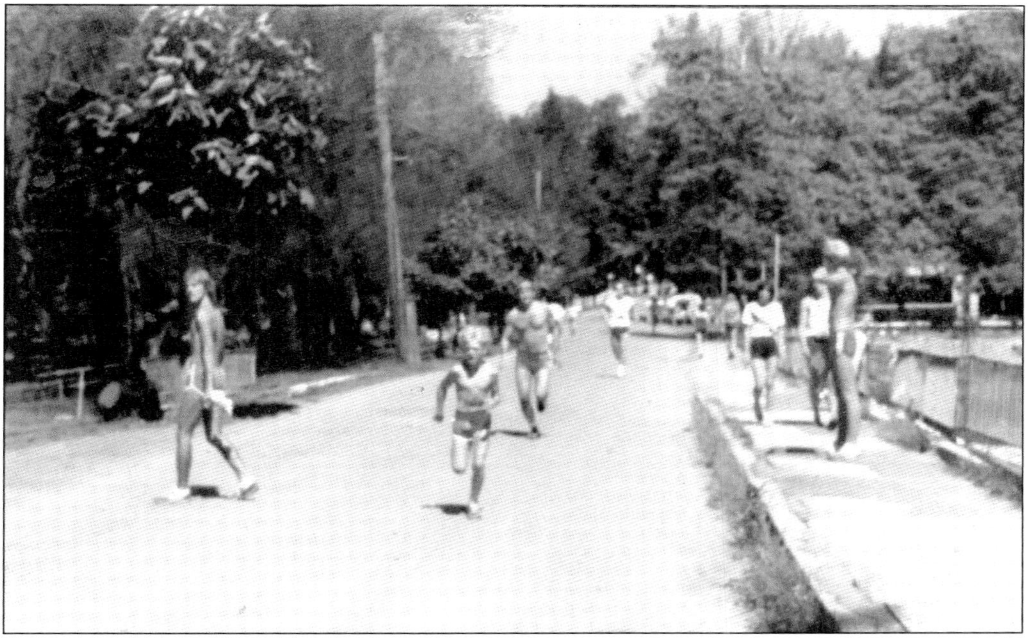

BAVARIAN RUN, LAKEWOOD PARK, 1979. Along with bike races and softball and golf tournaments, the Bavarian Festival held a half-marathon race around the Barnesville countryside. In the lead in the photograph are 10-year-old Matthew Lucyk and his father, E. J. Lucyk. Approximately 200 runners participated.

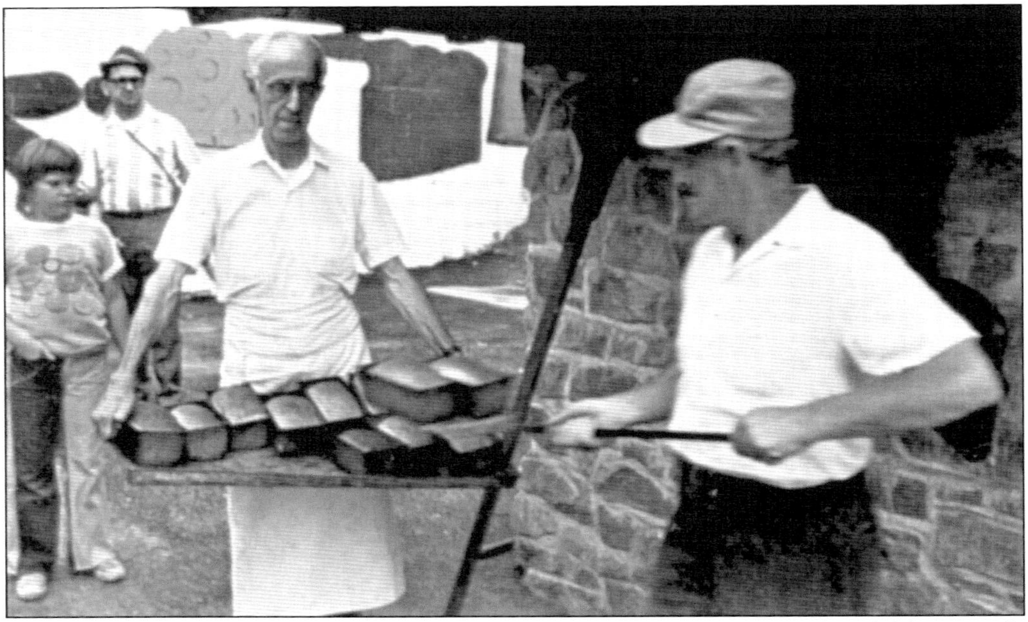

Bavarian Festival. No German festival would be complete without plentiful homemade baked goods. Hundreds of loaves of bread were baked in the stone oven located on the midway. (Courtesy of Dale Freudenberger.)

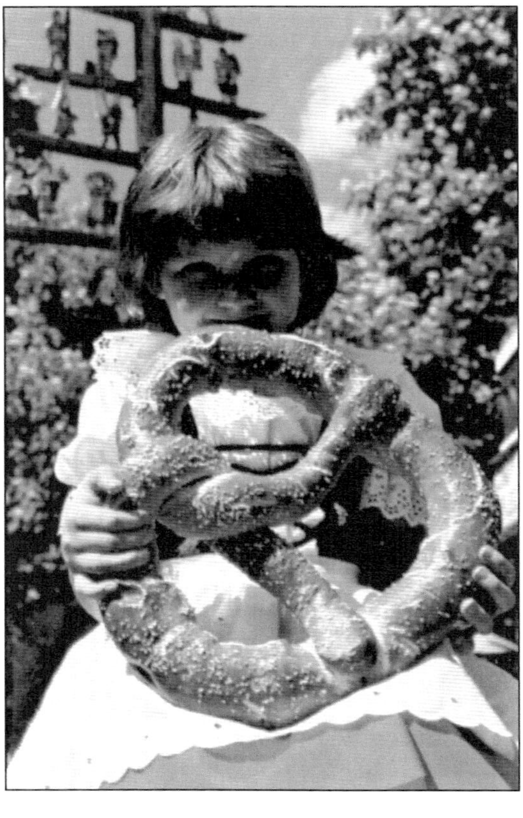

Bavarian Festival Necessities. Along with bratwurst, strudel, and knockwurst, soft pretzels were enjoyed through the park. Behind the fraulein is one of many carved maypoles placed around the park. (Courtesy of Dale Freudenberger.)

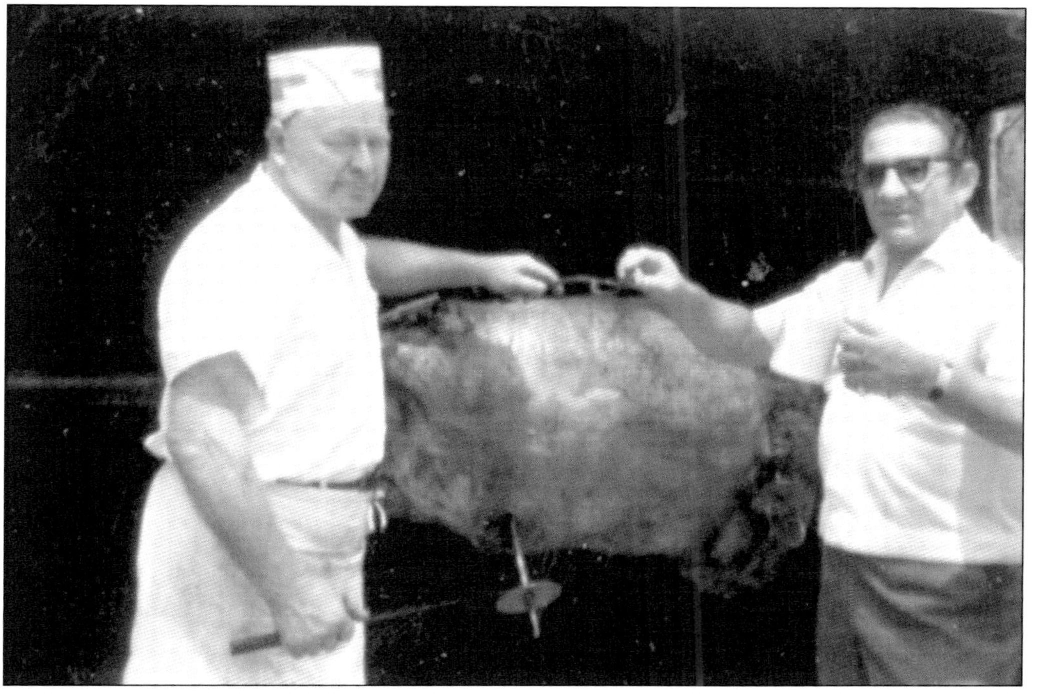

OX ROAST. The Bavarian chief cook tends to the fire along the midway where the ox was roasted. From there, the succulent meat went to the full-service restaurant for carving and enjoying.

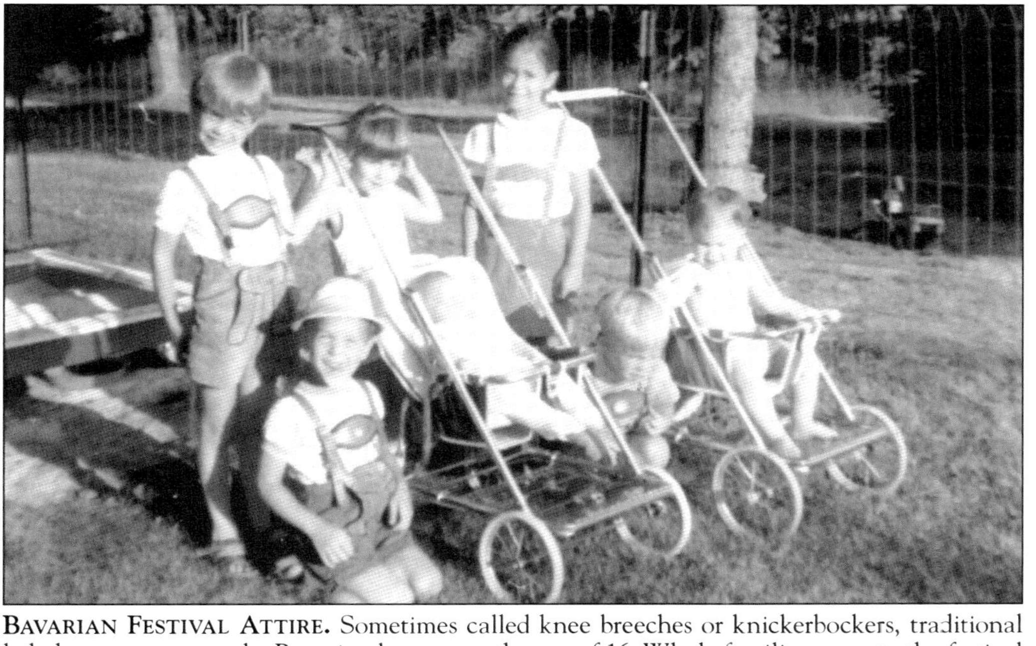

BAVARIAN FESTIVAL ATTIRE. Sometimes called knee breeches or knickerbockers, traditional lederhosen were worn by Bavarian boys up to the age of 16. Whole families came to the festival dressed in their "leather trousers." Pictured are, from left to right, cousins Richie Guinan, Tommy Connolly (kneeling), Margot Guinan, and Ceci Connolly. In carriages are Patrick Connolly and Shannon Guinan with David Koslosky in the middle.

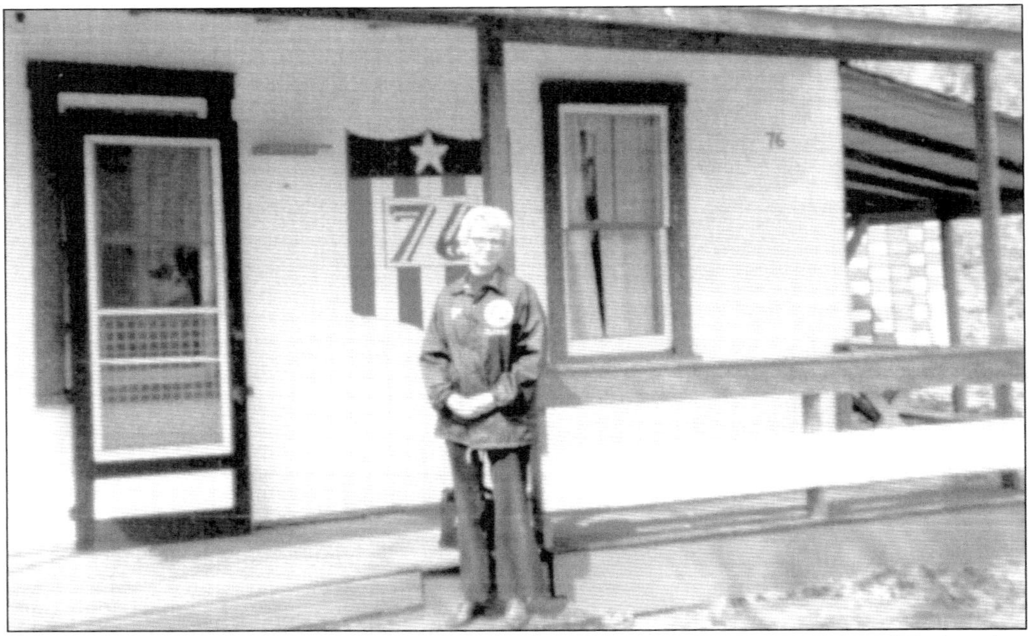

Starkey Clan. Some families celebrated their heritage once a year at Lakewood Park; other families celebrated everybody's heritage. Members of the Starkey family (Blanche Starkey above) enjoyed Lakewood so much they rented a cabin there for 15 years and picnicked with friends every weekend. (Courtesy of Wally and Blanche Starkey.)

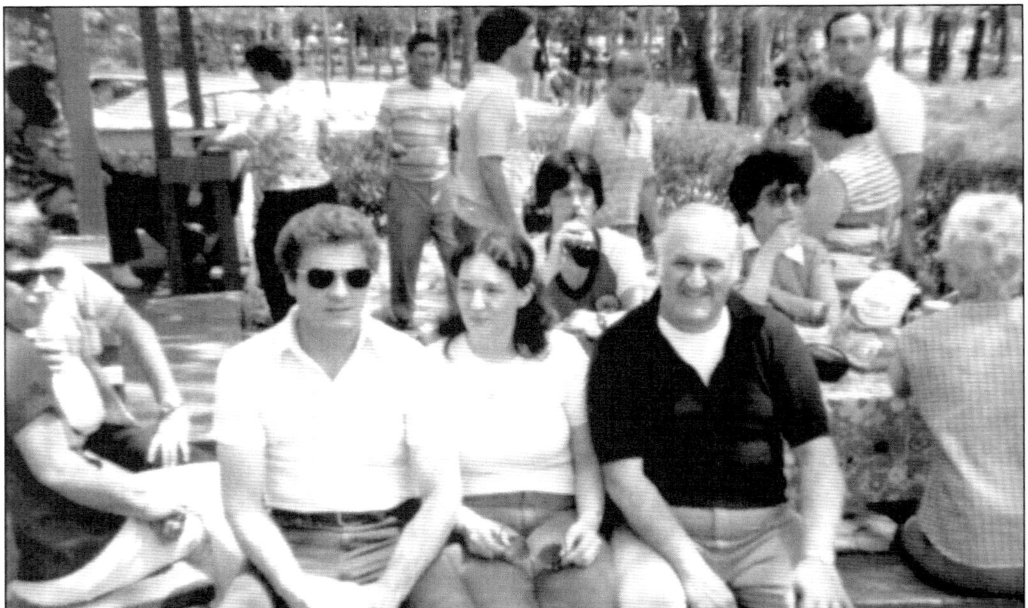

Old-Fashioned Fun. Passengers on the train knew to wave to the familiar faces at the Starkeys' cabin. The family had to pump its water and bring lots of warm blankets, but it was all part of the fun. Seated are, from left to right, John and Karen Klemovich and Dick Sheehan, friends who joined the Starkeys. (Courtesy of Wally and Blanche Starkey.)

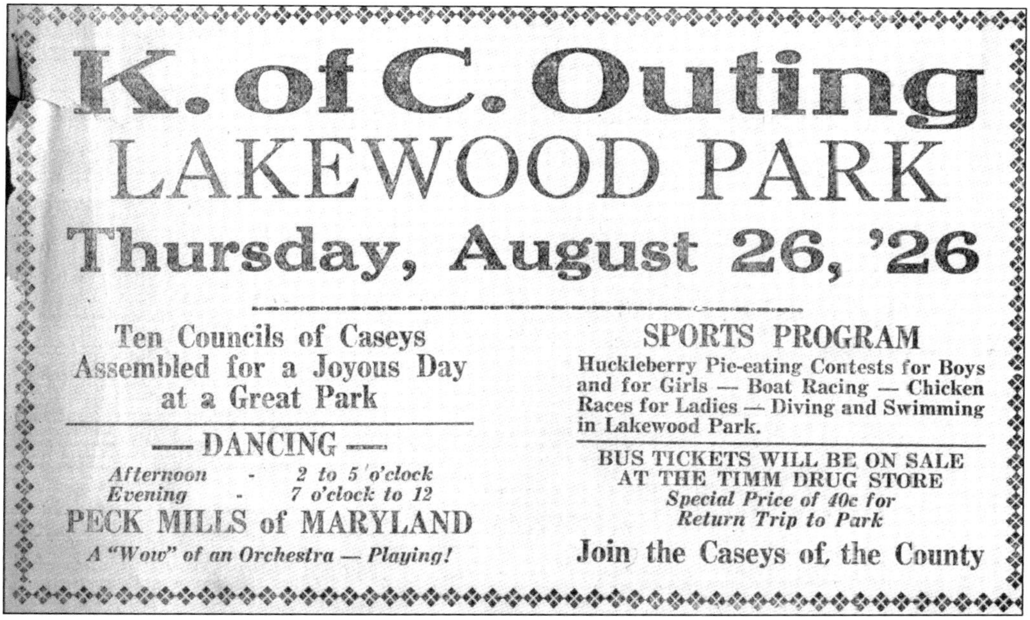

K. of C. Outing
LAKEWOOD PARK
Thursday, August 26, '26

Ten Councils of Caseys
Assembled for a Joyous Day
at a Great Park

— DANCING —

Afternoon - 2 to 5 o'clock
Evening - 7 o'clock to 12

PECK MILLS of MARYLAND

A "Wow" of an Orchestra — Playing!

SPORTS PROGRAM

Huckleberry Pie-eating Contests for Boys and for Girls — Boat Racing — Chicken Races for Ladies — Diving and Swimming in Lakewood Park.

BUS TICKETS WILL BE ON SALE
AT THE TIMM DRUG STORE
Special Price of 40c for
Return Trip to Park

Join the Caseys of the County

KNIGHTS OF COLUMBUS OUTING. As seen in this 1926 advertisement in the *Record American* newspaper, the Knights of Columbus (the Caseys), as well as many other religious groups, held multicounty gatherings at Lakewood.

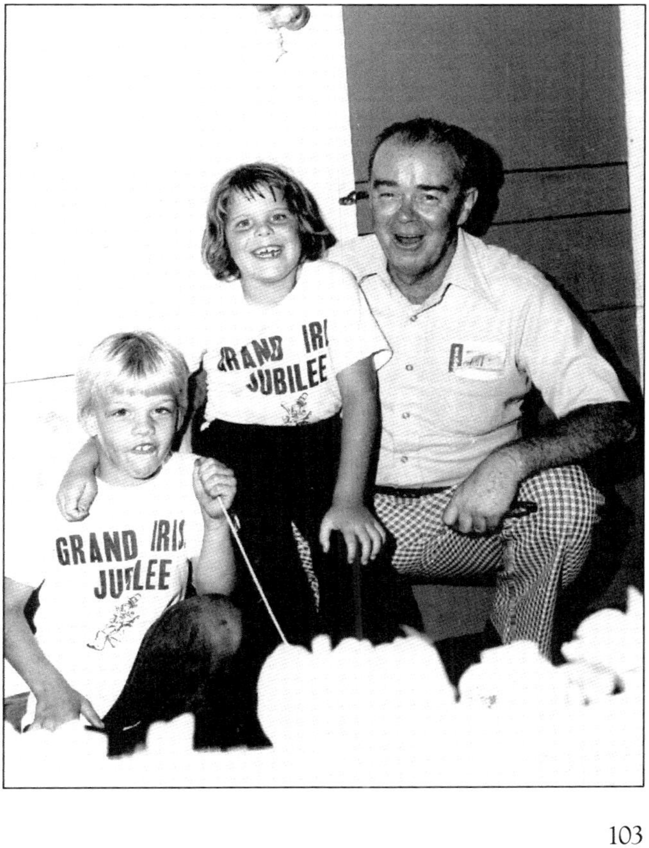

GRAND IRISH JUBILEE. Anyone who knew Frank Guinan knew his love for music. Listening to well-known Irish entertainers such as Paddy Noonan, Noel Kingston, and the Irish Balladeers inspired the beginning of his dream. After a trip to Ireland only hearing American pop music, he was determined to bring the traditional Irish music he loved to Lakewood Park in the form of an Irish music festival—thus, the Grand Irish Jubilee (1975–1982) was born. Guinan is pictured here with two of his grandchildren, Lisa Cunningham Fedor (center) and Matthew Lucyk.

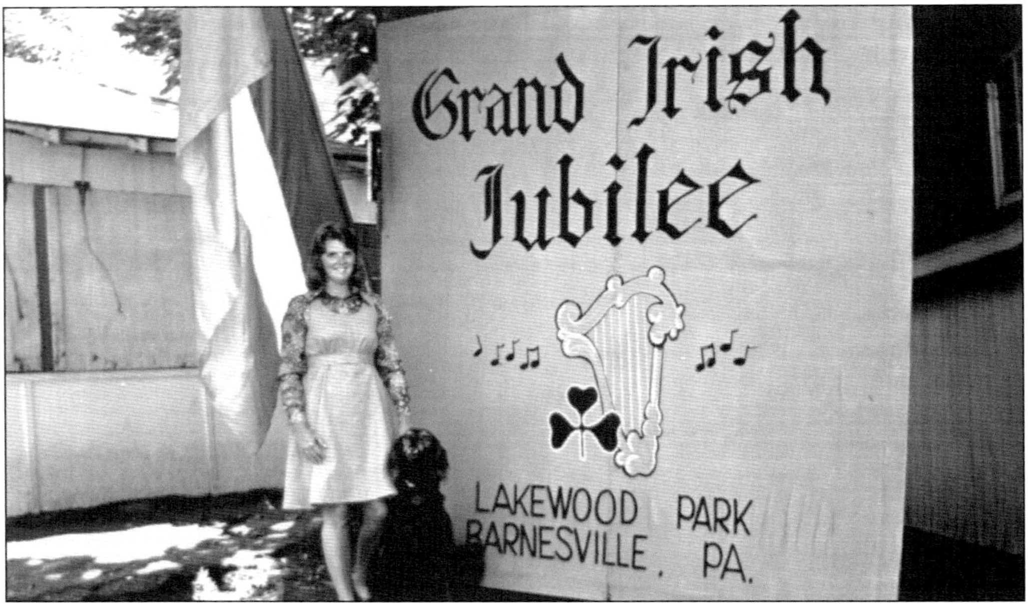

GRAND IRISH JUBILEE PROMOTION. Janet Cunningham and her friend Kelly Malone pose for some promotional pictures for the second Grand Irish Jubilee. The Grand Irish Jubilee, founded by Frank Guinan, quickly became one of the favorite ethnic days celebrated at Lakewood Park. The jubilee, defined by Guinan, was "Irish music, entertainment and dancing, plus Irish congeniality and family reunions."

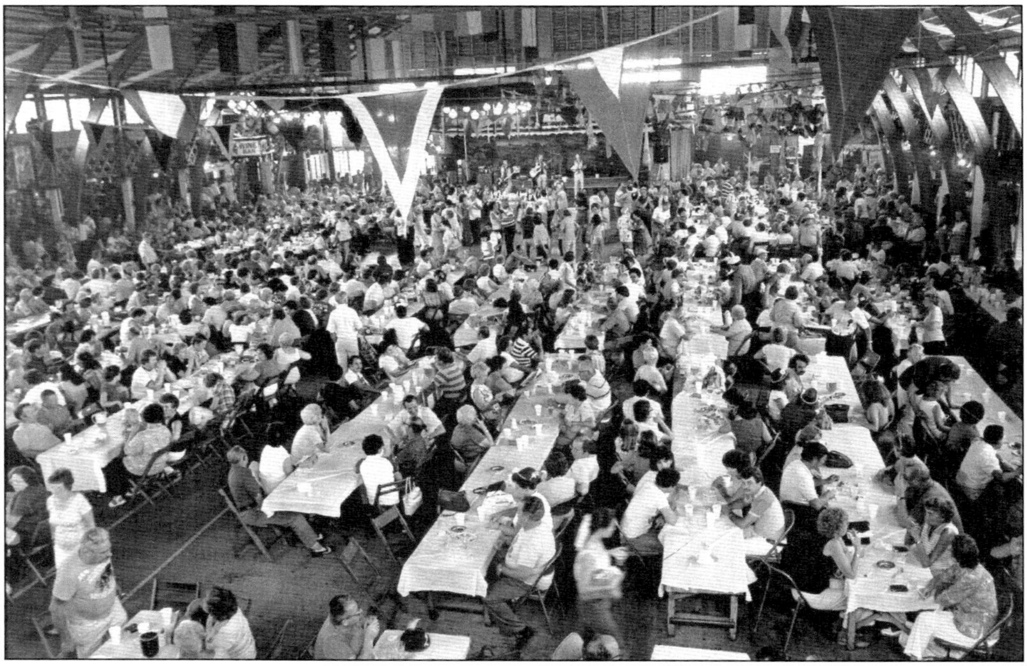

CROWDED GRAND HALL. This wide shot captures the typical Saturday crowd in the grand hall (ballroom) enjoying the music of Paddy Noonan, Mary McGonigle, Noel Kingston, and Martin Flynn.

MARY MCGONIGLE. "The Voice of Ireland," Mary McGonigle performs for her appreciative fans in the grand hall at Lakewood Park.

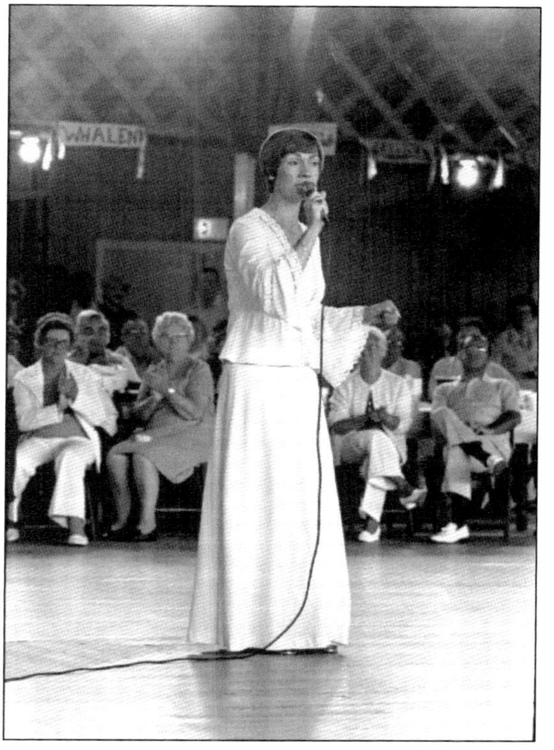

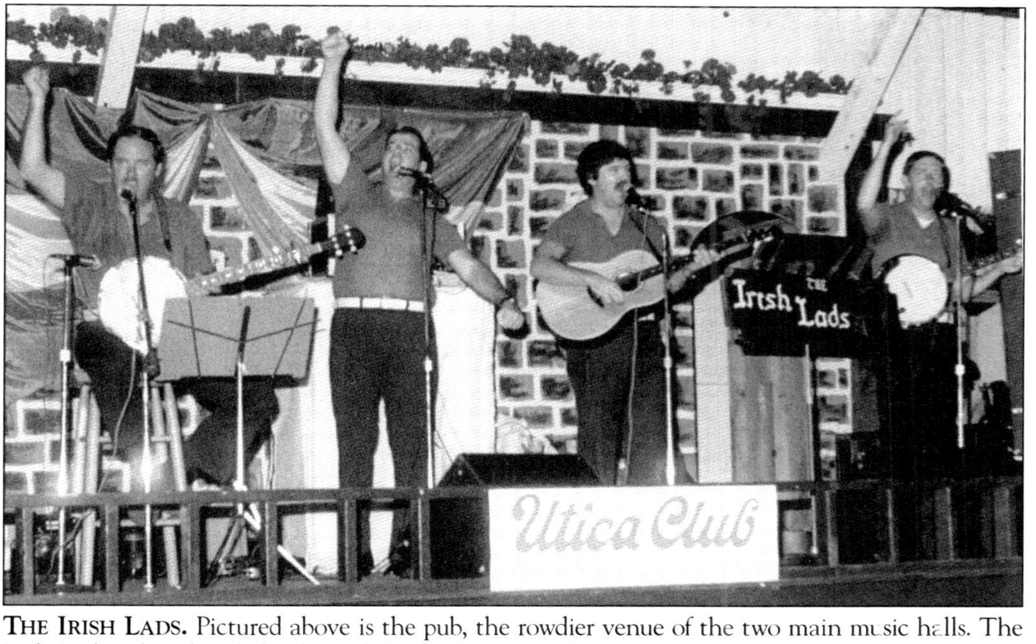

THE IRISH LADS. Pictured above is the pub, the rowdier venue of the two main music halls. The Irish Lads, who played the first jubilee for money collected in a hat on the midway, thrived on audience participation and usually concluded their performance with a rousing patriotic medley joined by a wildly enthusiastic audience. This picture shows the Irish Lads, from left to right, Mike Dolan, Neil Casey, Tom Boyle, and Ed Corcoran, performing "Cheer, Cheer for Old Notre Dame."

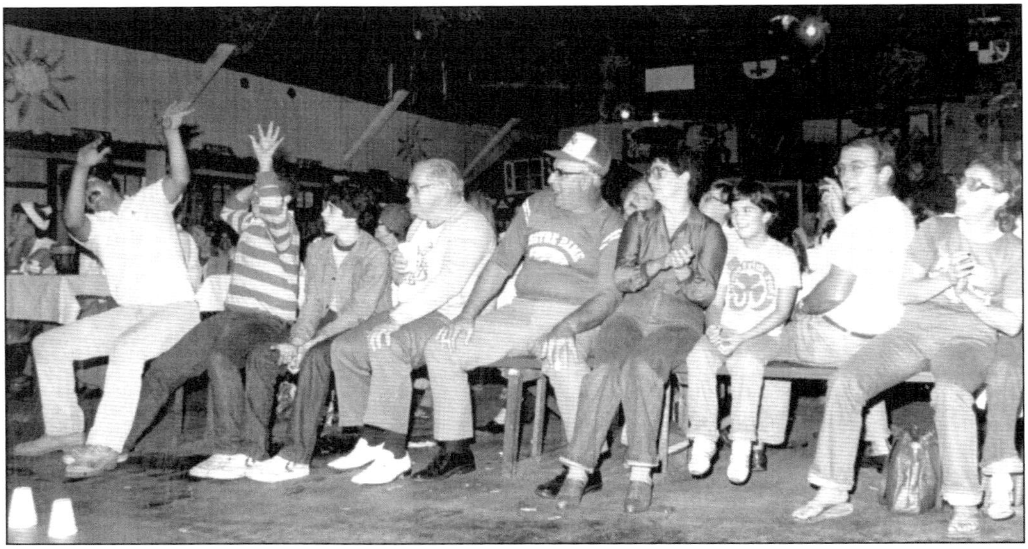

Fans at the Pub. Tom Boyle of the group the Irish Lads remembers the setting of this picture well. As he tells it, a couple from Boston the Irish Lads had met at one of their performances there appeared unannounced at his home during the jubilee with a tent they pitched in his yard. The next day they came to the jubilee and during a break placed Styrofoam cups on the floor and began dancing and jumping over them. In the picture are, from left to right, two friends from Boston, an unidentified fan, Tom Boyle's father, unidentified, Tom Whalen's wife Sandy, his daughter Jennifer, Tom Whalen, and unidentified.

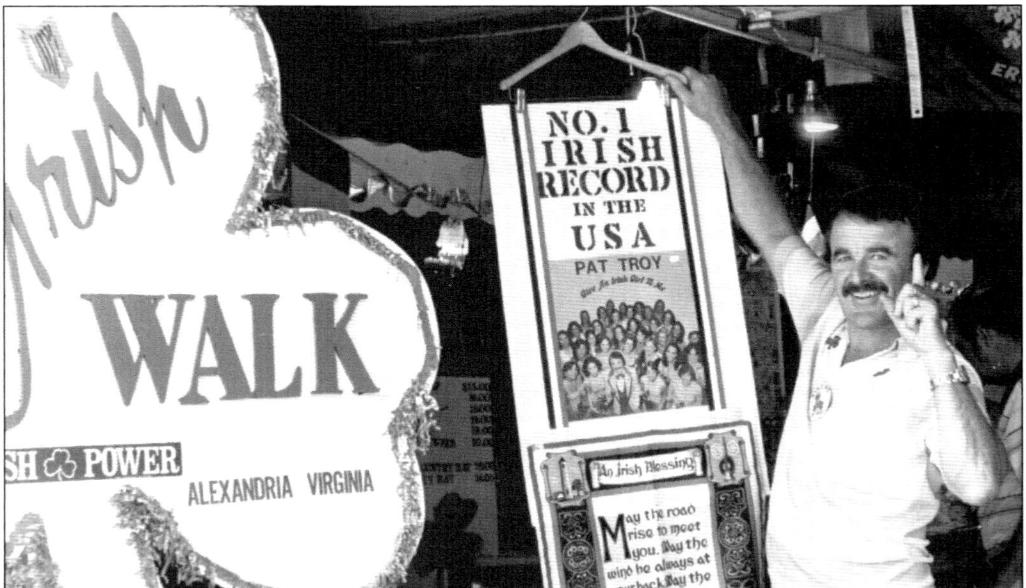

Pat Troy. One of the most popular figures at the Grand Irish Jubilee is pictured promoting his famous shop Irish Walk, located in Alexandria, Virginia. Troy brought his Irish Walk merchandise to the jubilee each year, filling the former Penny Arcade with hand-knit Aran sweaters, capes and jackets, Claddagh Irish wedding bands and friendship rings, Celtic crosses, Waterford crystal, family coat of arms, Irish albums, and cassettes.

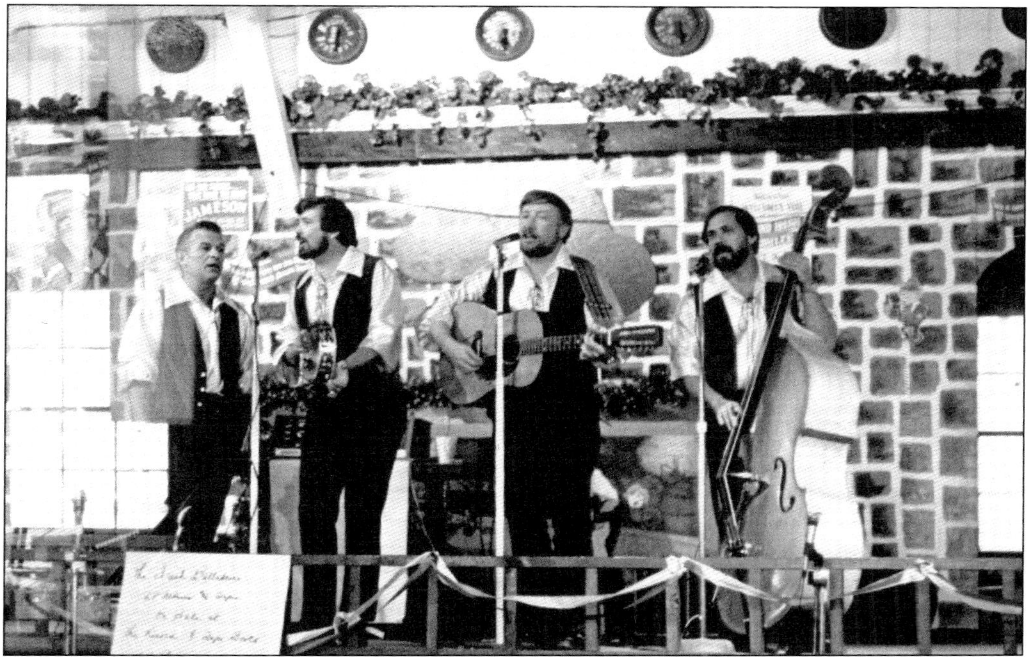

The Irish Balladeers. The Irish Balladeers perform onstage at the pub (original ballroom at Lakewood Park) on Saturday afternoon. The Irish Balladeers were an innovative Irish group from Scranton who appeared at the Grand Irish Jubilee every year.

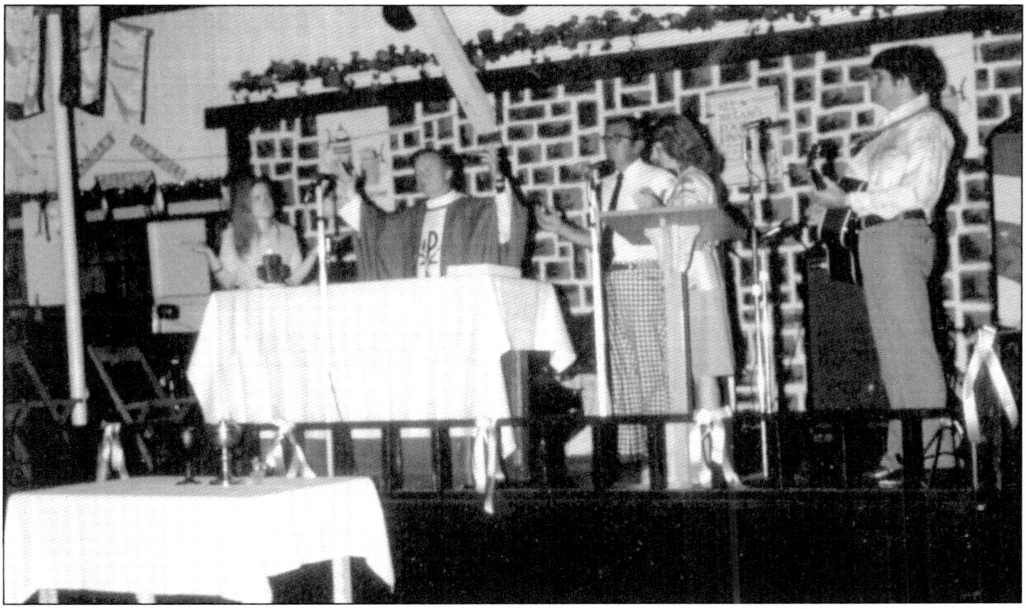

Mass at the Pub. Tradition at the jubilee dictated that shops close and entertainment stop while everyone attended noon mass at the pub, which had been miraculously transformed into a church chapel for the mass. Celebrating mass are Fr. Ed McElduff and, from left to right, McElduff's niece Mary Pat; Tom Whalen, reader and hall manager; Janet Cunningham, vocalist; and George Cunningham, guitar.

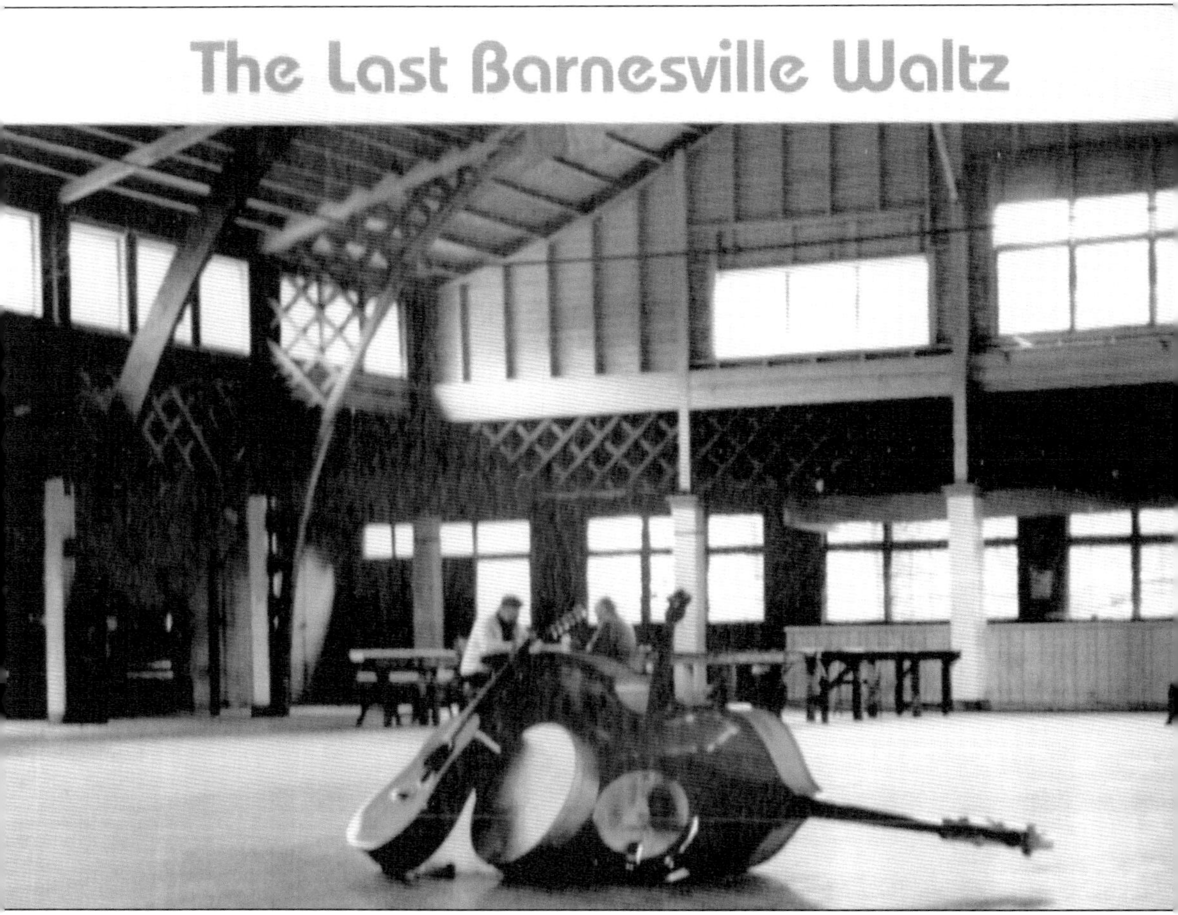

LAST WALTZ AT BARNESVILLE. This album cover is a photograph of members of the Irish Balladeers in the empty grand hall at Lakewood Park. The lead song on the album *The Last Barnesville Waltz* was written by the group shortly after the health of Frank Guinan precipitated the end of the Grand Irish Jubilee. It goes, "Now the old hall is shuttered and bare and only the memories remain." (Courtesy of Tom Whalen.)

Five

THE THEATER

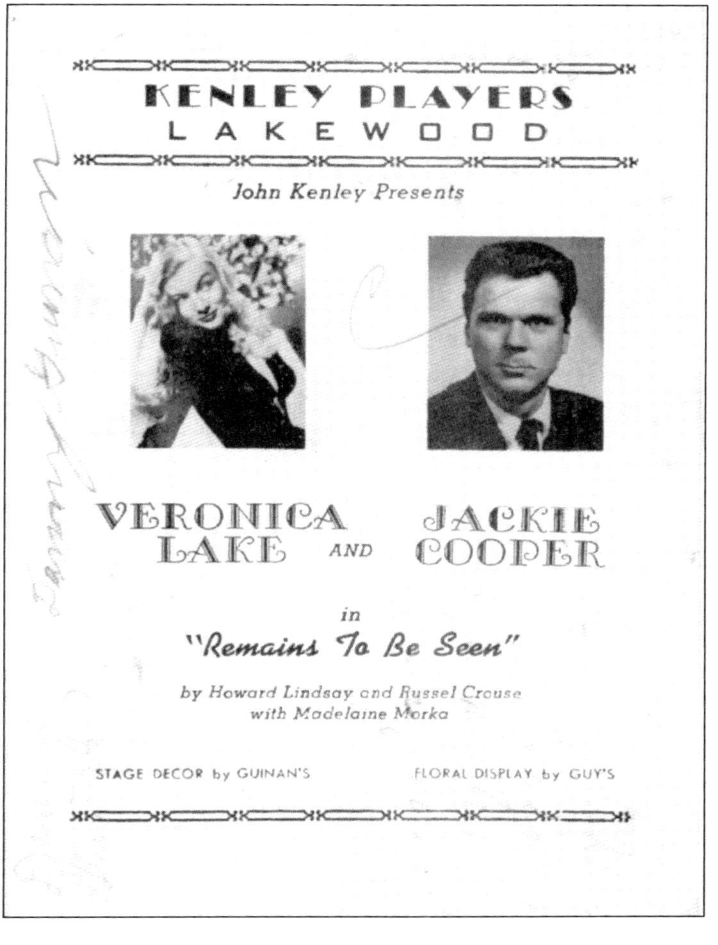

THE KENLEY PLAYERS. In 1947, Daniel Guinan II and his wife Margaret traveled to Deer Lake to meet John Kenley, legendary producer and director, and convince him to come to Lakewood Park with his Broadway-star summer stock productions. Daniel promised to build him a theater if he came. That day, on a handshake, the deal was sealed, and in 1949, the Kenley Players opened to a packed house at Lakewood.

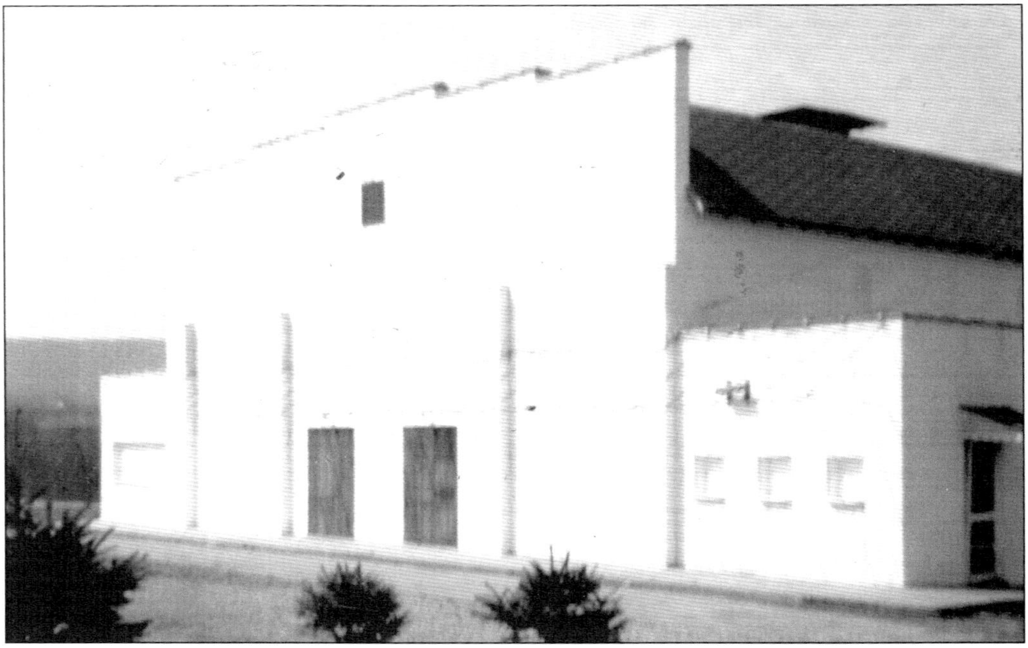

LAKEWOOD SUMMER THEATER. Construction for the theater began in 1948, and the theater opened for the summer season of 1949. The exterior was cinder block. The interior had a fully equipped stage and four backstage dressing rooms. There was plush seating for 638 on the main floor and 90 more in the balcony. Fully air-conditioned but not heated, the theater was only opened during the summer and early fall months.

JUNE 14,1949
KENLEY PLAYERS

1.	YES, MY DARLING DAUGHTER	*	ANN HARTING/TOM POSTON
2.	BURLESQUE		BERT PARKS/FRANK SUTTON
3.	LIGHT UP THE SKY		DIANA BARRYMORE
4.	DRESSED TO KILL		CHESTER MORRIS/TOM POSTON
5.	ANNA LUCASTA	* *	LIZABETH SCOTT
6.	HAPPY BIRTHDAY		JOAN BLONDELL
7.	MY SISTER EILEEN		BILLY GILBERT
8.	LET US BE GAY		KAY FRANCIS
9.	THE BAT		ZASU PITTS/TOM POSTON
10.	KISS AND TELL		PEGGY ANN GARNER
11.	THE BARRETTS OF WIMPOLE STREET	***	SUSAN PETERS
12.	HER CARDBOARD LOVER		TOM DRAKE/HAILA STODDARD
13.	ACCENT ON YOUTH		PAUL LUKAS
14.	THE PHILADELPHIA STORY	****	SARAH CHURCHILL/JEFF LYNN
15	PETTICOAT FEVER		SUNNY TUFF/ TOM POSTON

* Tom Poston was Lakewoods first Leading Man
** Lizabeth Scott is a Native of Sranton, Pa.
*** Susan Peters was tragically injured in a hunting accident and played the role from a wheelchair. She was married/ Divorced from the late Howard Hughes.
****Sarah Churchill was the lovely daughter of England's Prime Minister.

OPENING NIGHT, 1949. June 14, 1949, was opening night at Lakewood Park. *Yes, My Darling,* featuring Tom Poston of Newhart series fame, was the first of 15 dramas and comedies performed that year. Newspaper accounts of the opening describe a wildly enthusiastic capacity crowd. John Kenley spoke to the audience, promising more great theater and noting that the flowers that night were more lavish than at a Park Avenue wedding.

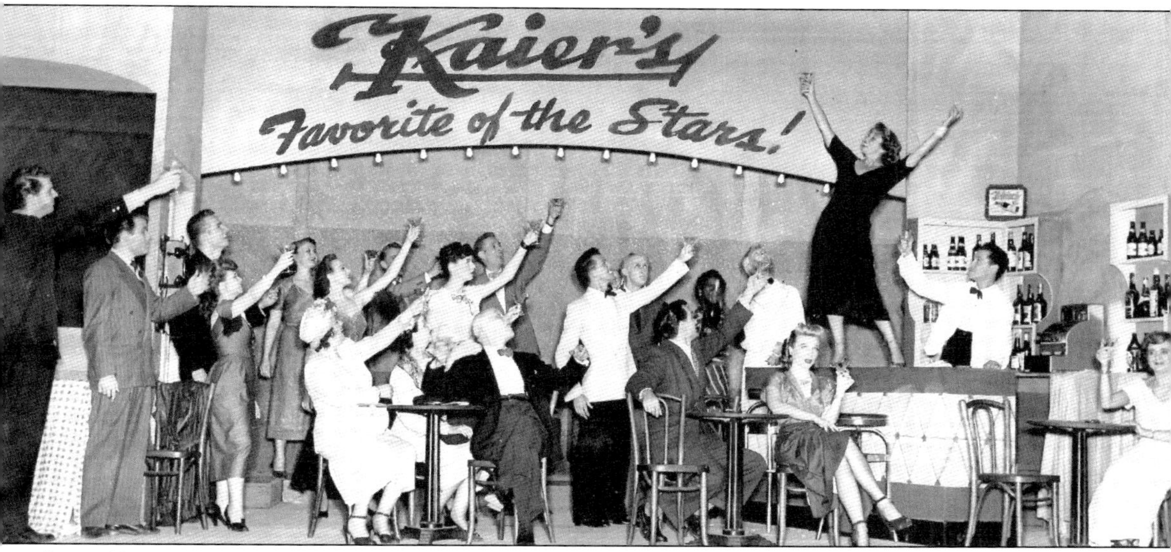

JOAN BLONDELL OF THE KENLEY PLAYERS AT LAKEWOOD STAGE. Joan Blondell appeared in the first season at Lakewood (1949) in the play *Happy Birthday*. Here she is on the bar on the Lakewood stage. The other actors are unidentified, but the picture exists because of the large Kaier's sign in the background. A regular advertiser in the Lakewood Theater programs, Kaier's Beer was brewed in nearby Mahanoy City and sold throughout the county. As a promotional gimmick, the sign was created by the Kenley Players crew as part of the nightclub scene in the play. (Courtesy of John B. Leiberman.)

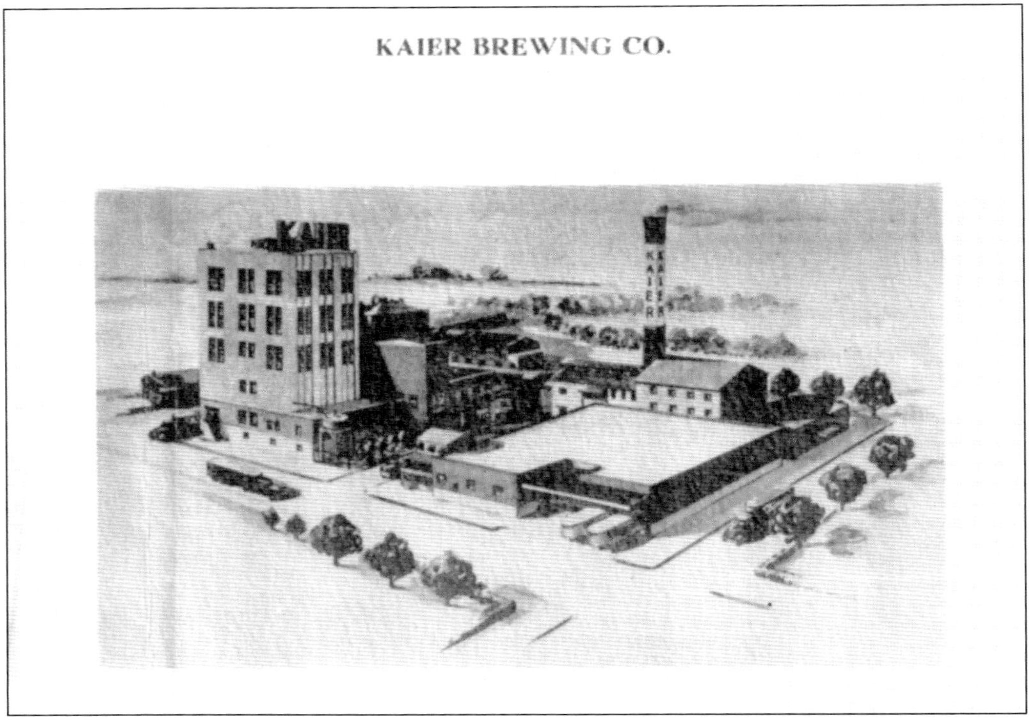

KAIER'S BEER ADVERTISEMENT. Above is one of the advertisements that appeared in all the theater programs. The line drawing is of the brewery situated on North Main Street in Mahanoy City.

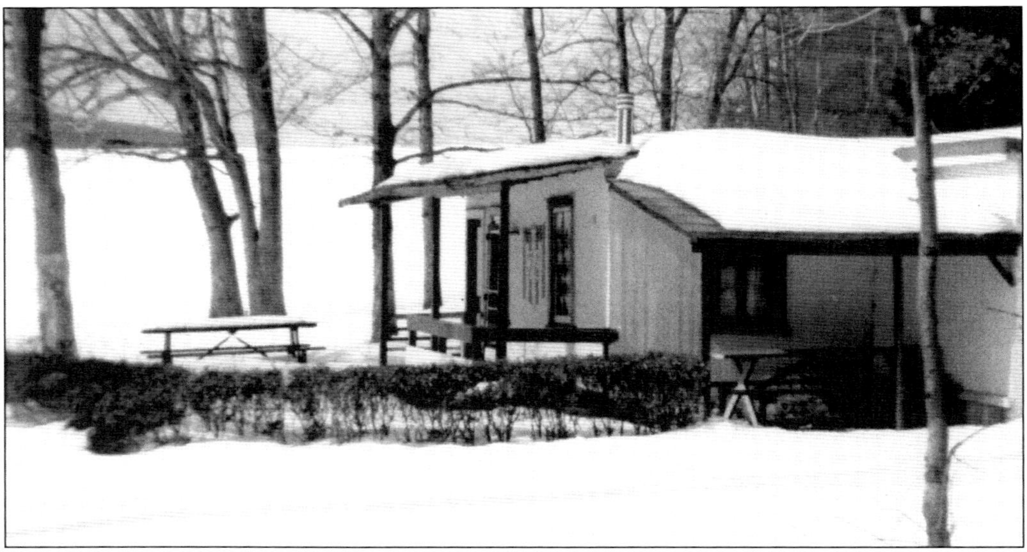

BUNGALOW AT LAKEWOOD. Throughout the history of Lakewood Park, employees and concessionaires lived in provided or rented cabins referred to as bungalows. Beginning in 1949 with the Kenley Players, apprentices and house actors who learned, worked, and performed at Lakewood were given housing at the park in this and at least four other houses. Kathy Guinan Connolly remembers staying in the Noll's bungalow and using a chamber pot during the night and public bathrooms by day. (Courtesy of Wally and Blanche Starkey.)

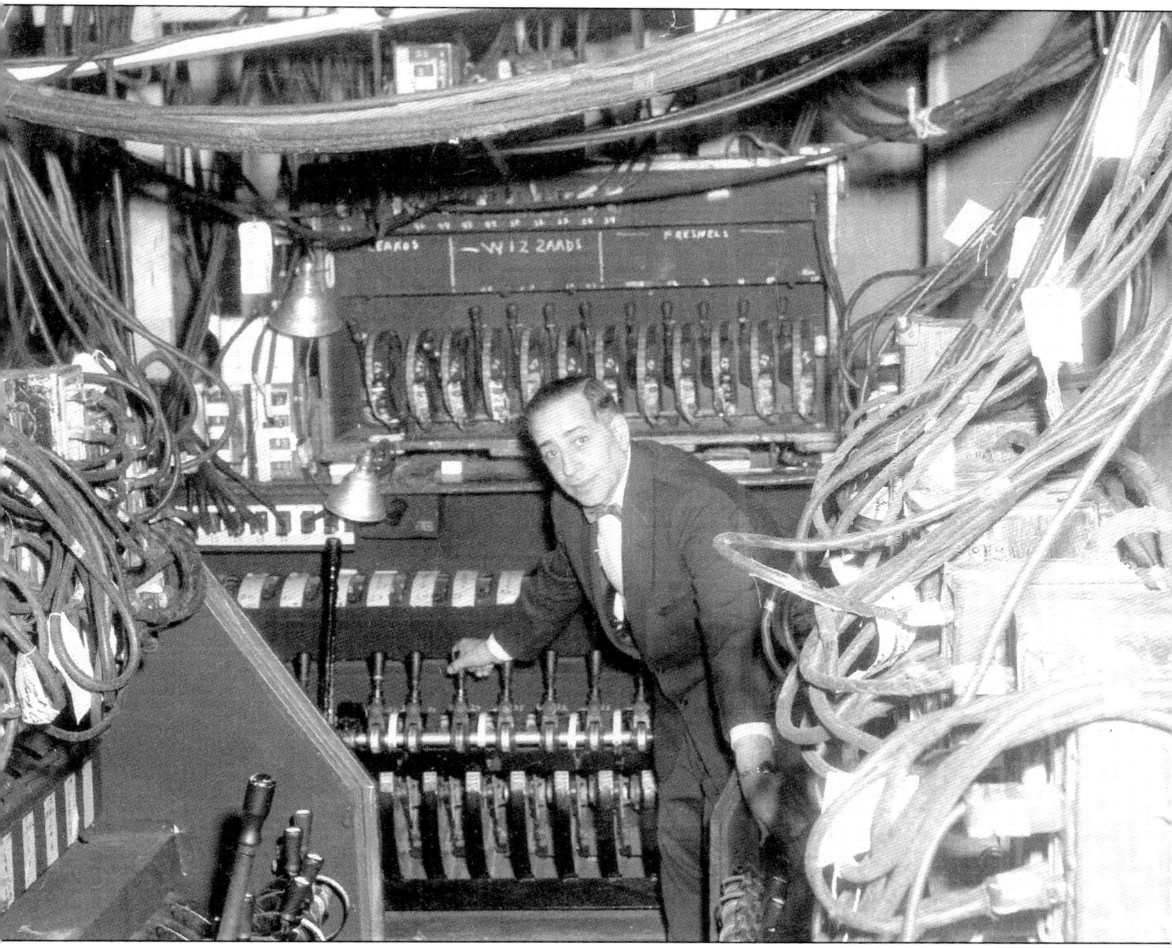

Bill Fanelli Backstage with the Theater's Electrical Panels. When John Kenley was putting together a stage crew, he went through the local International Alliance of Theatrical Stage Employees out of nearby Pottsville. The most senior member was Bill Fanelli, an experienced electrician, master carpenter, stage manager, and movie theater operator from Mahanoy City. Each week Fanelli and his crew built the stage sets from scratch; only the stars traveled from place to place in those days. Fanelli's talent was so great that they could not do without him, and he remained at Lakewood throughout the Kenley years and beyond. (Courtesy of Marjorie Fletcher.)

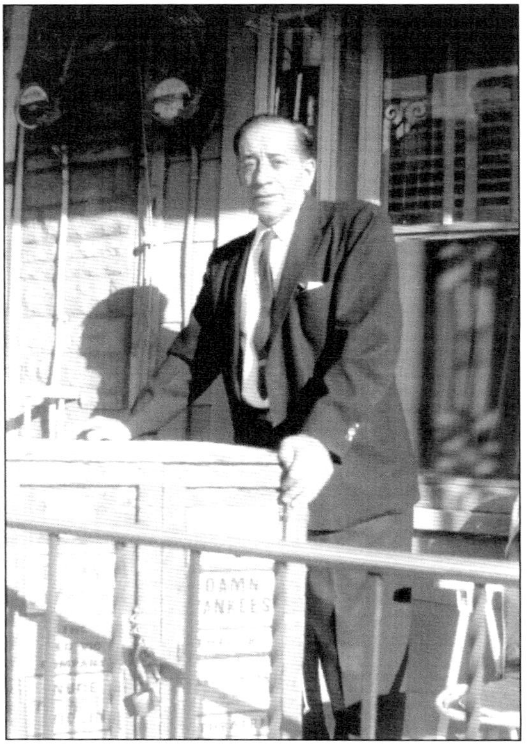

BILL FANELLI AT HOME WITH MASTER TOOLS AND EQUIPMENT. According to his niece Marjorie Fletcher, Bill Fanelli lived with his mother five miles away at the family homestead while working at Lakewood Park. He became friends with stars and apprentices alike and frequently brought many of the famous actors to his home for Italian meals cooked by his mother. Among the stars were Robert Alda and his son Alan Alda, who was an apprentice, Tom Poston, and Eva Gabor. (Courtesy of Marjorie Fletcher.)

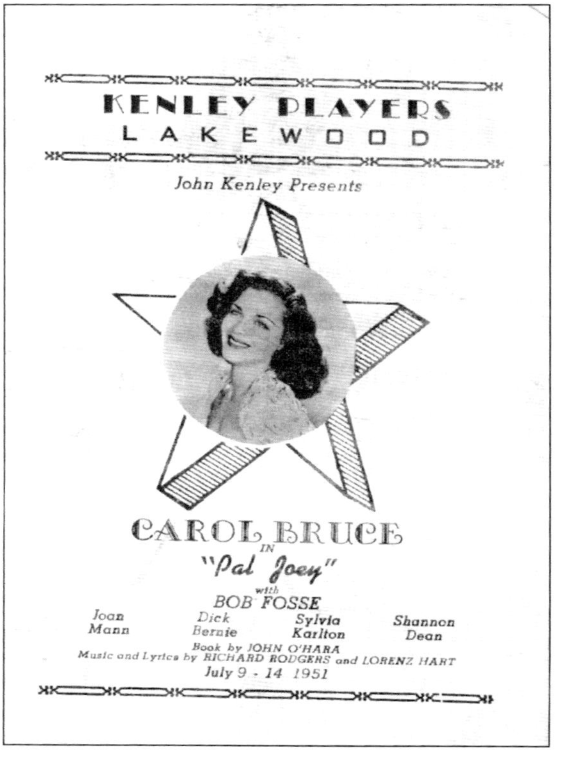

PAL JOEY WITH BOB FOSSE. In 1951, the Kenley Players put on the drama *Pal Joey*, written by Pottsville native John O'Hara. Bob Fosse, the legendary choreographer, appeared in the cast as Joey Evans long before he achieved Broadway fame.

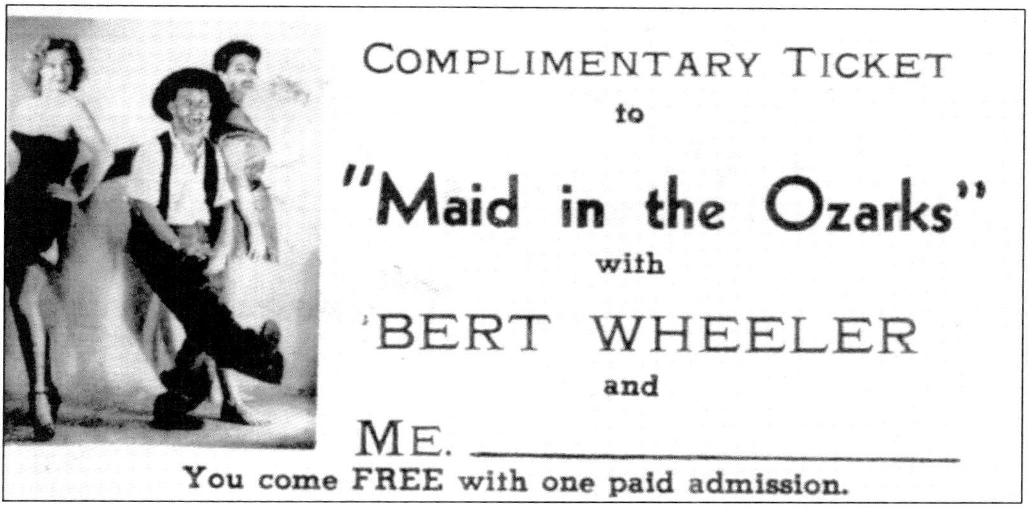

BERT WHEELER. In 1953, because of increasing production costs that required larger theaters, John Kenley moved his summer stock to Ohio. Charles O. Carey took over production and direction of the summer playhouse with Bert Wheeler starring in *Maid in the Ozarks* (1954). This was the only season for Carey in a year that featured Terry Moore, Tom Poston, Victor Jury, and Zachary Scott. (Courtesy of Marjorie Fletcher.)

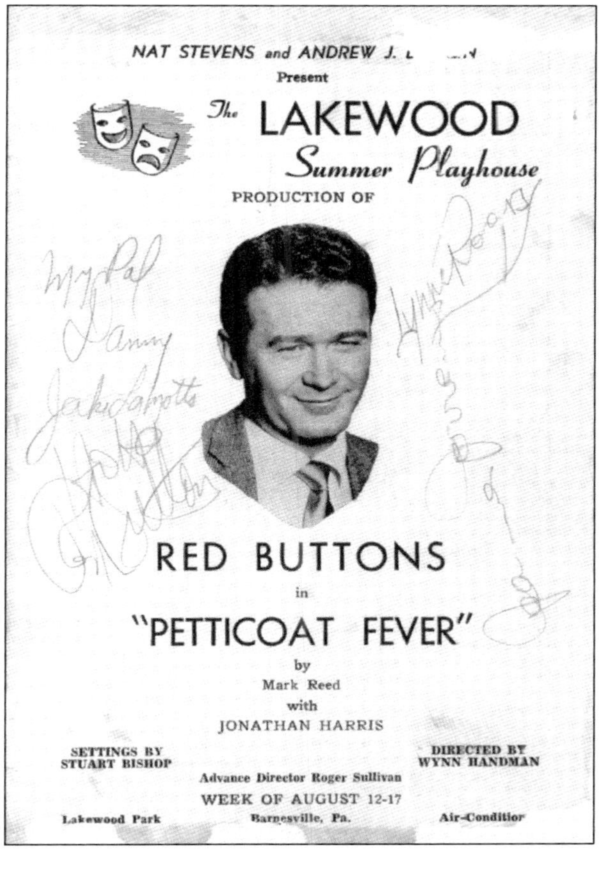

RED BUTTONS. This program from the 1957 season at Lakewood has Red Buttons starring in *Petticoat Fever* with Nat Stevens and Andrew Breslin as producers. Red Buttons started as a comedian and had his own very popular television show in the early 1950s. The year he appeared at Lakewood was the same year he won an Academy Award for best supporting actor for his dramatic role of Joe Kelly in *Sayonara* opposite Marlon Brando.

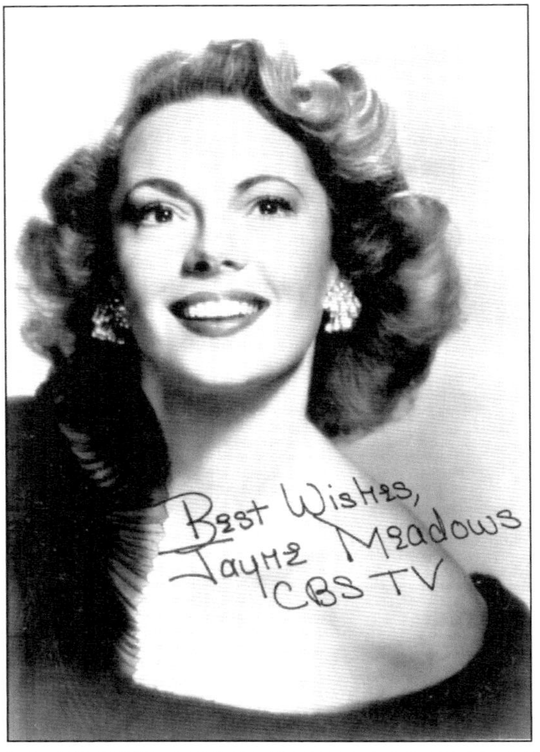

JAYNE MEADOWS. Movie actress, comedienne, author, and singer Jayne Meadows appeared at the Lakewood Theater in 1956 in *Tea and Sympathy*. At the time of her appearance, Meadows was in the fourth year of the popular television program *I've Got a Secret* and was appearing in all the major dramatic playhouses on television, including Hallmark, Kraft, Studio One, and *The Chesterfield Hour*. She was married to Steve Allen from 1954 to his death in 2000.

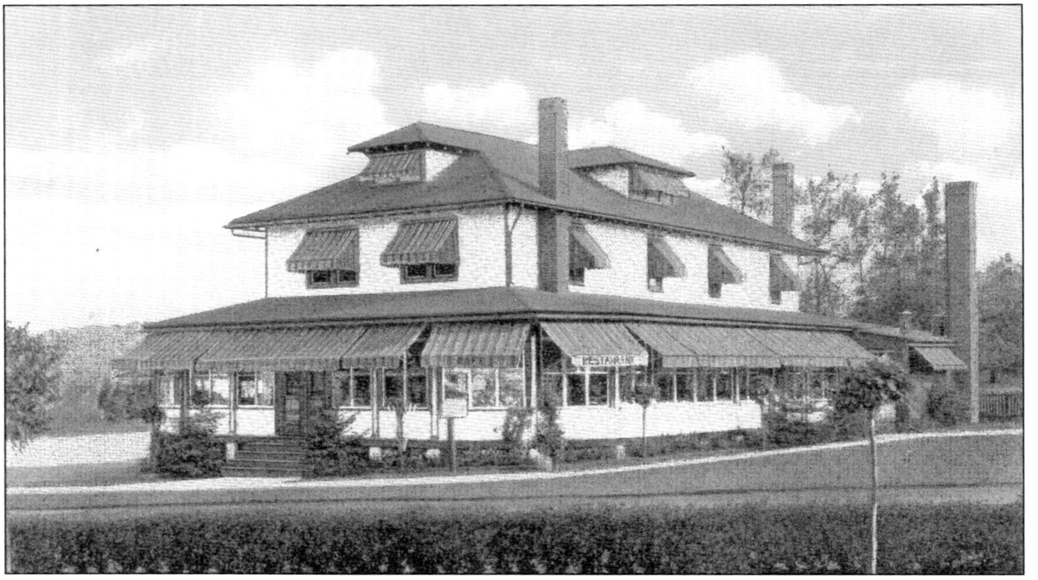

SCRAFFORD'S. This is a postcard of the original Scrafford's building that burned to the ground in 1940. Located in Hometown, approximately five miles from Lakewood Park, Scrafford's was an established business when the theater opened in 1949. Many stars stayed and dined at the rebuilt Scrafford's Hotel and Motel, enjoying home cooking and the congenial owners. Scrafford's always billed itself as "home of the stars." The business closed in the 1990s, and a McDonald's was built on its site.

EVA GABOR. Eva Gabor (February 11, 1919–July 4, 1995) was a Hungarian-born actress, best known for her role on *Green Acres*. She appeared in *Blithe Spirit* at Lakewood in 1956 and was as glamorous in person as she was on screen.

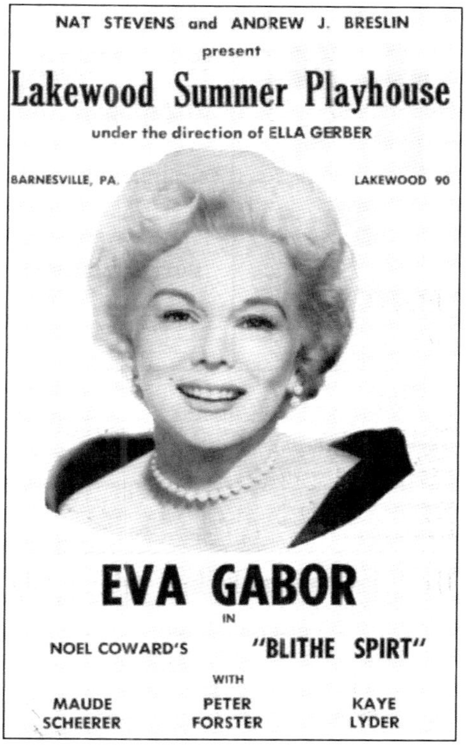

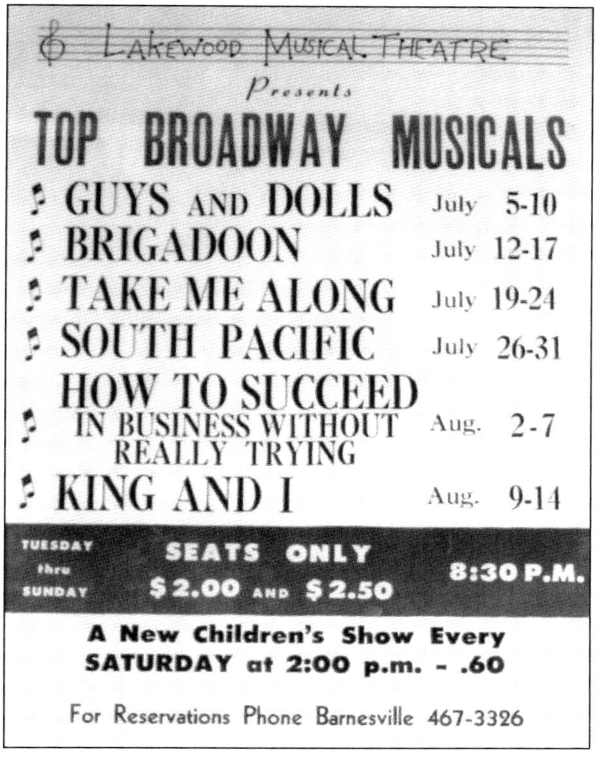

LAKEWOOD THEATER POSTER, 1966. This poster is from the first year local talents Rich Reimold and his wife Kathe of Hazleton took over production. The Reimolds tried hiring young and aspiring actors rather than stars, along with employing local residents as apprentices. The Reimolds produced three years of plays at Lakewood. Among the local residents who apprenticed were Amy Achley, Marle Becker, Mary Leiberman, Gayle Sisak Osenbach, Peggy Ward Coombe, and Rich Huebner.

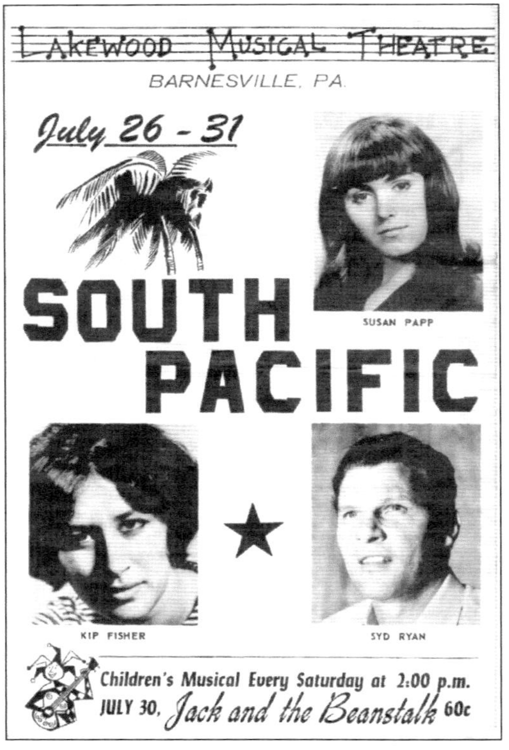

CHILDREN'S MUSICALS. Always popular at the Lakewood Theater were the special Saturday musicals for children put on by the apprentices. In July 1966, it was *Jack and the Beanstalk* that thrilled the young audience.

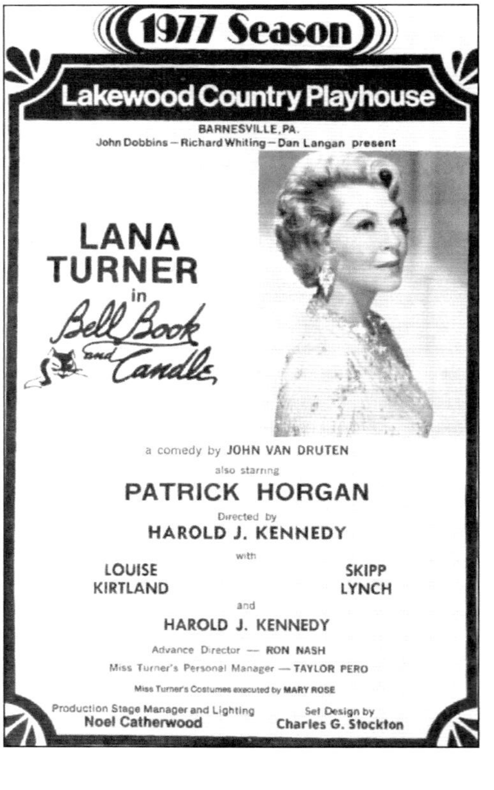

LANA TURNER. At the time Lana Turner appeared again at Lakewood Park in 1977, she was one of the top 10 actresses whose motion pictures had grossed more than any other in the history of film. In 1971, she had her stage debut in a comedy and continued through the 1970s with more comedies like the play she performed at Lakewood, *Bell Book and Candle*.

JOHN RAITT. John Raitt is most famous for his two Broadway leading roles: *Carousel*, offered to him by composers Rodgers and Hammerstein, and *Pajama Game*, in which he also starred in the movie version with Doris Day. Raitt starred in a two-actor musical at Lakewood, *I Do I Do*, in 1977. John Raitt is also the father of Bonnie Raitt, singer and songwriter.

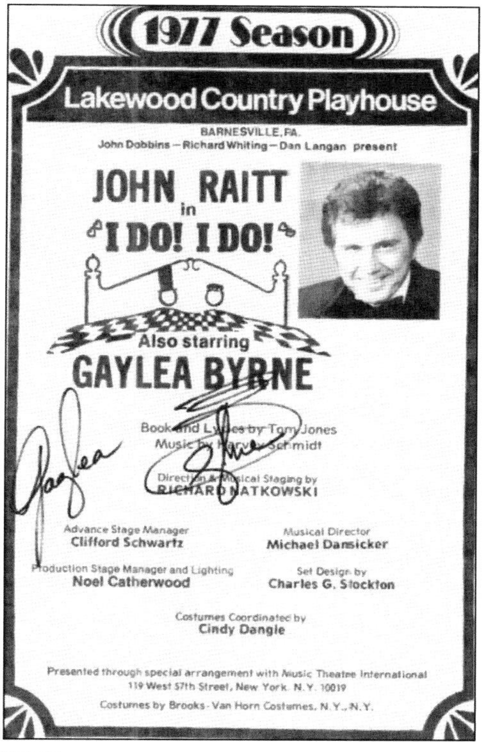

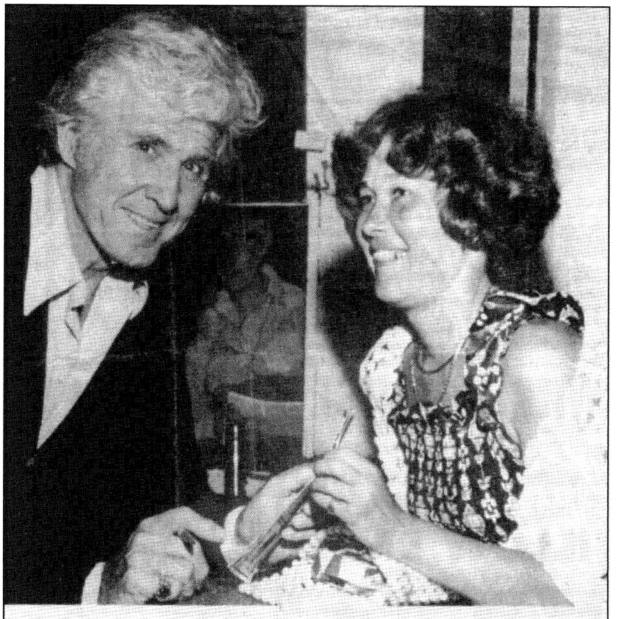

'I Do, I Do'

Peg Grigalonis, Barnesville, compliments John Raitt on his performance in "I Do, I Do" at Lakewood Playhouse Monday Evening.

June 1977

JOHN RAITT WITH PEGGY GRIGALONIS. Opening night for the 1977 season at the Lakewood Theater brought crowds and the press, which snapped this picture after the show. The year 1977 featured Lynn Redgrave, Phyllis Diller, Ann Corio, and Lana Turner.

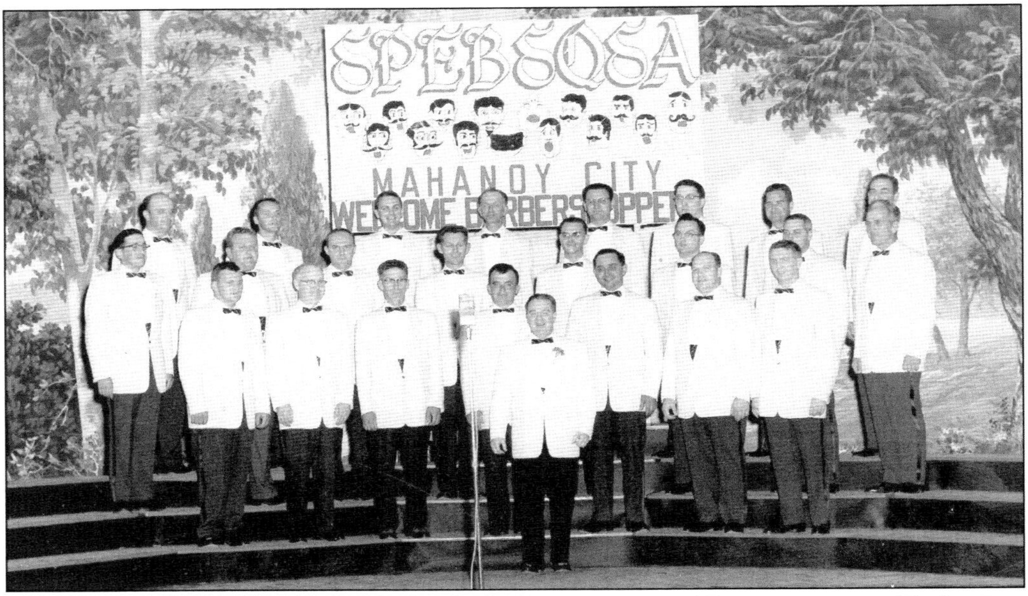

MAHANOY CITY CHAPTER. The Society for the Preservation and Encouragement of Barbershop Quartet Singing in America (SPEBSQSA) is a national organization for those who love to sing. The local chapter of the barbershop singers poses for a formal picture in its tuxedos. Front and center is Frank Guinan, founder and director of the local chapter. Behind him are, from left to right, (first row) John Dougherty, Puck Sullivan, Charles Humes, Jack Lane, Bill Owens, Ken Osenbach, and Jim Thompson; (second row) James Smith, Chugo Haley, Jack Lockwood, Ralph Burke, Charles Wagner, Jack Fowler, Haden Williams, and Louis Onorofsky; (third row) Dick Kirchner, Daniel Whitenight, John Murphy, Warren Davies, Bob Evans, Ted Evans, Marlin Koch, and Ed McLaughlin.

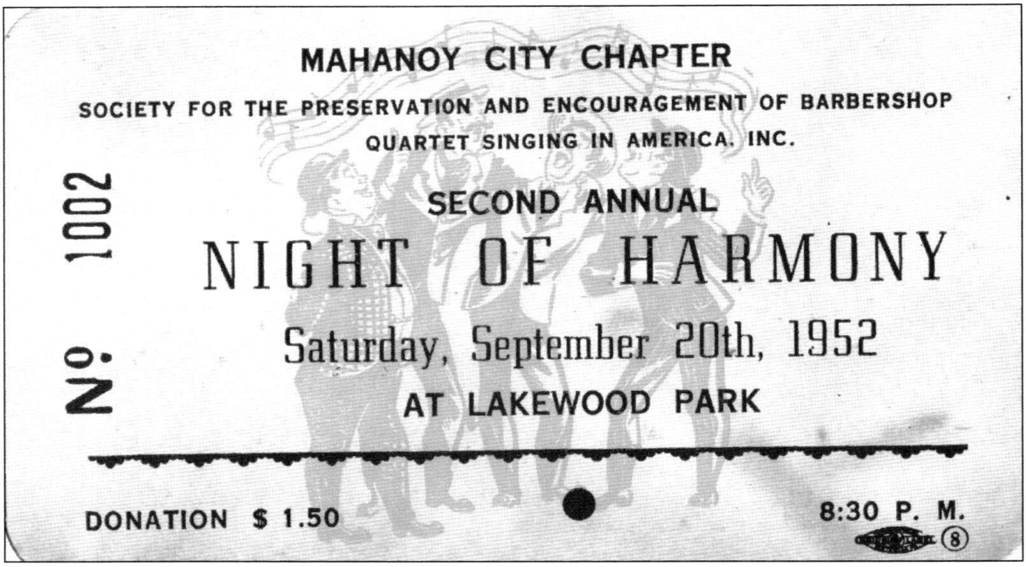

NIGHT OF HARMONY TICKET. This ticket from the second annual barbershop show in 1952 admitted the bearer to an hour of singing by national award-winning quartets from Pittsburgh, Buffalo, and other major cities, along with singing and antics from the local chapter.

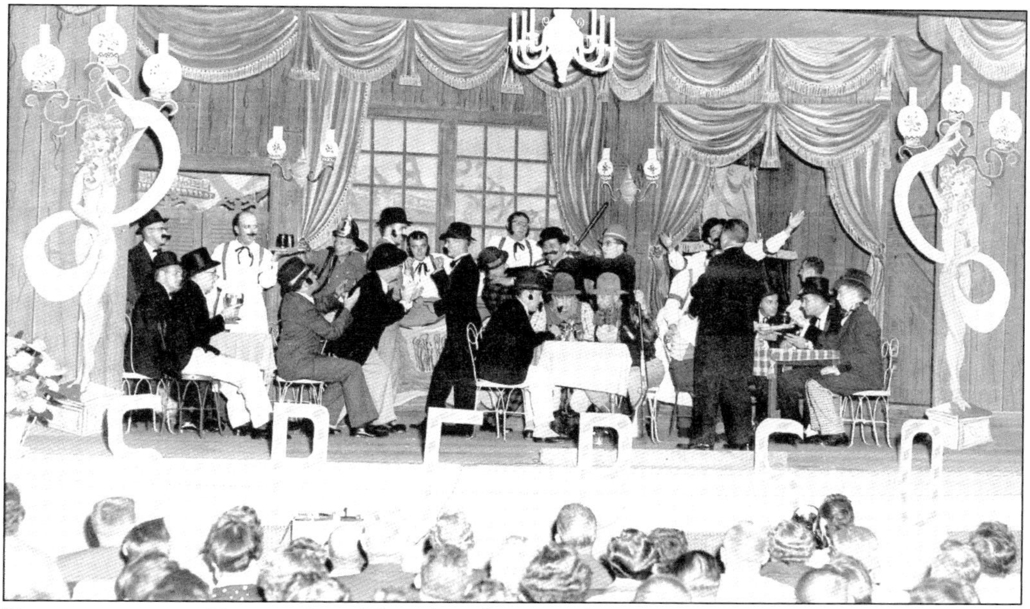

BARBERSHOPPERS FREEZE SET. This shot features the opening scene of a sold-out annual barbershop show at the Lakewood Theater. It was an anticipated treat for the audiences when the "freeze set" was first viewed. The curtain rose to enthusiastic applause and cheers, with the high expectation for a delightful night of harmony. The local chorus also hosted many national champion barbershop quartets throughout the years. One of the most memorial quartets, the Buffalo Bills, performed at the Lakewood Theater shortly before reaching fame for their appearances in the Broadway and movie version of the musical *The Music Man*.

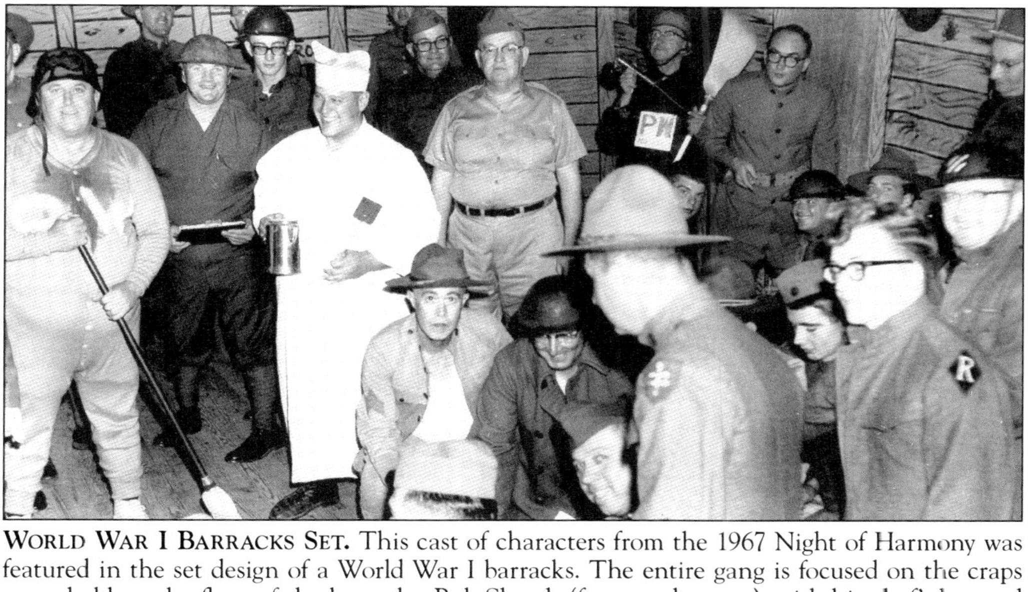

WORLD WAR I BARRACKS SET. This cast of characters from the 1967 Night of Harmony was featured in the set design of a World War I barracks. The entire gang is focused on the craps game held on the floor of the barracks. Bob Skeath (front and center), with his chef's hat and coffeepot in hand, is prepared to serve his fellow troops. Some of the other boys include Chugo Haley, Tom Anthony, John Dougherty, Larry Miller, Francis Hinkle, Jack Fowler, Jack Lane, Jim Langon, and Bob Evans. (Courtesy of the Bob Skeath collection.)

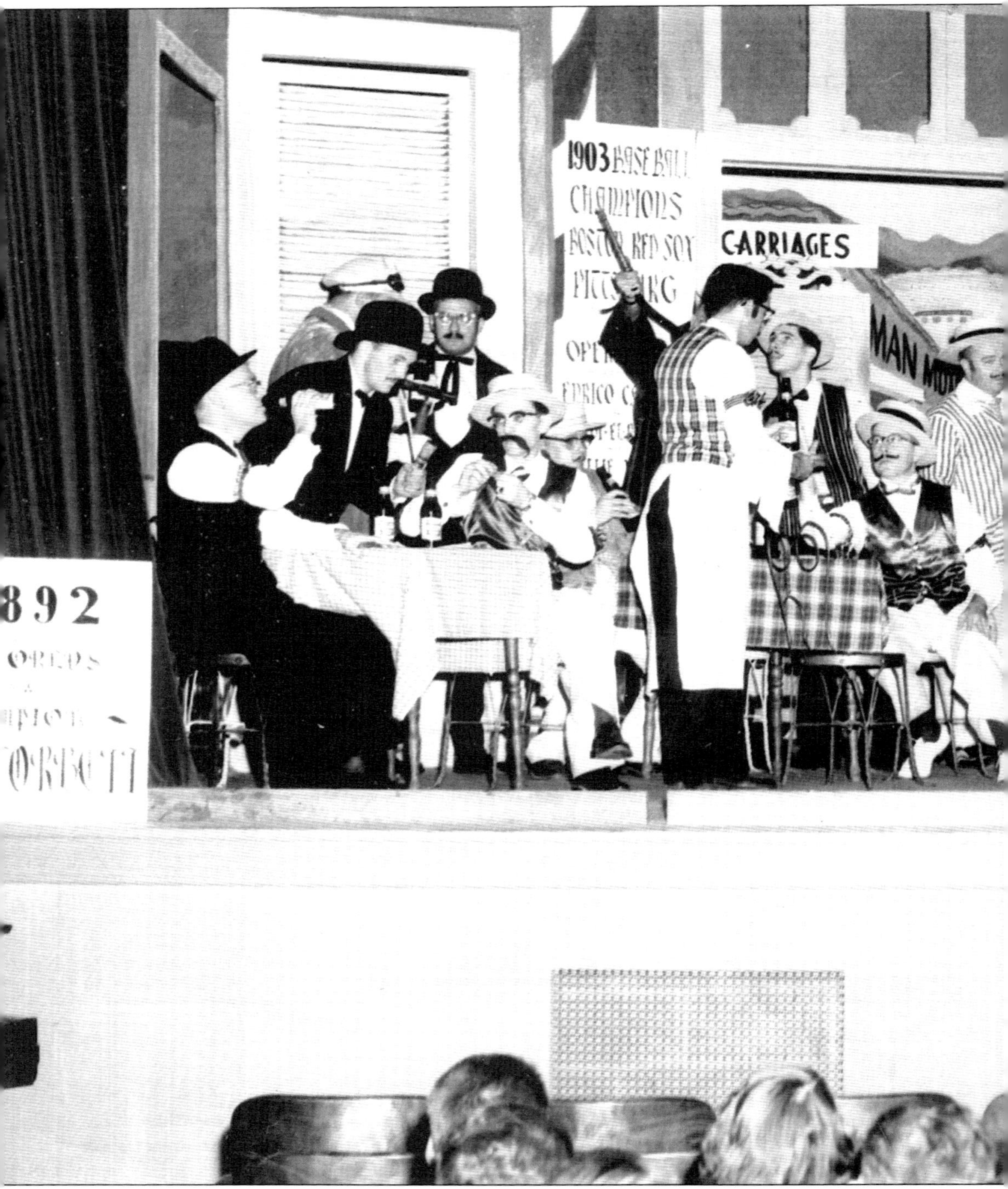

BARBERSHOPPERS AT THE SALOON. The elaborate sets used for the annual show were designed, constructed, and painted by Chugo Haley (pictured center stage) and the Mahanoy City barbershop chorus members. Haley used his artistic abilities to create the scene for that first heart-grabbing moment when the curtain went up. Seated at the table on the left are Puck

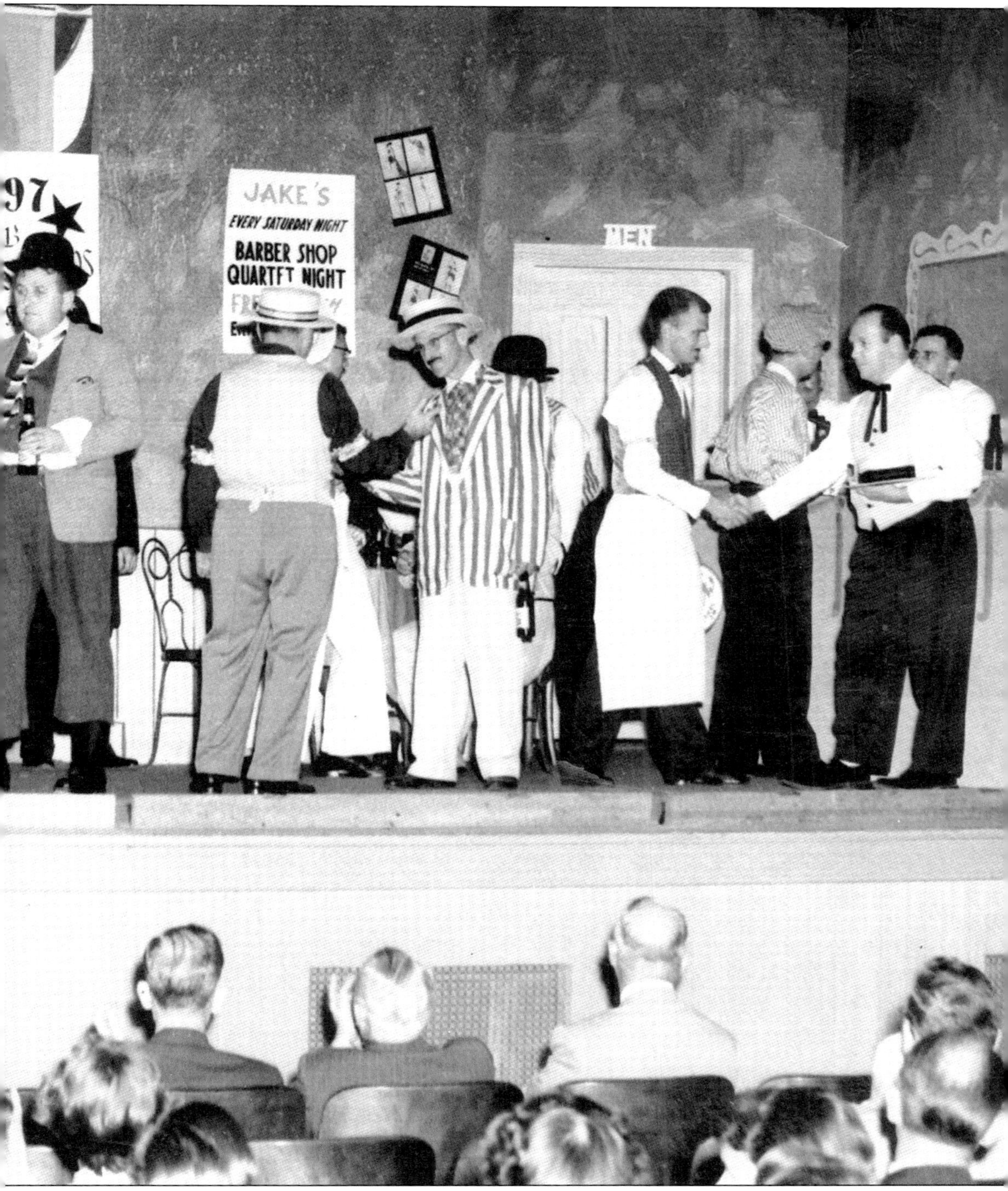

Sullivan and Dyke Campbell, wearing the bowler hat is John Dougherty, seated at table two is Kenneth Donnelly with Dave Bradbury behind him, entering the saloon is Frank Guinan, in the striped jacket is Charlie Humes, and shaking hands on the far right are Charles Wagner and Ken Osenbach.

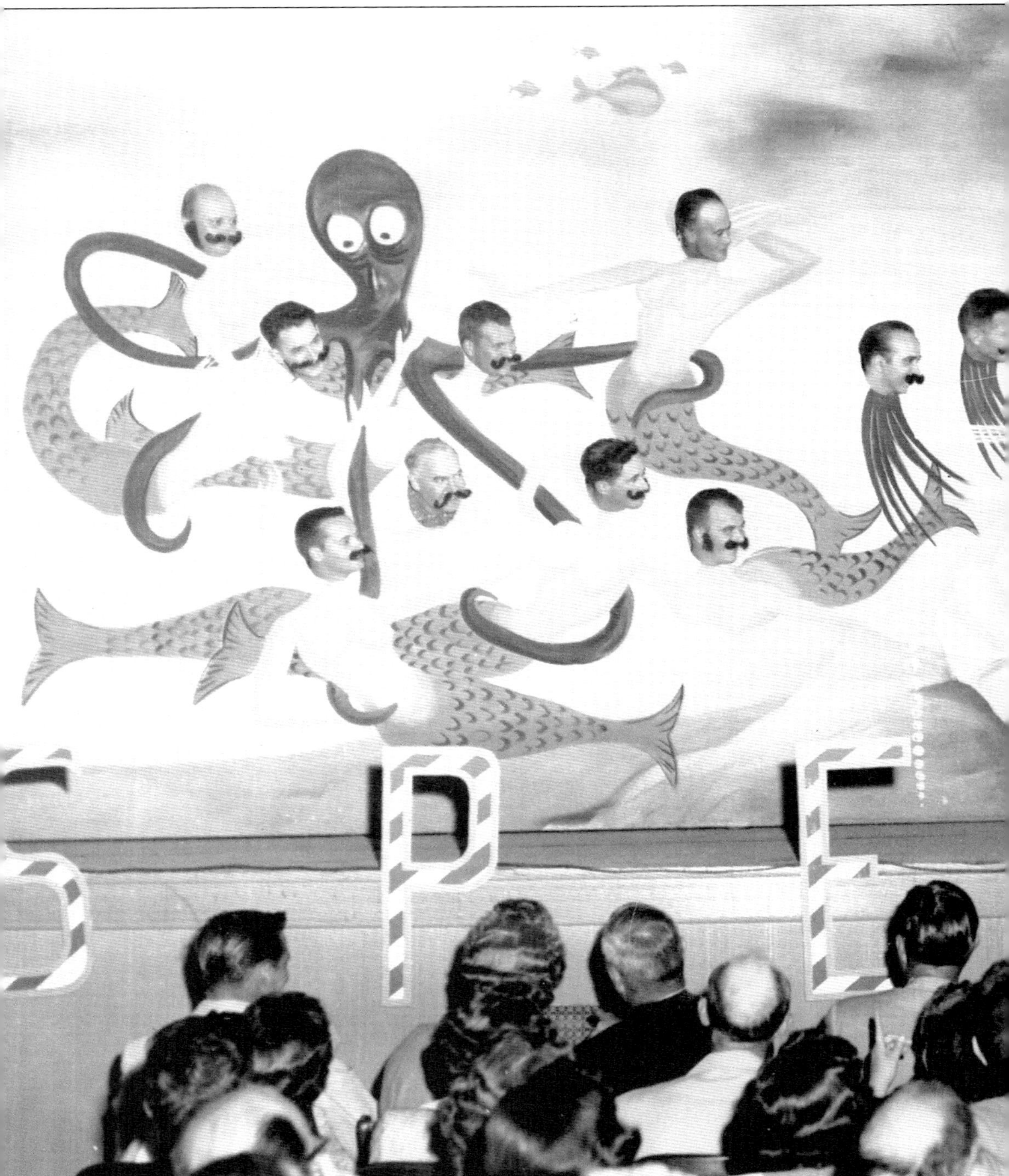

"Minnie the Mermaid." It is show time at the Lakewood Theater on opening night of the annual barbershop show in the year 1958. Frank Guinan as King Neptune (far right), god of water and the sea in Roman mythology, leads his school of mermaids in the song "Minnie the Mermaid." This sophisticated audience has grown to appreciate and anticipate the great opening

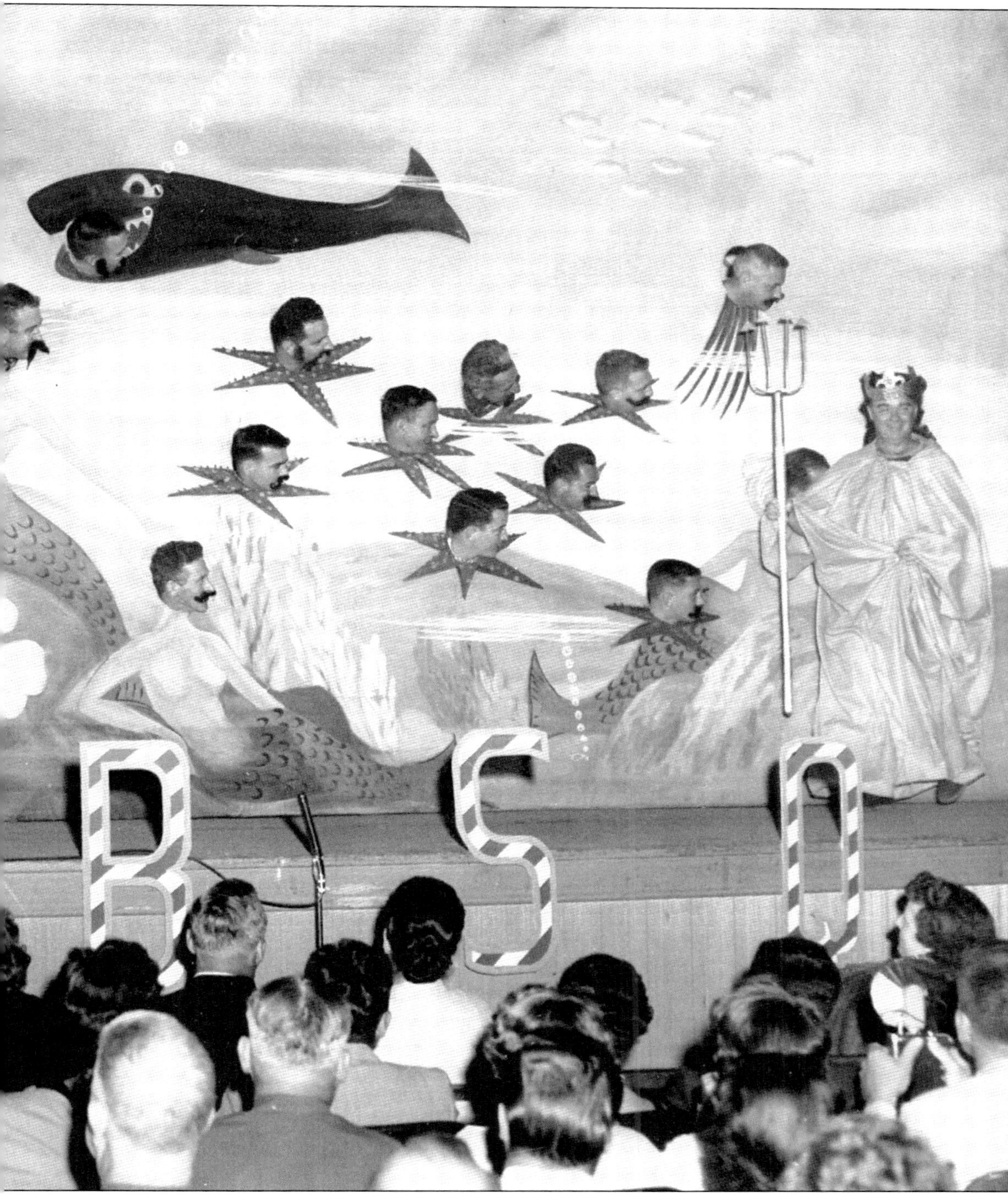

set and song with each annual barbershop show. This year's opener, "Minnie the Mermaid," and the underwater scene thrilled the audience. The thunderous applause was still echoing throughout the Lakewood Theater when a second surprise was unveiled (next picture).

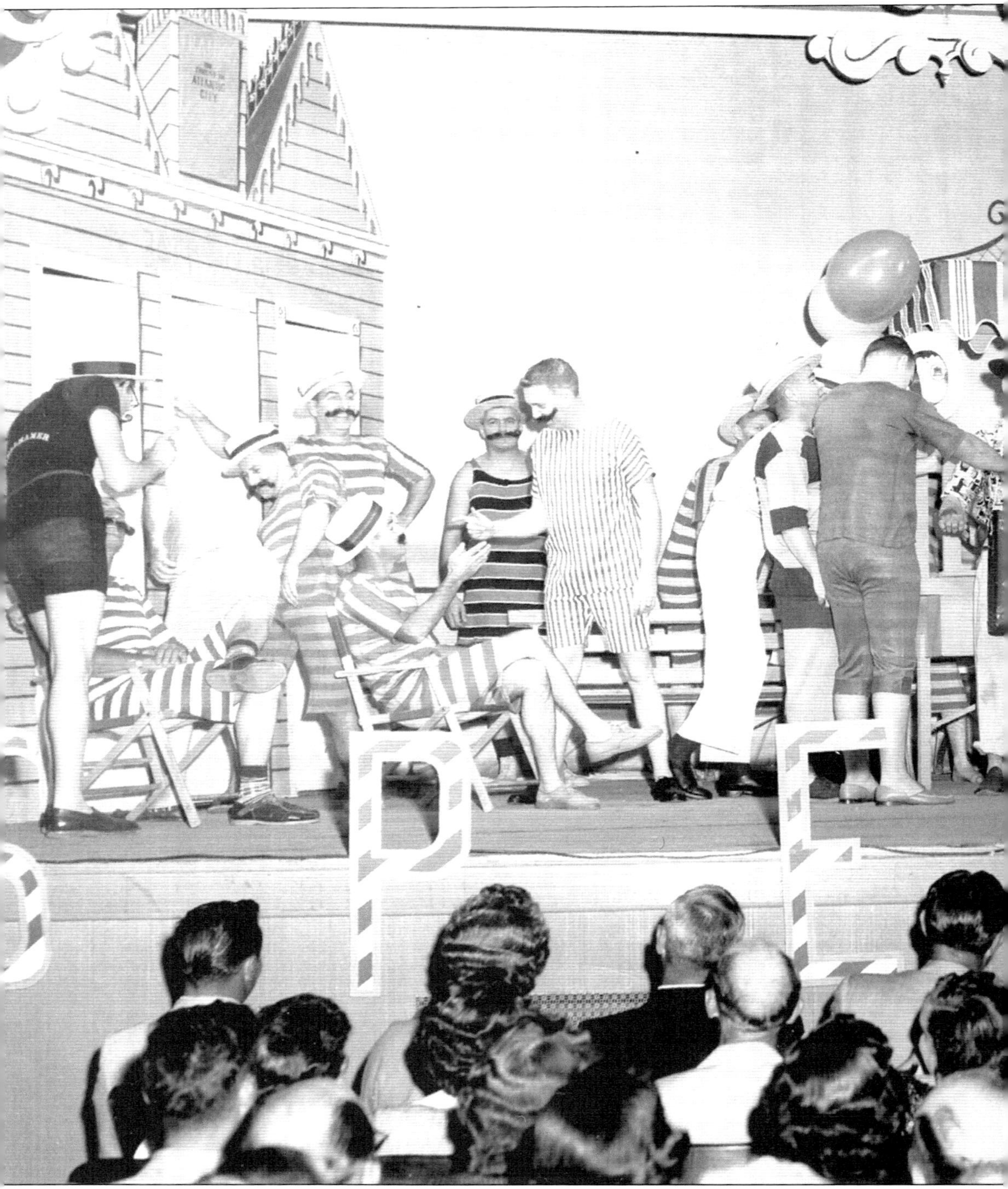

GAY NINETIES BOARDWALK. A second elaborate set had been prepared behind the closed curtain. When the heads of the mermaids withdrew and the curtain went up, the audience members howled with delight as they experienced yet another magnificent set, this one featuring the chorus on the boardwalk in their Gay Nineties swimwear, singing "By the Sea." This second

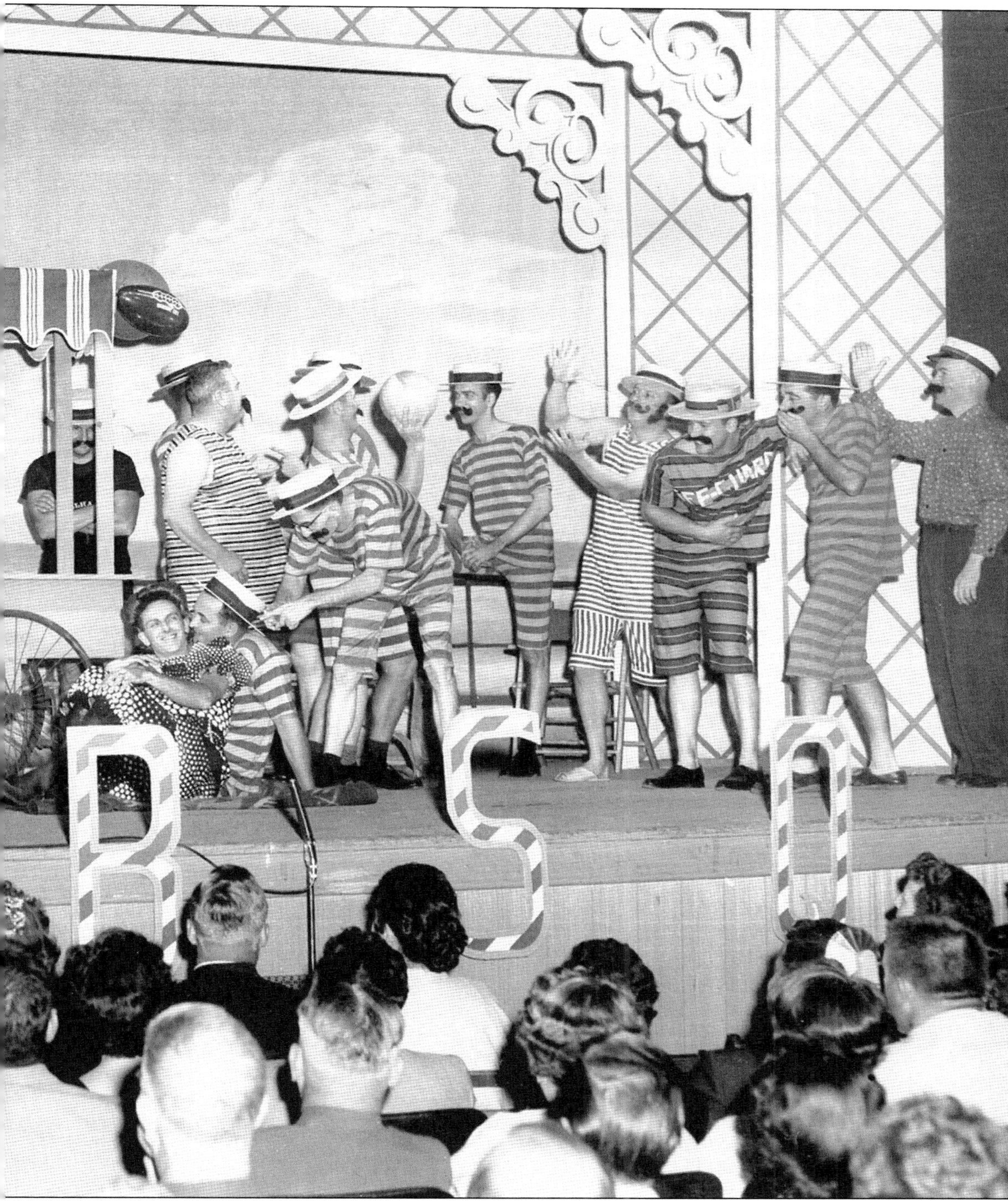

set was considered by the audience and the professionals alike to be a top production. It was this Gay Nineties set design that made the front page of the *Harmonizer*, one of the popular barbershop publications of that time.

Consistent with our mission to preserve history on a local level, this book was printed in South Carolina on American-made paper and manufactured entirely in the United States. Products carrying the accredited Forest Stewardship Council (FSC) label are printed on 100 percent FSC-certified paper.

MADE IN THE USA